A DREAM OF
WINGS

Americans and the Airplane
1875–1905

Tom D. Crouch

A DREAM OF WINGS

Americans and the Airplane

1875–1905

Smithsonian Institution Press • Washington • London

First time in paperback
New material edited by Jeanne M. Sexton
Cover design by Alan Carter

Printed in the United States of America
10 9 8 7 6 5 4 3 2 1
98 97 96 95 94 93 92 91 90 89

Library of Congress Cataloging in Publication Data

Crouch, Tom D.
A dream of wings.

Bibliography: p.
Includes index.
1. Aeronautics—United States—History.
I. Title.
TL521.C65 1989   629.13'00973   88-26512
ISBN 0-87474-325-7 (pbk.)

British Library Cataloguing in Publication Data is available
The paper in this publication meets the requirements of the American
National Standard for Permanence of Paper for Printed Materials Z39.48-1984

Published by arrangement with W.W. Norton & Company, Inc., New York
All photographs are courtesy of the Library of the National Air and Space
Museum, Smithsonian Institution. Portions of chapters 11, 12, and 13 have
appeared previously in *Smithsonian* magazine, which has kindly given permission
to reprint them.

For Nancy, Chris, Bruce, Abby, and Nathan
with all of my thanks

Contents

Preface to the 1989 Edition

It is good to have *A Dream of Wings* back in print. This book was originally intended to stand alone. It still does that, but *Dream* has also become the centerpiece of a trilogy. Having completed work on this volume in 1978, I turned my attention to the study of buoyant flight, producing *The Eagle Aloft: Two Centuries of the Balloon in America* (Washington, D.C.: Smithsonian Institution Press, 1984). Those two books, taken together with a recent arrival, *The Bishop's Boys: A Life of Wilbur and Orville Wright* (New York: W.W. Norton, 1989), present one scholar's vision of the roots of American aviation.

Today I find it impossible to read *Dream* without recalling the extent of my indebtedness to old friends and colleagues. The original acknowledgments stand, but the appearance of this new edition affords the opportunity for additional thanks to a few individuals who have played special roles in the history of this book.

The study began as a doctoral dissertation supervised by Professors John C. Burnham and Merritt Roe Smith, with substantial assistance from Professor June Z. Fullmer. Edwards Park, then an editor with *Smithsonian* magazine, set in motion the process of transforming a dissertation into a book when he accepted the final chapter as a magazine article in 1978. Ed Barber, now vice-president of W.W. Norton, read that article and stunned its author with a phone call soliciting the entire manuscript for publication as a book. Almost a decade later, Felix Lowe, director of the Smithsonian Institution Press and himself a superb editor, went to considerable lengths to bring the volume back into print.

In one sense, this is a better book than the original. A few typographical errors are missing and some of the footnotes are less confusing. The basic text, however, remains unchanged. While I have learned a bit more about the subject over the past ten years, I am still content with evidence presented and the conclusions drawn by the much younger and less experienced scholar whose book this remains.

Acknowledgments

Any author who has worked for six years on a book will find it difficult to thank adequately all who have offered advice and assistance. In the case of this volume, which began as a doctoral dissertation and has undergone several radical alterations, the task is especially difficult.

Charles H. Gibbs-Smith and Marvin W. McFarland, the doyens of early aeronautical history, have read and reread the manuscript, offering the sort of friendship and helpful comment without which the volume would be poorer. Paul E. Garber has offered similar service of the sort that is impossible to repay. John C. Burnham and M. R. Smith served as doctoral advisers and guided the initial development of the work, F. C. Durant III, my supervisor during the course of the work, has offered consistent understanding and encouragement. Melvin B. Zisfein and Howard S. Wolko have answered patiently any number of naïve questions on aerodynamics and aircraft structures.

My colleagues Richard P. Hallion, Claudia M. Oakes, and Donald Lopez have also read the manuscript and offered helpful counsel, while Eugene Emme and Thomas P. Hughes suggested basic alterations that improved the finished product.

A number of librarians and archivists have contributed to the project. Catherine Scott, Mimi Scharff, and other members of the NASM library staff have, as always, served as invaluable guides through the riches of their collection. William Deiss of the Smithsonian Institution Archive was of assistance in sorting through the Langley Papers. Father James McKevitt, archivist, University of Santa Clara, and the staffs of the Manuscript Division, Library of Congress, the John Crerar Library, the Cornell University Library, the Notre Dame University Library and Archive, and the National Archive also deserve thanks.

Others who have offered advice and assistance include Gregory Kennedy, Richard Hirsch, Mary Henderson, Rick Young, Phil Jarret, and Adrianne Noe. Phil Edwards of the NASM Library assisted in the selection of the photographs.

Special thanks go to Ivonette and Harold S. Miller of Dayton, Ohio. Mr. and Mrs. Miller, the Wright's favorite niece and the executor of their estate, opened their home to a young graduate student and patiently answered questions with friendship and hospitality. Octave A. Chanute and Elaine Chanute Hodges, relatives of another pioneer, have been generous with their time and friendship.

My wife Nancy and our children Christopher, Bruce, Abigail, and Nathan offered their support and understanding. Barbara Pawlowski put in long weekend and evening hours typing the manuscript and improving it in many respects. Ed Barber of Norton has been the most understanding of editors.

A DREAM OF WINGS

Americans and the Airplane
1875–1905

1

Huffman Prairie, 1904

Huffman Prairie is a forgotten place of American history. A low stone marker commemorating the events that occurred here lies hidden behind a tall chain link fence that rings modern Wright-Patterson Air Force Base, where thousands of Air Force employees stream in and out of the sprawling aerospace complex each day. Yet it was at Huffman Prairie, a meadow set in the rich farmland of southwestern Ohio's Miami Valley, that the old dream of aerial navigation became a reality for mankind.

Kitty Hawk had lured Wilbur and Orville Wright with the promise of ideal conditions for their aeronautical experiments. On the slopes of the Kill Devil Hills the Wrights had demonstrated in 1903 beyond doubt that their powered machine was capable of sustained flight under the control of a pilot. Nevertheless, they well realized that even the best performance of December 17, a straight-line flight of 852 feet in 59 seconds capped by a hard landing that damaged the forward skids and elevator, was scarcely calculated to convince skeptics that the age of flight was at hand. The brothers needed additional time to perfect their machine and to hone their piloting skills.

Immediately after their return from the Outer Banks, the Wrights began to search for a flying field near their Dayton home, a place where the world's first airplane could be transformed into a practical flying machine. Huffman Prairie was to be that place.

The Wright brothers arrived at this hummocky cow pasture with a new airplane in the spring of 1904. During the summer and fall of that year they gradually overcame the vagaries of wind and terrain and gained a degree of mastery over their craft. By August 1 they had completed 25 starts, including 4 flights of over 1,260 feet. Since this was approaching the maximum possible distance for a straight-line flight in the field, an attempt had to be made to turn the aircraft as it flew. Moving now beyond the limitations of 1903, the Wrights began to explore the full potential of their new technology. Progress was made almost daily in the skies over Huffman Prairie.

On September 20, 1904, the brothers had welcomed a rare visitor to their testing ground. For some weeks Amos Ives Root, a Medina, Ohio, apiarist and manufacturer of bee-keeping supplies, had been hearing fantastic stories concerning two minister's boys who were emulating the birds in a field near Dayton.

Wilbur (left) and Orville Wright and the 1904 flyer at Huffman Prairie, May 1904.

Fascinated by all things mechanical, he had come to investigate these rumors for himself.

As Root later reported in the pages of an unlikely journal entitled *Gleanings in Bee Culture,* his day at Huffman Prairie rivaled the fables of the Arabian nights. Wilbur made one short flight of a little over a minute that morning. In spite of a threatening sky, the Wrights and their mechanic, Charley Taylor, decided to attempt a second flight that afternoon. Wilbur would again be at the controls, while Orville and Charley operated stop watches and an anemometer on the ground.

The airplane moved swiftly down the launch track and into the air, flying the length of the field at an altitude of 10 to 15 feet. As he approached the fence at the far end of the meadow, Wilbur climbed to 25 feet and entered the first of a series of slow banking turns that would carry him back to the starting point in just over a minute and a half. During the course of this flight, covering some 4,080 feet, the Wrights had passed a great milestone. For the first time, a heavier-than-air flying machine had flown a complete circle.

Amos Root was stunned.

> When it first turned that circle, and came near the starting-point, I was right in front of it; and I said then, and I believe still, it was . . . the grandest sight of my life. Imagine a locomotive that has left its track, and is climbing up in the air right toward you—a locomotive without any wheels . . . but with white wings instead . . . a locomotive made of aluminum. Well, now, imagine this white locomotive, with wings that spread 20 feet each way, coming right toward you with a tremendous flap of its propellers, and you will have something like what I saw. The younger brother bade me move to one side for fear it might come down suddenly; but I tell you, friends, the sensation that one feels in such a crisis is something hard to describe.[1]

Root knew that he had witnessed a great moment in history. The winged locomotive that he had seen rise and circle the field would forever alter mankind's horizon. The long search for a fully controllable flying machine was at an end.

The 1904 flyer in the air, November 16, 1904.

But for Americans the quest was not new. It had begun seventy years before, in a building located 50 miles southwest of Huffman Prairie. In the spring of 1834 Cincinnati newspapers advised their readers to call at the Commercial Exchange, an exhibition hall located on Race Street, nearly opposite the old lathe factory below Third, where A. A. Mason, a steamboat mate and "ingenious citizen" of the town, had unveiled his "Aerial Steamboat." This ungainly craft, in which Mason proposed to make a public flight on July 4, was the first in a long series of unsuccessful powered flying machines that would be constructed in the United States over the next three-quarters of a century.

Enthusiastic local reporters described the "Aerial Steam Carriage" as a light boat hull some 10 feet long, the ribs of which had been covered with silk rather than planking. A 2-horsepower steam engine set in the center of the hull drove four "spiral silken wings" placed at the bow and stern. These helicopter blades were to draw the machine into the air, while two additional propellers, set horizontally at the rear of the machine, would propel the craft. A "moveable silken cover" was designed "to assist in counteracting the gravitating force, [and] at the same time . . . to assist in its propulsion forward."[2]

Mason and his "Aerial Steamboat" soon vanished from the pages of Cincinnati newspapers, but the seven decades that separate its unveiling from the first circular flight of an airplane in an Ohio cow pasture would be filled with other schemes for the conquest of the skies.

Throughout this period most Americans regarded the flying machine as little more than a chimera pursued by foolish dreamers. The poet J. T. Trowbridge provided a classic statement of this attitude in "Darius Green and His Flying Machine," one of the most popular story poems of the era. Like many another "country dunce," young Darius was convinced that "the air was also man's domain." Determined to conquer the skies, he set to work

> . . . with thimble and thread and wax and hammer and buckles and screws, and all such things as geniuses use. Two bats for a pattern, curious fellows! A charcoal pot and a pair of bellows. Some wire and several old umbrellas; a carriage cover, for tail and wings; a piece of harness; and straps and strings . . . these and a hundred other things.[3]

Encased in his contraption, the inventor leaped from the barn loft, only to thump into the yard below, surrounded by "a wonderful whirl of tangled strings, broken braces and broken wings, shooting stars and various things." For the thousands of Americans who chuckled over poor Darius' plight the moral was clear: If God had intended man to fly, he would have given him wings.

A wealth of educated opinion buttressed such popular skepticism. Had not Simon Newcomb, a leading American astronomer, argued that "the first successful flyer will be the handiwork of a watchmaker, and carry nothing heavier than an insect."[4] Another authority, Rear Admiral George Melville, the Navy's chief engineer, was even more forceful. "A calm survey of certain natural phenomena," he argued, "leads the engineer to pronounce all confident prophecies . . . for future success as wholly unwarranted, if not absurd."[5] John Le Conte, a well-known naturalist, had assured the public that "a flying machine is impossible, in spite of the testimony of the birds."[6]

But neither popular doubt nor the dour opinions of leading scientists could deter a significant number of nineteenth-century Americans who were irresistably drawn to the problem of aerial navigation. It was, after all, an age marked by enthusiasm for technology. There seemed no end to the wonders that poured forth from American laboratories and workshops. Messages, even human voices, passed for thousands of miles through thin strands of wire. Wax cylinders could be made to talk. The very image of life was captured on a ribbon of celluloid and projected on a screen time and again. A tiny carbonized filament enclosed in a glass bulb replaced the flickering light of torches, candles, and gas jets.

In view of what had already been accomplished, perhaps aerial navigation was not so wild a dream. Certainly the challenge was great, but so were the potential rewards. The man who produced a successful flying machine would surely find a place at the head of that pantheon of great inventors—men like Whitney, Fulton, Morse, Colt, Bell, and Edison, whose names were familiar to every schoolboy.

The first of a flood of fanciful aeronautical proposals were submitted to the patent office as local newspapers and national magazines reported on the scores of visionary citizens who were convinced that they alone possessed the secret that would open the great highway of the skies to mankind. It was an era in which every man was his own mechanic. The complexities of sophisticated high technology lay far in the future. Machines were comprehensible, familiar. Common sense, ingenuity, and perseverance were the tools with which these men attacked every technical problem from the repair of farm machinery to the design of a flying machine.[7]

These folk technologists developed an astonishing variety of bizarre and entertaining, plans for flight. None of them stood the slightest chance of realization. Indeed, so long as aeronautics remained the province of the Darius Green school of flight research, no serious progress would be made toward the age-old dream of flight.

The advent of the professional technologist to aeronautics

after 1860 was the great turning point that separated the work of A. A. Mason and his contemporaries from that of Wilbur and Orville Wright. The engineers brought self-confidence, professional organization and experience to the field, and they brought it first from Europe, where engineering involvement in aeronautics had begun early. But the final goal was achieved only after leadership had passed to the United States, where the foundation of a unique community of American technologists involved in flying machine studies had been formed as early as 1885. What follows is their story, the story of a handful of Americans who labored during the final quarter of the nineteenth century to bring forth the airplane. The visionaries and barnyard mechanics of the antebellum years had given way to a generation of talented engineers who struggled to lay a foundation for success. Their plans for flight ranged from bizarre contraptions based on little more than personal intuition to the carefully engineered gliders in which the most intrepid of these adventurers would risk, and occasionally lose their lives. Yet for all their diversity, they were bound by a shared belief that the time had come to navigate the ocean of air. To a man, they echoed the words of fellow enthusiast Charles Duryea, "Flying is within our grasp. We have naught to do but take it."[8]

2

An Engineer Discovers the Airplane

On the evening of April 2, 1903, members of the Aéro Club de France gathered for a "dîner-conférence" at the Hôtel de l'Automobile-Club, 6 Place de la Concorde, Paris. They had come to hear American engineer Octave Chanute, who would lecture on recent gliding experiments in the United States. As the French journal *L'Aérophile* reported, Chanute's appearance had caused a "great flutter in the aerial world." Recently retired from a brilliant career in civil engineering, Chanute had "worked with indefatigable ardour at this most difficult question of aerial navigation by heavier-than-air means."[1]

Speaking in French and employing a series of lantern slides, Chanute traced the rise of a hang-gliding tradition from the work of the German pioneer Otto Lilienthal through his own efforts with manned gliders in the summer of 1896. The most significant portion of the talk, however, was devoted to the gliding experiments conducted by Wilbur and Orville Wright, "bicycle makers of Dayton." His description of the extraordinary performance of the Wright 1902 glider both astounded and dismayed the audience. Here was compelling evidence confirming that, as the French-born aeronautical experimenter Louis

Mouillard had remarked in 1892, "You Americans are clearly in the lead in the aviation movement."[2]

Chanute's lecture was to have a profound impact on the development of the airplane. European interest in heavier-than-air flight was at a low in 1902. The French and Germans regarded the rigid airship as much more promising than the airplane, while the English had yet to move beyond the sport balloon. Chanute's revelations demonstrated that France, the land of the Montgolfiers, had lost its position of leadership in aeronautics.

Their national honor at stake, the French set to work in a vain effort to surpass the Wrights. The lineage of the first frail European craft to make forays into the air during the years 1906–1908 can be traced to this period of excitement following this Aéro Club meeting.[3] And it was indeed fitting that Octave Chanute should have been the man to introduce Wilbur and Orville Wright to the world. More than any other figure, Chanute was

Octave Chanute (1832–1910).

responsible for propelling American aeronautics from folk technology to the status of an engineering discipline. In so doing he
had set in motion a chain of events that led to the triumph of
December 17, 1903.

Chanute was a native Parisian, born to a family with roots
deep in French history. His father, Joseph Chanut, was a distinguished scholar and academician, the author of a standard history of France from the death of Louis XIV to the revolution
of 1830.

Joseph Chanut married Élise Sophie de Bonnaire on April 29,
1831. Octave, the first of their three children, was born eleven
months later on February 18, 1832. Late in 1838 Joseph resigned
his teaching position in Paris to accept the vice-presidency of
Louisiana's Jefferson College. He and Octave left for New Or-
leans immediately. Élise Sophie and the younger children were
to follow once a home had been established.

But the stay in Louisiana was a short one. By 1844 Joseph had
resigned his college post and resettled in New York, where he
became involved in what his son later characterized as "literary
pursuits."

Young Octave was thoroughly Americanized by the time he
entered his teens. His deep feeling for his adopted homeland
was clearly evident in a letter written to a French aeronautical
experimenter many years later. "I am a full-fledged American,"
he wrote, "even to the point of being prejudiced."[4]

The addition of the final -e to his patronym was one sign of
adaptation to the new environment. When schoolmates insisted
on dubbing him the "naked cat" (chat nu), he added the additional letter to suggest a more correct pronunciation to his
American friends.

It was while a student in New York that Chanute decided on
a career in engineering, a natural choice for a bright, ambitious
lad growing up in antebellum America. The continued economic growth of the United States obviously depended on the
creation of an improved transportation system to open the vast
markets of the West. The canal building boom that followed the
opening of the Erie Canal in 1825 was rapidly giving way to
enthusiasm for the railroad. Less than five years after the first

American-built locomotive had made a run on a 6-mile track near Charleston, South Carolina, in 1831, 1,098 miles of steam railroad track had been placed in service in the United States. By 1839 the figure had risen to almost 5,000 miles.

There were two avenues of entry into civil engineering, the profession that would direct the continued extension of this network of rails. In 1849, the year in which seventeen-year-old Octave Chanute entered the field, only four universities—West Point, Rensselaer Polytechnic Institute, Yale, and Harvard—offered formal programs of engineering education. For those who were too poor or, like Chanute, too impatient, apprenticeship offered an alternative.

In 1849 Chanute traveled to Sing Sing, New York, where the Hudson River Railroad was laying track. Presenting himself to Henry Gardner, the resident engineer, he was told that no positions were available. With the persistence that was always to mark his character, Chanute offered to work for nothing. Suitably impressed, Gardner put the young volunteer to work as a chainman, the lowliest member of a surveying crew. Within two months he was on the payroll at $1.12 a day. By virtue of his "careful and industrious application to his duties," Chanute rose quickly through the ranks. By 1853 he was a division engineer in charge of terminal facilities and maintainance of way at Albany.

In September 1853 he moved west to accept a position as division engineer in charge of track-laying operations for the Chicago and Mississippi Railroad. Over the next decade he was employed in various engineering positions by a number of Illinois-based railroads. While headquartered in Peoria during this period he met and married Annie James on March 12, 1867. Between 1867 and 1873 he served as chief engineer for several railroads being constructed into Kansas to tap the Texas cattle trade. In addition to his regular duties, he built a reputation as one of the finest consulting engineers in the West, responsible for the first bridge over the Missouri River and the Union stockyards in Chicago and Kansas City. The body of experience that Chanute built up in the areas of stress analysis, trussing methods, and the strength of materials during this period would prove invaluable when applied to the construction of gliders.[5]

Octave Chanute, age thirty-eight, appears in the cap in the upper left in this photo of workmen and divers taken during the construction of the Kansas City Bridge, March 2, 1869.

Chanute reached the pinnacle of his career in 1873, when he was appointed chief engineer of the reorganized Erie Railroad. During his twenty-year career as an engineer in Illinois and Kansas, he had played a major role in shaping the development of the West. The railroads and bridges he had constructed carried settlers into the region and distributed its products to the rest of the nation. Virtually every cow driven north from Texas passed through the stockyards Chanute had built. His services as a civic leader and consulting city engineer in towns from Peoria to Kansas City marked him as a man with a clear notion of the social responsibility of his profession.

Nor had his services gone unappreciated. At the time of his appointment to the Erie, western newspapers were filled with tributes to his character and achievements. The *Leavenworth Daily Times* praised him as "a gentleman in every respect," while the *Parsons* (Kansas) *Sun* protested "against New York taking

from us one of the ablest and best brain-men in the state." One
Illinois journal proclaimed him the "ablest as well as one of the
most popular men in the West." He was a "universal favorite,"
and "the best civil engineer in the West."[6]

In contrast, Chanute's ten years with the Erie were disappointing. The Panic of 1873 and the scandal surrounding the
financial machinations of Erie management thwarted Chanute's
attempts to improve the road. Nevertheless, by the time of his
resignation he had been able to double-track the entire line, to
standardize the gauge, and to so improve the grades and bridges
that the average size of Erie freight trains was doubled during
these years.

During this period Chanute also became heavily involved
in the work of professional organizations, particularly the revi-
talized American Society of Civil Engineers, of which he
was to become president. His early work on several ASCE
technical committees was especially noteworthy. In 1873 he
chaired one such group studying possible rapid-transit systems for New York City. Faced with opposition from local political bosses and vested-interest groups, Chanute and an associate, M. N. Forney, prepared a model report calling for the
construction of the elevated steam railways that were eventually put into service.

After ten years in New York Chanute resigned from the Erie.
Rejecting lucrative contracts for consultation in Latin America
and Asia, he returned to the West, settling in Kansas City,
where he established himself as a consulting engineer. From 1880
to 1885 he chaired another ASCE committee dealing with the
problems of wood preservation. By 1890 his reputation as an
authority in this field was so well established that he settled
permanently in Chicago, where he founded a firm specializing
in wood preservation.

As *Cassier's Magazine*, a leading engineering journal, commented, "The professional career of Mr. Chanute fairly repre-
sents that of the typical American civil engineer. . . ." It might
be more accurate to say that Chanute's career was a model, so
perfect that it was atypical.[7] He was clearly recognized as one
of the most successful men in his profession, having repeatedly

demonstrated his ability to solve a wide range of difficult technical problems. He was a leader of the movement to apply engineering methods to the solution of business and social problems. He was also deeply involved in the drive to increase the status and prestige of the engineering profession and to create a sense of national and international unity among engineers. Having accomplished all of this, he felt he could now relax and devote more time to the one engineering problem that interested him most—flight.

It is important to note that, in spite of the enormous impact Chanute was to have on aeronautics, he was never willing to regard the flying machine as more than an avocation. He conducted his flying-machine experiments, and encouraged others to do so, for the same reasons that lead men to pursue golf or bridge. Always the practical man of business, he was sometimes fearful that his infatuation with the subject might prove embarrassing or damaging. Yet, in private, he nursed a growing conviction that heavier-than-air flight was not only possible, but practical for mankind.

Chanute's interest in aeronautics was a direct result of the New York rapid-transit report of 1875. That assignment had exposed him to much public and professional pressure during the difficult early years in New York. The result was a period of exhaustion and depression that necessitated four months of rest and relaxation in Europe. It was while on tour that Chanute first discovered that some of his most distinguished colleagues in England and on the Continent were beginning to regard the airplane as a very real possibility. The connection between practical engineering and aerodynamic phenomena struck a responsive note in the mind of a man who had devoted his life to the design of rapid-transportation systems and large structures capable of resisting the onslaught of high winds. In his own words:

I gave some thought to the subject [aeronautics]. I was more disposed to do this because I had been aware for years that there were a number of observed wind phenomena, such as the lifting of roofs, the blowing off of bridges, and the tipping over of locomotives, which the known velocity and pressure of the wind at the time was insufficient to account for.[8]

Chanute's interest was piqued, but his return to business and professional responsibilities at home left little time for so frivolous an activity as aeronautical research. Not until 1885, when he was back in Kansas City with his engineering firm operating smoothly, could he once again pick up the threads of aeronautical research. Convinced that a clear understanding of what had been accomplished to date was required to chart a rational research program, Chanute began a comprehensive survey of flying-machine literature.

It became apparent to him that European aeronautical experimenters had made remarkable progress over the past three-quarters of a century. The process had begun with Sir George Cayley, "the Father of Aerial Navigation," whose career marked the first real watershed in the history of aeronautics. Born in Scarborough in 1773, Cayley was the first to provide an adequate statement of the basic problem, "viz—To make a surface support a given weight by the application of power to the resistance of air." By applying the methodology of science to flight research, he pointed the way for the next generation of aeronautical experimenters.

Nor were his efforts confined to the publication of his theoretical speculations. On the basis of his research he constructed the

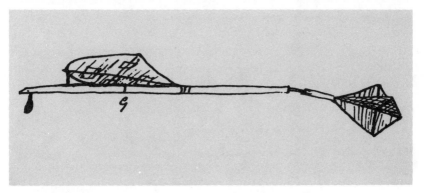

Cayley's model glider of 1804.

world's first successful flying model in 1804 and, in the half century that followed, three full-scale gliders capable of flight with a passenger on board. These machines suggested the modern configuration of the airplane as a vehicle with separate systems for lift, propulsion, and control. This basic, all-important notion was reinforced by the work of two Englishmen, William Samuel Henson and John Stringfellow. Their "aerial steam carriage" was firmly grounded in Cayley's work and fixed the image of a propeller-driven airplane with an enclosed fuselage, rectilinear wings, and a separate tail group soaring over the Pyramids, the Taj Mahal, or the Tower of London on the public consciousness.

The failure of a man of Cayley's genius to mount an effective, long-term effort to produce a glider capable of making repeated

A popular French treatment of Henson's aerial steam carriage.

flights was evidence of the need for a cooperative, well-directed flight research program involving many men with broad technical experience. The problems of flight were too overwhelming to be overcome by any individual, however talented. The first steps toward the creation of such a coordinated drive to achieve powered flight were taken after 1860, as professional engineers became interested in aeronautics.[9]

The need for a new ordering of the technical professions had become apparent as the industrial revolution of the eighteenth century forced a redefinition of mankind's relationship to the machine. The development of new devices, processes, and technical solutions to the economic and social problems that plagued an increasingly urban, regimented, and factory-oriented society could no longer be trusted to untutored craftsmen. While self-trained technicians like Eli Whitney, S. F. B. Morse, Samuel Colt, and Charles Goodyear continued to inject new ideas, techniques, and machines into industry, the leadership that directed the sustained growth of modern technology was drawn to an ever-greater extent from an expanding pool of trained engineers.

The craftsmen of an earlier era had learned to perform a limited number of specific tasks. The engineer, by definition, was trained to apply a broad understanding of general scientific and technical principles to the solution of a wide range of particular problems. During the course of his career, a nineteenth-century engineer could reasonably expect to become involved in a variety of projects ranging from surveying and bridge building to locomotive and ship design. The engineer was a self-confident generalist, always in search of new challenges, new areas in which to demonstrate his prowess.

It was this sense of delight in approaching a difficult technical problem that attracted engineers like Octave Chanute to aeronautics. The possibility of sending aloft a machine many times heavier than the air through which it would pass was staggering. Yet nature had solved the problem, and during the last quarter of the nineteenth century some of the most talented engineers in Europe became convinced that mankind could do so as well.

A sense of community became a major element directing the course of action for engineers involved in aeronautics. This cooperative ideal was expressed through both formal and informal organizations of professional technologists. Membership in professional societies was a familiar experience to engineers by 1870. The foundation of such groups had been one indication of the fact that these men were establishing themselves as distinct, useful, and highly trained professionals. Engineers interested in the flying machine simply transferred the system of professional communication and information sharing to which they were accustomed in their normal engineering pursuits to the study of aeronautics.

The history of the most important of these new groups, the Aeronautical Society of Great Britain, illustrates the way in which professional technologists approached the problems of flight. Established in 1866, the Aeronautical Society drew some distinguished amateur experimenters into membership during its early years, but professional engineers provided most of the guidance and leadership for the group. Francis Herbert Wenham, a well-known marine engineer and engine designer; Charles Brooke, a designer of self-recording instruments; Sir William Fairbairn, onetime president of both the Institution of Civil Engineering and the British Association for the Advancement of Science; Sir Charles Bright, a planner and supporter of the Atlantic cable; W. H. le Feuvre, president of the Society of Engineers; and Sir Charles William Siemens, a pioneer developer of both the telegraph and the dynamo—were among the prominent technicians who served on the council or ruling body of the society during the first two years of its existence. These men were not figureheads; they played active roles in directing the course of the organization.

Other leading engineers who served on society technical committees or offered papers at early meetings included James Nasmyth, the inventor of the steam hammer; Thomas Moy, an associate of the Institute of Naval Architects and the owner of a small engineering firm that specialized in the manufacture of steam engines and boilers; J. P. Bourne of the Institution of Civil Engineers; F. W. Young, an engineer with the Harbours and

Rivers Division of the Colonial Service, and A. Alexander, manager of the Camel Steel Works at Sheffield. While the total membership of the society numbered only 65 at the end of 1867, some of the finest engineers in England were enthusiastic participants in its activities.

The leaders of the Aeronautical Society planned informative lectures and technical meetings to attract young engineers into membership, and sponsored the first public exhibition of aeronautical technology to interest the general public in their activity, but the published *Annual Reports of the Aeronautical Society* proved to be the organization's most useful venture. For many years after the issue of the first volume in 1868, this series remained the primary source of trustworthy information on aeronautics available in English. The quality of the articles appearing in the *Annual Reports* was consistently high. The publication was aimed at a professional audience of scientists and engineers, not the lay public. The common denominator connecting most of the articles in the series was the attempt to extend contemporary engineering theory and practice into aeronautics. The authors of these pieces were not foolish dreamers or visionaries, but working engineers who perceived aviation as a solvable problem.[10]

European engineers also followed the English lead in establishing professional societies and aeronautical journals aimed at an audience of technical specialists. *L'Aéronaut,* which began publication in Paris in 1869, was followed by *Revue de l'Aéronautique* in 1888. German engineers also developed aeronautical journals during the two decades after 1860.

The immediate effect of this activity was to encourage a dialogue that enabled technical professionals to fix known points of reference. Basic data that could serve as a starting point for active experimentation was prepared as the first step toward the development of a successful heavier-than-air flying machine.

As scattered engineers began the task of translating the data accumulating in their newly established journals into an operating airplane, the basic dimensions of the task emerged. A completed flying machine would represent the successful amalgama-

tion of solutions to problems in the basic areas of aircraft structure, aerodynamics, and propulsion.

The technology of aircraft structures—the choice of materials
and assembly techniques to be used in building a safe airframe
—was the least critical of these three areas. Most experimenters
chose to employ standard materials whose properties were
thoroughly understood. Nor was innovation in construction
technology encouraged. Procedures long accepted as standard in
carpentry and the building trades were to prevail in aeronautics
as well. Civil engineering contributed basic data on trussing
systems, strength of materials, and the properties of various
structural forms under stress. But, for the most part, structural
problems were solved empirically.

Would-be flying-machine builders paid more attention to propulsion technology. Attitudes toward the engine problem varied between two extremes. One group of experimenters saw the
development of a suitable power plant as the single most important difficulty. These men dedicated their efforts to the perfection of the aero engine and tended to move to the construction
of full-size machines or test beds based on minimum aerodynamic research. Others believed that once the more difficult
aerodynamic problems had been overcome, a suitable engine
would be relatively easy to obtain.

The choice of power plant varied. Steam was the early candidate. As late as the last decade of the nineteenth century, the
enormous body of experience with light-weight steam engines
and boilers made them the logical choice for an experimental
aeronautical power plant.

The potential of the internal combustion engine was more
difficult to recognize. Prior to 1895, most serious experimenters
were forced to conclude that the new engine technology was too
experimental and unreliable for use in a life-or-death flight situation. There was an additional, though unrecognized, danger in
the gasoline engine. As S. P. Langley was to discover, the experimenter who braved the relative unknowns of the lightweight
petrol engine, in addition to developing an airframe, added
years to his search and needlessly compounded his problems.
The ability of the Wright brothers to design and build their own

gasoline engine with relative ease would have been impossible a decade earlier.

Finally, a few enthusiasts focused on extremely lightweight power plants suitable for brief periods of operation. Compressed air and carbonic-acid gas engines were the most common choices in this category, particularly with model builders or those who chose to take to the skies in very light proto-airplanes that were essentially powered hang gliders.

By the last quarter of the nineteenth century much thought was also being given to the means of translating the power of the engine into forward motion. The oars, sails, flapping wings, and paddle wheels of an earlier epoch had almost universally given way to the propeller, but few enthusiasts were willing to invest time and energy in studies of propeller efficiency. Thus, the inadequate conception of the "air screw" boring through air was retained until overthrown by the brilliant Wright treatment of the propeller as a rotary wing generating a forward lift vector.

It was in aerodynamics that the first generation of aeronautical engineers made their most significant contributions. The design of a proper wing was the central concern. Cayley had demonstrated that the whirling arm, ballistic pendulum, and other instruments devised by eighteenth-century ballisticians could provide general data of value in guiding flying-machine builders. The development of new instruments, most notably the wind tunnel, introduced by F. H. Wenham and John Browning in 1871, was to prove far more important, however, for it opened new approaches to the study of aerodynamic phenomena underlying wing design.

In many respects Wenham can be seen as the prototype of the investigators who would achieve the success of 1903. He advocated the construction of gliding machines with which a pilot could gain experience in the air prior to adding an engine. Such machines were to be thoroughly grounded in engineering data obtained by means of the most advanced experimental apparatus. His use of the wind tunnel, for example, directly inspired the Wright brothers' later application of this device.

The wind tunnel made it possible to estimate the wing-surface area required to support a given weight. As this minimum area began to appear too large to deal with as single wing, both Cayley and Wenham suggested the use of multiple surfaces. Biplane, triplane, multiplane, and tandem wing configurations made their appearance in the plans of the most realistic experimenters. Only in this manner could the needed surface area be embodied in a machine that would remain reasonably small, light, and maneuverable.

Attention was also focused on the correct shape for a wing. Cayley had tentatively suggested that an arched surface was more efficient than a flat plane, but it remained for professional technicians to establish the virtue of the cambered wing after 1860. Wenham initiated this process by arguing that all bird wings were arched. He also noted that the center of maximum pressure fell toward the thick leading edge. This belief helps to explain Wenham's choice of long, narrow (high aspect ratio) multiplane wings for his own glider of 1858–1859.

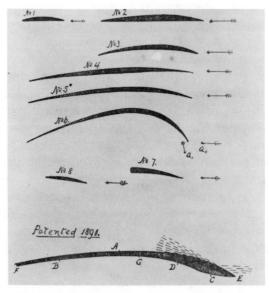

Sample airfoils developed by Horatio Phillips.

Horatio F. Phillips, following Wenham's lead, turned his own ingenious steam-injection wind tunnel to the study of cambered surfaces in the 1870s. The wing shapes that emerged from these tests represent an important step toward the modern airfoil. Phillips emphasized the two-surface wing section in which the lower side of the airfoil was given a gentler curve than the top side. This, combined with a gradual rise to maximum thickness near the center of pressure, one-third to one-half the distance behind the leading edge, resulted in several sections with a distinctly modern appearance. Phillips applied his wing theory in the construction of a multiplane slat-wing test bed that made short, tethered, unmanned hops from a circular track in 1907.

With work under way on the development of an effective wing, attention was turned to the other great aerodynamic problem—control. As in the case of power-plant research, there were two basic attitudes toward stability and control.

Unlike a vehicle operating on land or water, an aircraft in flight is free to rotate about three axes of motion. The craft can "pitch" its nose up or down to initiate a climb or descent, or "yaw" its nose to the right or left in a flat turn in one plane. The third, or "roll," axis is employed when the machine, by raising one wingtip and lowering the other, rotates about an imaginary line drawn through the center of the fuselage.

The implements for controlling motion in yaw and pitch had appeared long before 1860. Eighteenth-century balloonists had suggested the adaptation of the ship's rudder for steering their proposed aerial craft. It was but a short step to a "horizontal rudder" or elevator that could be employed to regulate altitude. In his basic glider model of 1804, Cayley had used a cruciform tail that combined rudder and elevator.

Control in roll (lateral control) was quite another matter, for no analogy like a ship's rudder could be drawn from older technologies. A search of nineteenth-century patent records and aeronautical literature indicates that a few imaginative men were giving thought to the problem, but these few suggestions for roll control attracted little or no comment. Nor was the need for control in the roll axis recognized by many of the nineteenth-century pioneers.

In order to realize the importance of banking an aircraft to make a turn, one had first to break free of the older notions of control that applied to surface vehicles. It was necessary to adopt, as C. H. Gibbs-Smith, English aeronautical historian, has suggested, the altitude of the "airman," and eschew that of the ground-based "chauffeur." Few men possess the imagination or insight required to break the traditional mode of thinking.

Most experimenters chose simply to ignore the possibility of active pilot control in roll. Following the lead of French experimenter Alphonse Pénaud, they sought to perfect a mechanism that would guarantee absolute inherent lateral stability. This would mean that a flying machine would proceed on a straight and level course, with the pilot intervening only when changing direction or altitude. Thus, a simple mechanism such as building dihedral into the wings, which would provide some measure of stability in roll, was substituted for an active control system. The rudder alone would be used to swing the aircraft around in a slow, flat turn, perhaps assisted by some device that could increase air resistance on the pivoting wing.

A number of factors explain this emphasis on automatic stability. Many students of the atmosphere were convinced that upper-air gusts and currents shifted so rapidly as to defeat human reflexes. They believed that a mechanism that could "sense" these changes and automatically maintain the craft on an even keel was required. "Gust dampers" might be provided, for example. These were hinged sections of the trailing edge of each wing that would automatically "give" when struck by wind gusts to return a raised or lowered wing to a horizontal position.

Just as important, however, is the fact that few experimenters really sought to develop a finished aircraft, complete with adequate controls. Most felt that the first task was to demonstrate a simple straight-line flight with a man on board. Once this had been accomplished, they argued, full attention could be given to control.

It was apparent to Octave Chanute that profound changes had occurred in aeronautics as a result of the entry of the engineers into the field. The boundaries of the problem were being mapped. An organized dialogue among men trained to attack any technical problem with powerful analytical tools had prepared the ground for active flight researchers. Flying machines produced by inventors in the mainstream of aeronautics would no longer be the product of a single mind working in isolation. They would represent a distillation of the experience of other professionals in the field.

Chanute believed that if progress was to be made with the flying machine, engineering involvement in flight research would have to expand. American engineers should join their European brethren in the search for a flying machine, and Chanute was in an ideal position to introduce his colleagues to aeronautics. As a leading American engineer, he received frequent invitations to address college and university groups as well as local technical societies. Moreover, his seniority in national organizations gave him the opportunity to plan aeronautical programs for meetings that would draw an elite audience.

He began cautiously, uncertain of the reaction of his colleagues to his interest in flight. The Buffalo meeting of the American Association for the Advancement of Science in August 1886 seemed to offer a perfect opportunity to broach the subject of aeronautics to his technically sophisticated peers. Chanute, then serving as vice-president of the AAAS, was responsible for planning the Section D ("Mechanical Engineering") portion of the program. The fact that his old friend Robert H. Thurston was to serve as vice-chairman for this session made the possibility of including an aeronautical program at the upcoming Buffalo meeting even more appealing.

Thurston, one of the nation's leading engineering educators, had been named director of Cornell University's Sibley College of Engineering in June 1885. Like Chanute, he was very interested in the airplane as an engineering problem. In 1884, he had surveyed the field for the journal *Science,* concluding with the remark that "the art of aerostation is much nearer a practical state than scientific men generally suppose."[11] Thurston was more than willing to cooperate with Chanute in using the Buffalo meeting as a means of introducing American engineers to aeronautics.

The two men invited Israel Lancaster, an amateur naturalist and aeronautical experimenter, to address Section D on the subject of "The Soaring Bird." A description of Lancaster's experiments with a series of flying models would form the core of the talk.

Lancaster's enthusiasm for aeronautics had grown out of his observations of bird flight. He was one of a family of farmers who had settled on the Illinois prairie early in the 1850s. While still very young, he became interested in the mechanics of bird flight.

For over twenty years Lancaster continued to farm and pursue his bird studies. He developed elaborate methods of approaching nesting birds, going so far as to cover himself with yards of muslin painted green and brown. By 1876 he had developed an excellent reputation as an ornithologist and was a confirmed believer in the possibility of human flight. The solution of the riddles facing flying-machine inventors could, he argued, be found in the soaring bird, a "model from the workshop of nature, launched in mid-air, which man could profitably take as a pattern to work from in attaining atmospheric dominion." So great was his confidence that he remarked, "the only thing remaining undone . . . [is] a matter of mechanical construction, requiring neither great expenditure of money, time or skill."

Lancaster built a series of "soaring effigies," or models, to demonstrate that his principles of bird flight could be translated into a flying machine. These effigies were to excite more interest among scientists and engineers than the theory on which they were based. Their inventor described the construction of the small craft in detail:

> Take a stick of wood one inch square and eighteen inches long, and point one end. Slit the other end three or four inches and insert a piece of stiff cardboard six inches wide and one foot long. This will represent the body and tail of the bird. Fasten on both sides near the pointed end a tapering stick two feet long, with the outer ends slightly elevated, and fasten to these and the body a piece of cardboard two feet long. Have the tail vertical instead of

horizontal as in the bird. Round off the outer corners of the wings three or four inches.[12]

The imitation bird was now complete with the addition of a swinging pendulum to provide stability. Lancaster claimed that flights of up to fifteen minutes covering over 500 yards had been made with these "effigies." He had constructed "hundreds" of the small models, all of which had demonstrated the ability to soar, "although none had been able to fly out of sight." Many enthusiasts, including Chanute, took a genuine interest in the "effigies" and attempted to match Lancaster's experimental results, without success.

Nevertheless, the models convinced their inventor that his theories were valid. He saw no reason why they could not be applied on an even larger scale. While Lancaster did not build a full-size craft himself, he did describe how it might be constructed.

A wing area of 200 square feet would, he believed, be sufficient to support 300 pounds in the air. The pilot would lie prone, face down, in a "fine bamboo case" 6 feet square and "rigid without joints or any other movable part." Control would be by means of levers in the cockpit, which would permit the operator to "break" the edge of the wing. His feet would fit into stirrups operating the rudder. When complete, the airplane would be hauled into the air between two sturdy poles 100 feet high and 100 yards apart. Once the pilot had become accustomed to the control of the machine in the wind, he could release the craft to begin his first free flight.[13]

At the time of the Buffalo meeting, Chanute was still unwilling to reveal the full extent of his personal interest in aeronautics. In his opening remarks to Section D, he did little more than point to the airplane as an interesting research topic, the solution of which probably lay far in the future. In a real sense, Lancaster was to be Chanute's means of testing the waters.

When Lancaster accepted the invitation to speak, Chanute, without consulting the lecturer, arranged for him to give two talks. The first of these was the presentation to Section D on the afternoon of August 18 on the subject of the "Soaring Bird." The second, to be offered on August 23, was listed in the official program as a demonstration of the flying characteristics of the effigies.

The first lecture was received with less enthusiasm than Lancaster and his sponsors had hoped. The *Buffalo Courier* reported that the assembled scientists "unanimously joined in reviling and laughing at him." The basic and very obvious weaknesses of Lancaster's theory made it impossible for those present to pay serious attention to the speaker's discussion of the application of his principles in the construction of the "effigies." A reporter commented:

> Some of the members of the Association seem to be in a quandary as to whether Mr. Lancaster is a crank, or a sharp practical joker who has been giving the great association of America's savants guff.[14]

Lancaster, having faced the ridicule of the members once, was naturally loathe to do so again. Word of the fiasco of August 18 passed among the scientists, and the small room chosen for the demonstration of the "effigies" was packed by a "big rush" of curiosity seekers at the appointed time on the twenty-third.

Lancaster may never have intended to test his models, or the combination of his experience earlier in the week and the temper of the crowd gathered to hear his second presentation may have convinced him to change his initial plans. Whatever the cause, the "effigies" were nowhere to be seen at the second meeting. Instead, a large testing apparatus was explained while the scientists who had come to witness the promised flights seethed.

When it became apparent that the "birds would not soar" that day, one scientist leaped to his feet and offered one hundred dollars to any man who could fulfill Lancaster's claims. Another countered with an offer of one thousand dollars for a successful flying model. The situation quickly degenerated into chaos, with President Morse of the AAS attempting unsuccessfully to bring order.[15]

Chanute, who was not present on the second occasion, later

tried to explain Lancaster's failure to fly his "effigies" as advertised. The small room, packed with people, would have made a convincing demonstration impossible, he argued. The absence of the steady breeze in which the small craft had performed most successfully might have led to failure and even more ridicule.

In spite of the disappointment of the Buffalo meeting, Chanute's first attempt to draw the attention of his colleagues to the subject of aeronautics was to have far-reaching consequences for the development of aeronautics in America. For one of those in attendance was Samuel Pierpont Langley, director of the Allegheny Observatory, who left the meeting determined to prove or disprove the possibility of manned flight. Thus, Chanute's activity had already set in motion the first of a series of ripples that would quickly result in the establishment of a major aeronautical research effort.

3

Experiments in Aerodynamics

Samuel Pierpont Langley was fifty-one when the American Association for the Advancement of Science met at Buffalo in 1886. His manner was aloof, even regal, as one might expect of the man whom many would soon come to regard as the unofficial chief scientist of the United States.

Langley was physically imposing, a bulky figure with broad shoulders and a full chest that indicated endurance and determination. A firm jaw was hidden behind a neatly trimmed brown beard and mustache that were rapidly turning to white.

Some time before, a reporter had noted that two "large and protuberant eyes and heavy eyelids" dominated Langley's face. The same observer had remarked on his "queer expression," which seemed to alternate between a "smile of contempt" and "an air of languid sadness."[1]

Of all the men attending the meeting, he must have been regarded as one of the least likely to take a serious interest in the problems of aerial navigation. Yet, during the decade after 1886 Langley was to establish himself as a second focal point of aeronautical research in the United States. Just as his own entry into the field had been triggered by Chanute's activity, so Langley's

Samuel Pierpont Langley (1834–1906).

effort would inspire and attract other talented engineers to the problems of flight.

Langley was born in Roxbury, Massachusetts, on August 22, 1834, the son of a wealthy produce merchant. He attended Boston Latin School and graduated from Boston High School in 1851. Unlike many of his upper-middle-class Boston contemporaries, he chose not to enter Harvard. Instead he moved west to Chicago and St. Louis, where he became a civil engineer and an architectural draftsman for a dozen years.

Little is known of Langley during this period, but we can assume that he was dissatisfied with his situation, for in 1864 he returned to Boston and his first love—astronomy. With the assistance of his brother John, a Harvard-trained chemist, he constructed a 7-inch reflecting telescope in his father's barn before embarking on a tour of European observatories in order to expand his knowledge of contemporary astronomy. Langley returned to Boston in 1865 and immediately accepted a position as assistant under Joseph Winlock at the Harvard Observatory.

The experience of his tour and the academic polish gained at

Harvard prepared him to accept his first fully professional job as assistant professor of mathematics and director of the observatory at the United States Naval Academy. Langley gained invaluable administrative experience at Annapolis, where his primary duties involved the total reorganization of the observatory and staff following the Civil War. In 1866 he moved to the Western University of Pennsylvania in Pittsburgh, where he was named professor of physics and director of the Allegheny Observatory. He remained at Allegheny for twenty years, building a reputation as one of the finest scientific administrators in the nation.[2]

Like a number of other midwestern observatories established during the mid-nineteenth century, Allegheny was the product of local enthusiasm for culture and self-improvement. Founded in 1859, it had floundered for six years under the direction of local amateurs before Langley's arrival as the first salaried professional.

The first task of the new director was to prepare a reasonable budget for the observatory. Realizing immediately that his plans for establishing a major astronomical center in Pittsburgh would require much more than the meager funds which an impoverished western university could provide, Langley developed an ingenious scheme in which he contracted to sell the exact time to railroads. Such a service was to prove invaluable to railroad officials, who wished to provide accurate time for their passengers, and to employees charged with maintaining schedules and ensuring safe operations. Langley determined the time by means of star sights taken at the Allegheny Observatory, then transmitted the results to stations on subscribing railroad lines twice a day. Eventually, the subscription list was expanded to include other businesses and city governments. The income from the time service, supplemented by the generous financial assistance of William Thaw, a local philanthropist, enabled Langley to purchase experimental equipment and launch a substantial program of astronomical research.

Langley was attracted to astrophysics and the study of the sun from the outset of his research career. By the 1870s many, if not most, problems of interest to astronomers required a command of mathematics that Langley did not possess. As he admitted, unlike many of his university-educated colleagues, he could not claim "eminence in mathematics or theoretical astronomy."[3] He was a skilled observer and a talented experimenter, however, and recognized that his strength in these areas could be put to maximum use in solar research, where the acquisition of basic data was still the most important task.

Langley's view of the purpose of science was also an important factor leading to his interest in the sun and, later, in aeronautics. He regarded science as a utilitarian enterprise. Surely an improved understanding of the sun, "the source and sustainer of life," would ultimately benefit mankind.

As early as 1870 he began a series of visual observations of the sun's surface. The publication of the resulting detailed drawings of solar prominance and sun spots brought him early recognition. But his reputation as an experimental astrophysicist was based not on these studies, but on his successful measurements of the heat produced by the sun.

Langley was particularly fascinated by the relationship that bound the sun and its enormous output of energy to conditions in the earth's atmosphere. The bolometer, an instrument he perfected by 1887, was the most accurate device known for measuring heat radiation and opened new avenues to an understanding of the nature of the sun.

This portion of Langley's career was capped when he was awarded the Rumford medals by both the Royal Society and the American Academy of Arts and Sciences in 1886. By 1887, when he was invited to serve as assistant secretary of the Smithsonian Institution under the ailing Spencer Fullerton Baird, Langley was regarded as one of the most eminent astrophysicists in the United States and heir apparent to the most prestigious scientific post in the nation.

But the course of Langley's career had been drastically altered by his attendance at Lancaster's Buffalo lecture. As he later was to recall:

The subject of flight interested me as long ago as I can remember anything; but it was a communication from Mr. Lancaster, read at the Meeting of the American Association for the Advancement of Science in 1886, which aroused my then dormant attention to the subject.[4]

Langley's aroused attention first focused on a preliminary survey of the aeronautical literature. He later remarked that, with the exception of the work of Wenham and Pénaud, "fact had not yet been discriminated from fancy."[5] This introduction to the approaches that had been adopted for the study of flight convinced him that no one had attacked the problem from the point of view of the experimental physicist. "Nature had solved it [flight]," he argued, "and why not man. Perhaps it was because he had begun at the wrong end and attempted to construct machines to fly before knowing the principles on which flight rested."[6]

In aeronautics, as in astrophysics, Langley chose to function as an experimenter, not as a theoretician. Through precise measurements made with cleverly contrived instruments, he would probe the laws of aerodynamics just as he had worked to understand the sun. He was always careful to emphasize that this new line of research was purely scientific. His goal was to study the possibility of heavier-than-air flight, not to conduct the engineering research that would be required to construct a flying machine. His experimental program would not result in an airplane, but would "find the principles on which one should be built."[7]

For 250 years the disciples of Newton had argued that heavier-than-air flight was an impossible dream because the resistance encountered by a flat- or plane-surface wing moving through the air would vary with the square of the sine of the angle of incidence at which the wing met the air. In simple terms, this meant that if the Newtonians were correct, a successful flying machine would require an enormously powerful engine to overcome the resistance of wings large enough to support the craft in flight. The weight of such an engine would require even larger wings, which in turn would require an even more powerful engine to drive them through the air. This spiraling relationship would make it very difficult, if not impossible, to achieve success with a flying machine.

Langley was determined to investigate the validity of this Newtonian hypothesis. He would discover "just how much horse-power was needed to sustain a surface of a given weight by means of its motion through the air."[8]

An understanding of this basic goal explains Langley's use of flat planes in conducting his aerodynamic studies rather than the curved or cambered wing surfaces recommended by Cayley, Wenham, Phillips, and other experienced investigators. These men were engineers intent on discovering the most efficient wing section for a flying machine. Langley had no immediate interest in solving this or any of the other difficult practical problems associated with the development of an airplane. Rather, he sought to provide an experimental test of the theoretical objections to flight. As the sine-square rule had been postulated on the basis of a flat plate, Langley's test of the rule would have to employ plane surfaces as well. As Langley explained: "I have not asserted that planes such as are here employed in experiment . . . are the best forms to use in mechanical flight . . . since this involves questions as to the method of constructing the mechanism, of securing its safe ascent and descent . . . [and of] our ability to guide it in the desired horizontal direction, . . . questions which, in my opinion, are only to be answered by further experiment, and which belong to the inchoate science of *aerodromics*, on which I do not enter."[9]

The board of trustees of the university and observatory could hardly be expected to fund a study so far removed from astronomy. In fact, to spare the institution and himself any possible embarrassment in the event of total failure, Langley consistently referred to his "work in pneumatics" in communications to the trustees as well as in annual reports and in public statements. Every effort was taken to ensure that the real nature of the aerodynamic experiments at the Allegheny Observatory would be withheld from the general public.

With the approval of the board, however, he was free to begin a search for the funds to support the construction of special test equipment and the hiring of extra assistants. William Thaw, a wealthy Pittsburgh philanthropist and long-time supporter of the observatory, agreed to underwrite the effort.

Langley's next step was to devise the apparatus necessary to investigate those areas that he felt would be most fruitful in illustrating the possibility of human flight. The basic item of equipment would be a large whirling arm. This device had been employed by aeronautical investigators since the seventeenth century. Cayley, Wenham, Lilienthal, and others had all turned to the whirling arm as a means of testing the reaction of aerodynamic surfaces in motion through a fluid. As Langley remarked, the sole function of the "whirling table," as he preferred to call it, was to "sweep through the air," with the experimental shapes and appropriate instruments on the end of the arms.[10]

Before proceeding with the construction of such a large and expensive item of equipment, two smaller models were built in order to provide the experience that could be applied in the design of the full-scale machine. The first of these tables was a light-weight version with no internal power supply. John Brashear, a talented local instrument maker, was commissioned to produce a series of models powered by strands of rubber which could be used both as test surfaces and power source for the table. Brashear had long provided the Allegheny Observatory with high quality prisms, defraction gratings, and optical equipment. In later years he became a respected astronomer in his own right. The models constructed for Langley consisted of tubular frames containing plane surfaces. Two propellers powered by rubber-band motors drove the surface and the free swinging arm to which it was attached so slowly that the results obtained were of little value. This early table was destroyed during a wind storm.

The second small whirling table was constructed inside a large darkroom in the observatory building. This machine was turned by an electric motor that not only increased the speed of operation, but allowed the experimenter to vary the rotation at will. Langley and his staff made full use of this machine in the design of the final large table. In addition, they employed it to run preliminary tests of inclined planes.[11]

Design of the great whirling table began in the summer of 1887. A Pittsburgh machine shop was awarded the contract for construction. Langley specified that the two 30-foot arms were to pivot on a vertical shaft driven by underground belting that led to a gasoline engine housed in an observatory building. This original power plant was soon replaced by a more reliable steam threshing engine. A system of pulleys allowed the operator some measure of control over the speed at which the table revolved.

When running at top speed the tips of the arms approached 70 miles per hour. The speed was measured by a series of four electrical contacts over which the arms passed. The horizontal arms were placed 8 feet above the ground to avoid accidents while the table was in motion. A lever was provided to lift the vertical shaft out of the pulley transmission, so that the arms could turn freely. This was necessary when an electric motor was applied to turn model propellers placed on the tips of the arms. These propellers would then be used to turn the whirling table without the application of external power. In this way the efficiency of various "wooden windwheels" could be tested.

An octagonal fence was built completely around the table protecting the tests from some of the effects of gusty winds, and removing the entire area from the eyes of inquisitive observatory visitors.

In order to add to the variety of tests that could be run on the great whirling table, secondary pivots were added at the mid-

Langley's great whirling arm at the Allegheny Observatory.

point of both arms. In effect, then, each arm could serve as a smaller table driven by an extension from the central hub. The finished table was in place by September 1887. Langley was now prepared to begin the experiments designed to demonstrate that much more lift could be derived from a flat plane in motion through the air than had been predicted by the Newtonian formula.

A dynamometer chronograph was employed to record the lift, resistance, "and other phenomena" produced by the attached planes. In addition to the plates, small model aircraft with wings of tin or cork were occasionally run on the table and the results recorded for comparison with those obtained when simpler surfaces were "flown."

Auxilliary items of equipment were devised to extend the utility of the great table. Langley identified the first of these pieces of apparatus as the "suspended plane." It consisted of a flat plate suspended vertically on a spring within a wooden frame which could be attached to the end of the 30-foot arms. The plane was free to swivel at its center, so that when the table was in motion the plate would turn from the vertical position to a natural angle of inclination. It was also free to move up and down on wooden rollers that ran in tracks on either upright. As the speed of the arm increased, the plane would, Langley hoped, be forced toward the top of the frame by air pressure. The various movements of the device were recorded on a strip of paper by an attached stylus. The "suspended plane" was intended to provide a rough notion of the conditions that had to be present to allow the plane to "soar." In addition, it was thought to demonstrate changes in the center of pressure on the plate as the speed of rotation of the table varied.

The "indicator" or "resultant pressure recorder" was a second instrument intended to record the total pressure on a flat surface and to give some indication of the lift engendered at different speeds. In this case a horizontal plane was held in a swivel clamp at the end of the arm. A series of rods ran through gimbal joints and springs to a stylus that traced the pattern of the movements of the plane on a revolving drum.

The term "counterpoised plane" was applied to a device that

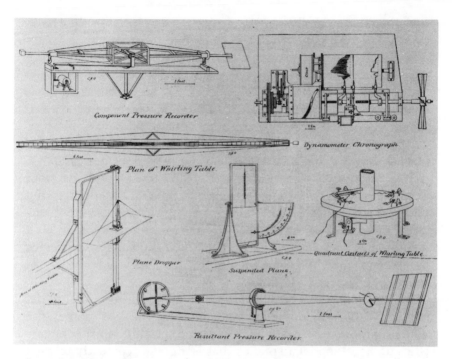

Component Pressure Recorder

Dynamometer Chronograph.

Plan of Whirling Table

Plane Dropper

Suspended Plane.

Quadrant Contacts of Whirling Table

Resultant Pressure Recorder.

Some of the instruments Langley ran on the whirling arm.

resembled the suspended plane. The central feature was a lead weight placed on one edge of the plane that served to prevent gross perturbations when the instrument was run on the arm. Its primary function was to check the changing angle of incidence and center of pressure under varying conditions.

The rolling carriage was a small wheeled cart, 8 1/2 meters long. A spring stop was placed at the back of the carriage, so that the device moved backward only under pressure. A flat plate was attached broadside to a rod at the front of the carriage. When the arm was placed in motion, the pressure forced the cart back against the spring. The motion was recorded on a drum driven by a clockwork mechanism.

The "plane dropper" was introduced to test Lancaster's contention that a plane in horizontal motion could mysteriously support its own weight. The device was a simple upright wooden frame with grooved tracks on the inside edge of each upright. Planes of different width could be placed in the tracks on ebonite rollers so that they were free to move up or down. The time required for each surface to drop from top to bottom was recorded while the frame was at rest. The plate was then lifted back to the top and allowed to fall while the frame was sweeping horizontally through the air. If the time of the fall while in motion was significantly slower than when at rest, Lancaster would be at least partially vindicated. Langley reported that the fall was indeed slower in the second case.

The "component pressure recorder" was used perhaps more frequently than any other item of equipment. It consisted of a plane that could be inclined at any angle, and was used to determine the speed at which the surface could maintain its own weight. The speed at which "soaring" was achieved as the device moved through the air on the end of the arm was recorded on the standard revolving drum.[12]

In addition to the tests conducted with the instruments described, other phenomena were investigated. As noted, the whirling table was employed to test the aerodynamic characteristics of small model airplanes that Langley incorrectly termed aerostats. The dynamometer chronograph was also pressed into service to study the power transmitted by various propeller forms. Langley went so far as to test the flying qualities of stuffed frigate birds and condors acquired from the Smithsonian Institution. He was disappointed to discover that far more power was needed to lift these museum specimens from their supports than their live counterparts required.

Throughout his career, Langley was in the habit of establishing the basic program of experimentation, design, and supervision, then turning the actual work of conducting the investigation over to assistants. Frank W. Very, an assistant at the Allegheny Observatory, was placed in charge of the aerodynamic experiments. Joseph Ludewig, a general mechanic and handyman, assisted Very. Once the work was under way, Very was normally responsible for setting up a run on the whirling table and overseeing the operation of the equipment and instruments. Ludewig ran the engine and the transmission and built many of the test surfaces and items of equipment. Brashear remained on call to construct especially delicate models and to ensure that the instruments were properly calibrated and functioning.[13]

Langley, who had accepted the additional duties of assistant secretary of the Smithsonian Institution in 1887, spent a great deal of his time in Washington. When he was in Pittsburgh, administrative and social responsibilities claimed most of his time and energy. After Baird's death, he moved permanently to Washington, while work on aerodynamics continued under his direction both at the Smithsonian and at the observatory. This does not mean that the staff at Allegheny was given a free hand in conducting the work in aeronautics, however. The director, who consistently applied his personal drive for perfection to his employees, remained in contact with Very by mail and telegraph. Langley demanded frequent reports on the progress of the experiments and freely criticized his assistant's decisions. Very naturally chafed under these conditions. On one occasion, Langley blamed his staff for an accident that resulted in slight damage to the whirling table and the destruction of a propeller test rig. Very answered his employer's accusation in no uncertain terms.

> I am ready to carry on for you any experiments which I can comprehend and which do not overpass the possible, but if they must be made with such flimsy apparatus as that which you have designed for this, and if I am to be held responsible for all, I prefer to be relieved from the necessity of conducting *such* experiments.[14]

Although the problems between the two men were resolved on this occasion, Langley's relation with his staff would remain difficult at best until the end of his career.

The experiments in aerodynamics were conducted between 1887 and 1891. At the conclusion of the tests, Langley was convinced that he had accumulated a sufficient body of data to prove that the reaction of aircraft in a fluid stream was superior to that expected under the sine-square rule. Langley knew that although he had not yet taken the first step toward a practical airplane, he had demonstrated the scientific validity of questing after a flying machine.

Langley presented his research results and conclusions in *Experiments in Aerodynamics*, published in 1891. His most important observation was a simple affirmative statement:

> The most important general inference from these experiments, as a whole, is that so far as the mere power to sustain heavy bodies in the air by mechanical flight goes, *such mechanical flight is possible with engines we now possess.*[15]

In addition to accomplishing his primary objective, the demonstration of a favorable ratio between power and lift, Langley believed he had uncovered an unexpected phenomenon that would make the realization of the final goal less difficult. "Actual experiment shows, I repeat, that the faster the speed, the less the force required to sustain the planes."[16]

In essence, Langley argued that the faster a surface moved through the air, the lower were the power requirements necessary to maintain it at that speed. The "Langley Law," as this relationship between power and speed came to be known, was accepted by those who did not bother to retrace the experimental steps or the mathematics involved in its formulation. Those who did give the matter serious consideration realized that the "Langley Law" was very misleading. Otto Lilienthal, the Wright brothers, and others who conducted studies similar to Langley's rejected the secretary's findings in this regard.

Following Langley's death in 1906, the Smithsonian Institution planned to honor him with a special plaque emphasizing the "Langley Law" as one of his major achievements. Wilbur Wright, upon learning of the content of the proposed text, sent a quiet letter to Charles D. Walcott, the new secretary, suggesting that such action could only reflect negatively on Langley's reputation in aeronautics. The elder Wright argued that Langley's early work contained some "unfortunate lapses from scientific accuracy." He considered it "both unwise and unfair to him [Langley] to specially rest his reputation in aerodynamics upon the so-called Langley Law, or upon the computations that gave rise to it, as they do not seem to represent his best work."[17]

In general, the professional reaction to *Experiments in Aerodynamics* was guarded. Lord Rayleigh, for example, who reviewed the volume for *Nature,* was willing to accept the American's experimental evidence, but he pointed out that man was really no closer to flight as a result of Langley's efforts. The English scientist, however, recognized that "sufficient maintaining power is not the only requisite, and it is probable that difficulties connected with stability and with safe alighting at the termination of the adventure will exercise to the utmost the skill of our inventors."[18]

But even the most knowledgeable reviewers could hardly be expected to treat the book critically. No one had run a series of experiments as extensive as Langley's. There was simply no basis for comparison. The secretary was widely regarded as a careful researcher, and there was an inclination on the part of men like Rayleigh to offer the American the benefit of the doubt.

The prevailing opinion was clearly evident at the meeting of the British Association for the Advancement of Science at Oxford in August 1894. On this occasion a joint meeting of the physics and mechanics sections was held to consider the problems of flight. Hiram Maxim served as chairman for the session. Samuel Langley and Cyrus Adler, the Smithsonian librarian, who were touring Europe at the time, attended. Langley was invited to present a short paper summarizing his thoughts on aerodynamics. Following his presentation, Lord Kelvin rose and demonstrated Langley's errors in computation on the blackboard. Lord Rayleigh then commented that while he recognized the validity of Kelvin's arguments, the case was far from closed. After all, he remarked, Langley had performed the investigations, and "if he . . . succeeded in doing it [flying] he would be [proven] right."[19] In essence, the possibility that the experiments at the Allegheny Observatory did represent an accurate assessment of the physics of flight overshadowed the logical and mathematical inadequacies of the volume.

By the turn of the century a sufficient body of aerodynamic evidence had been accumulated to demonstrate that Langley's most basic findings were in error. In retrospect, precise readings were impossible to extract from a device like the whirling table. The combined effect of vibration, centrifugal force, belt slippage, and wind gusts invalidated the data. Still, the work did serve a very useful purpose. The fact that a man of Langley's stature believed in the possibility of the flying machine was enough to convince most laymen that aeronautics was no longer the pastime of fools.

Langley felt that he had little to lose by continuing his aeronautical work beyond the initial scientific phase into a genuine engineering effort aimed at the development of an airplane. Having announced the results of his preliminary tests, he was already on record as a believer in the possibility of flight. A practical demonstration with a flying model could only, as Rayleigh suggested, serve as proof of the accuracy of Langley's data. Just as important, Langley now felt confident that he could provide such a demonstration.

Prior to beginning work in aerodromics, the engineering portion of the effort, Langley undertook a study of the internal currents and eddies that compose the wind. His work evidences his continuing interest in Lancaster's findings. He realized that the gravitational force Lancaster used to explain the extraordinary flights of his "effigies" was out of the question. Langley felt that it was more likely that the phenomenon of soaring was the result of the "internal work of the wind."

His investigations of forces, currents, and other irregularities in the wind began as early as 1887 and were conducted at the same time as those with the whirling table. Anemometers, light planes, and other measuring devices were raised on high poles, first at the Allegheny Observatory and later at the Smithsonian, in order to determine whether or not updrafts were sufficiently strong and frequent to sustain a flying machine. The results of the experiments were reported in a paper read to the National Academy of Sciences in 1888. It was later published in the *American Journal of Science,* and finally appeared as a separate volume, *The Internal Work of the Wind,* in 1893.

As a result of his studies, Langley's enthusiasm for flight grew. He foresaw a day when very large passenger-carrying airliners would ply the skies of the world, soaring almost constantly. He argued that such a machine would be able to fly around the world, using the engine only during rare moments of calm. It is noteworthy, however, that he abandoned this belief very quickly once he began his experiments with large powered flying models.

The experiments in aerodynamics and the wind studies were preliminaries that had little effect on Langley's conception of the successful flying machine. His first real efforts in pursuit of a practical airplane design were made as early as April 1887, when he ordered the construction of the first of a series of small flying models powered by twisted rubber strands. In deciding to proceed in this fashion, Langley was heavily influenced by the example of Alphonse Pénaud, who had reported some success with such models. The secretary clearly hoped to build on the Frenchman's experience.

This work was carried on while the aerodynamic and wind experiments were being conducted. During the early years at the Allegheny Observatory, Brashear and Ludewig prepared the models, with Very providing the experimental data on the power derived from various types and weights of rubber. After the move to the Smithsonian, C. B. Nichols, a carpenter in the museum shops, was placed in charge of construction.[20]

A total of thirty to forty craft were built during this three- to four-year period. So many major design modifications were made in these original craft, however, that the total number of basically different models probably approached 100. One of the earliest of these "aerostats" was typical of the entire series. The fuselage was constructed of two pieces of wood, each 1 meter long. A bundle of rubber weighing 300 grams powered two four-bladed propellers 30 centimeters in diameter. The two superposed wings were built of light pine covered with paper. The total lifting surface was to be 3,600 square centimeters. When complete, the model weighed 1 kilogram. This craft "soared" or lifted its own weight on the whirling table at a speed of 10 miles per hour, but in actual flight, "its propellers were utterly insufficient to sustain it."[21]

Serious efforts to lighten the structure included the replacement of the wooden fuselage members by hollow metal or shel-

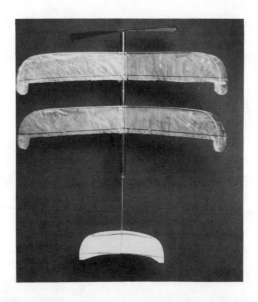

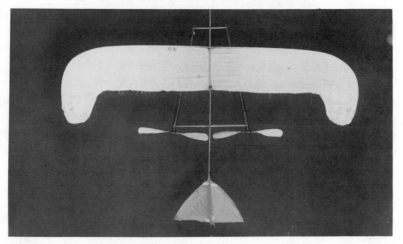

Two of Langley's rubber-powered aerodrome models.

lacked paper tubes. Langley later remarked on the great variety of forms tested.

> . . . nearly 40 were constructed, some with two propellers, some with one; some with one propeller in front and one behind; some

with plane, some with curved wings; some with single, some with superposed wings; some with two pairs of wings, one preceding, and one following; some with the Pénaud tail, some with other forms.[22]

Every combination of wing, fuselage, propeller, and tail surface was tried. Not until March 28, 1891, however, was the first model light enough to actually fly. The longest flight obtained with any of the late models lasted from six to eight seconds and covered 80 to 100 feet. The secretary was particularly disappointed to discover that he could not even approach the 13.5-second average flying time claimed by Pénaud. He discovered that only when the wing area approached 4 square feet could he hope for flights of even limited duration. This proportion of lifting surface to weight was, as he noted, far greater than that enjoyed by birds.

Langley concluded that little would be gained by continuing the experiments with rubber-powered models. These flights had been "so erratic, and so short, that it was possible to learn very little from them."[23]

He concluded that the problem lay not in the models themselves, but in the inadequacy of the rubber-band motors. Other power plants were investigated, including carbonic-acid gas engines, but all were rejected as either unreliable or too heavy. A light steam engine seemed the only alternative.

By late 1891, Langley had decided that if he was to continue work toward a flying machine, the size and complexity of his models would have to be increased and a suitable light steam engine acquired and placed in the craft. This was one of the two major turning points of the secretary's aeronautical career. He was now treading new ground. In his earlier studies he had attacked questions raised by other investigators and had proceeded within a frame of reference familiar to both physicists and engineers. The step from these preliminary experiments to the construction of a very large and expensive steam-powered "aerodrome" was a difficult one to take. Langley was fully aware of the fact that he had little experimental evidence suggesting that such a craft could be flown. He was a nonengineer facing a technical problem that many experts considered insoluble.

The primary consideration, however, was the apparent finality of such a step. Langley was a public figure, administering a quasi-governmental agency at least partially supported by public funds. The reputation for good judgment, fiscal responsibility, and sound scientific preparation that had fitted him for this position of trust could now be called into question. It must have been obvious to Langley that once he had announced his decision to build and fly a large model, he had to succeed. Anything less than an unquestionable flight of some length would be regarded as a failure, in which case the secretary would almost certainly be discredited. Samuel Langley was sure that he stood on firm ground. His decision would culminate in disaster in the cold waters of the Potomac twelve years later.

4

Chanute and *Progress in Flying Machines*

If America's first serious program of aeronautical research—Langley's—rose from the ashes of Israel Lancaster's dismal performance at Buffalo in 1886, so also was the gathering a turning point for Octave Chanute. Disappointed, discouraged, even frightened by the negative reaction to Lancaster's presentation, he was torn between his own growing enthusiasm for flight and a fear that, if widely known, his interest might expose him to ridicule.

This indecision was apparent during a visit to the home of friends in Kansas City in 1891. The after-dinner conversation had turned to hobbies, and Chanute was asked how he spent his leisure time. "Wait until your children are not present," he replied, "for they would laugh at me."[1]

Chanute was finally able to resolve this dilemma as a result of an offer from his old friend Matthias Nace Forney, an engineer and technical journalist with whom he had become involved during the work on the New York City rapid transit system. In 1886, when Forney merged the *American Railroad Journal* and *Van Nostrand's Engineering Magazine,* he asked Chanute's assistance in gathering fresh material of interest to readers.

Chanute extended his best wishes for "all possible success" and replied that he would be willing to prepare a piece on either wood preservation or air resistance in locomotive design. Forney, who was aware both of Chanute's interest in aerodynamics and his fear that a premature declaration of enthusiasm might damage his professional reputation, urged him instead to prepare a series of articles tracing the historical development of the flying machine and informing readers of the current state of knowledge in the area. He argued that such a series, carefully researched and presented in terms that would appeal to engineers, could only do the author credit.

Chanute was cautious, but he found the excuse to expand his investigation of aeronautics and to present his findings in detail from such an ideal platform too attractive to dismiss.

> "Why have you put such temptation in my way," he remarked, "by proposing such an excellent subject for a book, and such a good plan? I thought that I was through with literrary [sic] work, and I meant to devote my time to putting my affairs in shape for my declining years . . . but here you have to come and propose a piece of work I should like very much to do."[2]

Following a meeting with Forney in New York, the Chicagoan agreed to begin work on the articles, with the understanding that the series might not be ready for several years.

Chanute attacked the task of researching the articles with his usual energy. The circle of aeronautical acquaintances that he had been building since 1875 expanded rapidly as his clipping service kept him informed on current aeronautical activity around the world. In this manner he discovered and contacted scientists, engineers, technical educators, journalists, and experimenters interested in the possibility of the flying machine. Within a short period of time he began a program of letter writing and information gathering that quickly bore fruit. Chanute rapidly gained a reputation as a clearinghouse for information within the community of aeronautical investigators. Isolated enthusiasts came to rely on a letter from Chanute to bring them up to date on activities in other parts of the world.

Chanute's entry onto the international aeronautical scene came at a propitious moment. A decade earlier, few efforts had been made to translate the growing number of impressive engineering studies of the aeronautical problem into working machines. By the early 1890s, this was to change as a number of European technologists began actively experimenting with full-scale or model aircraft.

Three basic practical approaches to the development of the airplane had emerged from this effort. Some experimenters chose to forge ahead and construct full-scale machines with few intermediate steps. Confident that all aerodynamic problems could be solved on paper, they concentrated their attention on the development of a suitable aeronautical power plant.

Hiram Maxim was the best known of these figures. An expatriate American living in England, Maxim developed an enormous engine test bed designed to operate on an 1,800-foot runway. Trials of the craft in 1892 and 1893 were marred by accidents and breakage, culminating in the end of the tests when the craft, which was held in place by an upper rail, rose slightly and crashed.[3]

Clément Ader, French pioneer of the telephone, also constructed a full-scale machine with little previous model or glider testing. His *Éole* of 1890 made a short, uncontrolled, powered hop. His second craft, *Avion II,* was never completed, and his *Avion III* of 1897 refused to leave the ground. In both cases the problem of control had been given little serious attention. This approach to the problem of flight was naïve, and while Maxim and Ader aroused interest and generated publicity, they contributed little to the progress of flight technology.

A second experimental tradition that evolved during the latter half of the nineteenth century called for the use of model aircraft to investigate flight problems. Surely, these men reasoned, if an efficient powered model could be flown, then the creation of a man-carrying craft would involve nothing more than "scaling up" the original. Models seemed ideal. Being small, they would be reasonably inexpensive, could be flown repeatedly, and did not risk a pilot's life.

Sir George Cayley had first pointed to the utility of the model

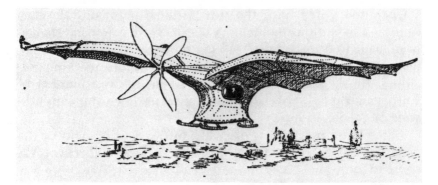

Clément Ader's Éole.

with his glider of 1804. Between 1850 and 1875 a number of enthusiasts, including Félix du Temple, Gustave Trouvé, Victor
Tatin, and Thomas Moy, who would become Chanute's European patent agent, succeeded in producing at least tentative
flights with models powered by clockwork mechanisms, compressed air, and steam engines.

The most influential model maker of the period, however, was
Alphonse Pénaud, a French marine engineer who introduced
the use of twisted rubber strands as a model power plant. Pénaud, who was active during the decade of the 1870s, was also the
first to construct a model embodying a useful degree of inherent
stability, an absolute necessity for any pilotless aircraft. S. P.
Langley's early work with rubber-powered models was heavily
influenced by Pénaud.

Lawrence Hargrave, the Australian pioneer, while not basically a modeler, was a member of this group. Hargrave, who
built and flew several interesting models, is perhaps best known
as the inventor of the box kite. Like Pénaud, he was interested
in problems of automatic stability.

But Chanute believed that the full-scale manned glider provided the most promising approach to the flying machine problem. Cayley and Wenham had pioneered in this field. Wenham's
high-aspect-ratio multiplane of 1858–1859 in which the pilot lay
prone was, technically, one of the most influential designs of the
entire pre-Wright epoch. The South African John Household,

the French-Egyptian experimenter Louis Mouillard, and the American John Joseph Montgomery also built and flew hang gliders before 1890. After 1891 the spectacular glides achieved by the German Otto Lilienthal would electrify the aeronautical world.

These early pioneers had forged bold new paths toward flight, but none had been able to carry his work to its logical conclusion. While models were flown, no experimenter attempted to scale up his craft to man-carrying dimensions, nor were any of the glider builders successful in adding power plants to their machines. Men had taken tentatively to the air, but an obvious plateau had been reached far short of complete success.

Geographic isolation, a lack of close immediate communication, and personal rivalry and jealousy were the principal retarding factors. James Means, American aeronautical enthusiast and publisher of the influential *Aeronautical Annual,* commented on this situation:

> Maxim speaks of Lilienthal as a parachutist, and likens him to a flying squirrel. . . . Lilienthal, after alluding to the unwieldiness of Maxim's machine, says, "After all, the result of his labors has been to show us how not to do it." If any two men should be friends rather than foes, these are the two. Each has certain ideas and publications which the other lacks and it is the greatest of pities that they cannot clasp hands over the watery channel.[4]

To an extent, Chanute's ongoing correspondence with many of these European pioneers was to correct the sense of isolation that had retarded progress in aeronautics. He recorded and analyzed the efforts of every flying-machine experimenter he could uncover. Because he was one of the few men interested in collecting information rather than conducting experiments, Chanute became the world's leading authority on the flying-machine problem in a remarkably short period of time.

This process was not one-sided, however, since Chanute was drawn into active work with many of his European correspondents. In a number of cases he provided not only information and

Louis Mouillard (1834–1897).

moral support, but technical advice and, on occasion, financial
assistance. His relationship with Louis Mouillard was typical.

Mouillard, born in Lyons in 1835, had abandoned a promising
career in art to immigrate to Algeria, where he became a farmer
until forced to flee because of political problems in 1865. He then
settled in Cairo, where he taught art in a government military
academy until 1871, when all Frenchmen were dismissed from
the public employ. Subsequently he worked in a variety of mer-
cantile positions, eventually entering into a partnership with a
woman operating a small herb and drug shop. During the closing years of his life he was able to supplement this meager
income performing clerical work for the Egyptian government.

Like so many enthusiasts of the period, Mouillard's interest
in flight was initially aroused by observing the birds. In fact,
many of his most important publications concentrated on this

subject rather than his work with gliding machines. As might be expected, his airplane designs were governed by this preoccupation.

Mouillard's training in art had not prepared him for work in the sciences or technology. He once remarked candidily to Chanute, "I must confess that I have the deplorable habit of paying little attention to writing pertaining to pure mathematics, because of the difficulty I have in understanding them."[5]

In the late 1850s, while still residing in Algeria, Mouillard had constructed three gliders. The third, a tailless monoplane made of curved agave sticks screwed to muslin-covered boards, is the most interesting of these machines. The pilot stood in a hole between the wings, which were then strapped to his shoulders. Straps were provided for his legs and arms which were free to control the dihedral of the hinged wings. In this hang glider, the pilot shifted his weight to change the center of gravity and control the machine.

Mouillard carried his 33-pound craft to an isolated road early one morning in order to avoid ridicule.

> I strolled onto the prairie with my apparatus up on my shoulders. I ran against the air and studied its sustaining power, for it was almost a dead calm: The wind had not yet arisen, and I was waiting for it.
>
> Nearby there was a wagon road, raised some 5 feet above the plain. It had thus been raised with the soil from the ditches about 10 feet wide dug on either side.
>
> Then came a little puff of wind, and it also came into my head to jump over that ditch. I used to leap across easily without my aeroplane but I thought that I might try it armed with my aeroplane; so I took a good run across the road, and jumped at the

A simple sketch of the glider flown by Louis Mouillard in the 1850s.

ditch as usual. But, oh horrors! once across the ditch my feet did not come down to earth; I was gliding on the air and making vain efforts to land, for my aeroplane had set out on a cruise. I dangled only one foot above the soil, but do what I would, I could not reach it, and I was skimming along without the power to stop. At last my feet touched the earth. I fell forward on my hands, broke one of the wings, and all was over; but goodness! how frightened I had been![6]

Mouillard had flown 138 feet over the ground at 11 to 14 miles per hour. He commented that while he had been "too much alarmed" to appreciate the experience, he would never forget "the strange sensation produced by this gliding."

A later glide in the same machine came even closer to disaster.

I had no confidence, as I have already stated, in the strength of my aeroplane. A violent wind gust came; it picked me up; I became alarmed, did not resist, and allowed myself to be upset. I had one shoulder sprained by the pressure of the wings, which folded up against each other like those of a butterfly when at rest.[7]

The experimenter had hoped to continue his studies, but poverty and the move to Cairo in 1865, where his new quarters and urban life style severely limited his work area, forced him to abandon his work for a quarter of a century.

Chanute first wrote to Mouillard in 1891 in an effort to collect information for his articles and speeches. Mouillard was delighted to learn that he was still recognized as an authority in the field and began a remarkable correspondence with Chanute that was to continue until the Frenchman's death in September 1897.

Their early letters were very general, covering Mouillard's past work and his hopes for the future. They discussed the uses to which a perfected machine might be put. Mouillard remarked: "I would not like to play the clown or be a smuggler; in short, I would not do anything improper. I certainly would like wealth, but honestly obtained, money of which one can be proud." He continued to list areas of potential utility, including hunting for precious metals in remote areas, hunting for whales, and flying to the North Pole.[8] Chanute, always the realist, replied, "In answer to your question about the lucrative uses of your machine, if it succeeds, it always seemed to me that profit would consist in selling the machine either to the Government (especially in Europe, where war is imminent) or to the fans who want novelty."[9]

Mouillard believed that secrecy had been the major stumbling block in the path of success. "The greatest danger to aviation," he opined, "is the spirit of mystery in which those who take up the study of aeronautics generally cloak themselves." Chanute argued for the necessity of protecting the inventor's own interests by maintaining silence until his ideas were patented. In January 1892 Chanute, with his usual generosity, sent Mouillard money to cover the cost of patenting his aircraft in France and America. The United States Patent Office, however, rejected the application on the grounds that "as a whole it is not practical since the machine cannot rise without a balloon. In other words the project is not useful according to the meaning of the law. No evidence will be considered sufficient to demonstrate the efficiency of the project and to cause the patent office to rescind its objection, unless it is a model in full operation which would be capable to make an ascent and to be controlled."[10] Chanute was, however, able to bring his considerable influence to bear, and the patent was eventually granted.

Chanute continued to seek a solution to Mouillard's basic financial problem. As early as 1891 he offered to pay Mouillard's expenses for a trip to the United States to assist in developing a lubricating process suggested by the Frenchman, but these plans had to be abandoned because of Chanute's growing concern that Mouillard might be stranded in this country with no job should the business arrangement prove unsuccessful. During the fall of 1892 Mouillard was drawn deeper into the life of the American aeronautical community when, through Chanute's good offices, he received 300 francs for an article in *Cosmopolitan* and 150 francs for a summary of his book, *L'Empire de l'Air*, which appeared in the *Annual Report of the Smithsonian Institution*.

Intrigued by Mouillard's drawings and description of a proposed new aircraft, Chanute inquired as to how much such a machine would cost if constructed in Cairo. Mouillard replied that he believed 2,500 francs would suffice.

Before offering to pay such expenses himself, Chanute attempted unsuccessfully to interest James Scott, the owner and editor of the *Chicago Herald*, in supporting Mouillard. When this failed, Chanute himself agreed to provide 2,500 francs with which Mouillard could build the glider.[11]

Mouillard promptly reported that he had found a secluded nunnery in the desert where he could build and test the glider in secret. True to form, he began to send letters to Chanute containing the most impractical suggestions for improving the original machine. As usual, the American served as the best of sounding boards and a stabilizing influence. To Mouillard's suggestion that rockets be added to the finished glider, Chanute responded, "I told you not to depend on rockets for they do not always push straight." When Mouillard expressed a preference for aluminum in the construction of the machine, Chanute answered, "I tell you frankly, that for an experimental airplane which is certain to be remodeled time and again, I would use bamboo which you should find excellent."[12]

A year later, in May 1895, Mouillard reported that he was still working on the glider. In July of that year Chanute sent a second 2,500 francs. Finally, in December 1895, Mouillard sent a photo of the completed craft to his Chicago friend. Chanute was obviously disappointed and replied that "I . . . can at last judge your airplane by myself. I think that you made it too big and heavy, and that you copied the bird too closely."[13] The craft was tested without success in January 1896.

The most important feature of the machine was a set of hinged planes, or "annularies," sections of the trailing edge of each wing that could be independently lowered by the pilot. Mouillard was convinced that these, when properly utilized, would prove the key to success. He commented to Chanute that "I must greatly increase their importance. This device is indispensable. It was their absence which prevented Lilienthal from going farther, it is this which permits going to left and right."[14]

Mouillard's U.S. patent clearly indicates that these devices were intended to serve as "steering air brakes." He argued that

The Mouillard glider financed by Chanute.

by dropping the hinged "annulary" on either wing, the increased air resistance would force the nose of the craft into a yawing turn in that direction. By dropping both surfaces simultaneously, he hoped to reduce the forward speed of the machine.

In later years Chanute would argue that these "steering air brakes" were protoailerons and could have been used to control the craft in the roll axis, to maintain lateral balance, or to bank for turns. The "annularies" did bear some resemblance to the simple "down only" ailerons of the sort used on the classic Farman III airplane of 1909, but the similarity is apparent only with hindsight. In 1897 neither Mouillard nor Chanute had the slightest notion that control in roll would even be necessary in a flying machine. They hoped to achieve nothing more than flat skidding turns in one plane by varying the air resistance of either wing.

In fact, that is exactly what would have occurred, with disastrous results. As the speed of one wing was reduced, the airflow would obviously be reduced as well. This wing would drop, while the unaffected wing rose and pivoted, forcing the craft into a spin with no means of recovery available.

Chanute's association with Mouillard was unique only in de-

gree. He was to become less heavily involved in the efforts of
many of the best-known European aeronautical workers.

Following the crash of Hiram Maxim's gargantuan engine
test bed near London in 1894, Chanute attempted unsuccessfully
to create a financial syndicate that would enable Maxim to relo-
cate and begin work on a new craft in Chicago. He offered
advice to Otto Lilienthal on the market potential for sport gliders in the United States and, with James Means of Boston, spear-
headed an unsuccessful movement to attract the German experimenter to America for a season of exhibition gliding. He assisted
Lilienthal, Mouillard, and others in obtaining U.S. patents.
Maxim, Mouillard, Lilienthal, and Lawrence Hargrave were all
repeatedly indebted to Chanute for his assistance in placing
their work with American publishers and for arranging to have
their papers read at technical meetings.[15]

In some cases, notably that of the Englishman Percy S.
Pilcher, Lilienthal's leading European disciple, Chanute exer-
cised a major technical influence. Pilcher's most advanced ma-

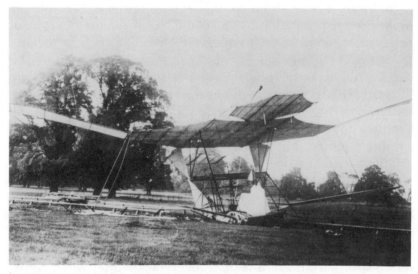

The elephantine Maxim aircraft.

chine, a powered triplane hang glider, grew directly from Chanute's work.[16]

With the passage of time, other Americans drawn into the aeronautical community were to follow Chanute's example by building close contacts with old-world experimenters. Lawrence Hargrave is typical of the isolated figures for whom such contact had real psychological value. Throughout his career, isolation was the Australian's principal problem. Sydney was far from being a hotbed of aeronautical enthusiasm. In fact, Hargrave seems to have been subject to more local criticism than his brethren in other nations, where, in large measure, experiments with flying machines were becoming accepted as a matter of course. He once commented: "The people in Sydney who can speak of my work without a smile are very scarce."[17] A trip to England and continued contact with Europeans indicates that he attempted to ally himself with the greater aeronautical community, but he was to discover that Americans exhibited more interest in his contributions. Hargrave spoke appreciatively of this fact in a letter to A. F. Zahm, an important American experimenter and an associate of Chanute: "I feel stirred with enthusiasm and thankfulness . . . that my work has been grasped and appreciated by Americans."[18]

Hargrave numbered the most prominent American aeronautical figures among his correspondents. In Langley, for example, he found a man who was eager to discuss developing engine technology. Hargrave also recognized that American aviation competitions were an important factor in publicizing individual efforts. He sent a series of his box kites to take part in a contest planned by the Boston Aeronautical Society in 1895 and was disappointed when this event was canceled for want of other participants. And when he decided to place his most valued models and kites in a museum for permanent preservation, he chose an institution in America.

Chanute's contact with these European experimenters gave him the confidence necessary to make his first public statements on aeronautics. During a European tour in 1889 he met with Continental aviation enthusiasts, who persuaded him to attend a Paris conference on aeronautics and present a paper on the

Lawrence Hargrave (1850–1915).

physical basis of aerodynamics. His remarks so impressed the group that Chanute recognized, perhaps for the first time, his own position of leadership in the field. He had expressed his belief in the possibility of flight before a distinguished audience and had not only escaped ridicule, but had been congratulated on his performance.

Chanute returned from Paris convinced that the time had come for a serious attempt to interest his countrymen in the problems of flight. The Toronto meeting of the American Association for the Advancement of Science in 1889 offered Chanute an opportunity to explain his views on manned flight as an engineering problem to a gathering of eminent American scientists and technicians. His attitude before the Toronto meeting was very different from that at Buffalo three years earlier. Those attending could have no doubt that Chanute's closely reasoned, mathematically based arguments for the possibility of flight indicated that he was now a sincere believer in the future of the flying machine.

The reaction of those present was quite unlike that which had greeted Lancaster's paper in 1886. The depth of the presentation and Chanute's reputation as an authority on the problems of engineering analysis that were so closely related to the questions under discussion ensured that his remarks would be well received. While Chanute's paper was printed only as an abstract in the proceedings of the Toronto meeting, the demand for the full text was so great that he was able to keep several manuscript copies in circulation among colleagues for many months.

A third speech, this time before Robert H. Thurston's students at Cornell University's Sibley College of Engineering was to cement the Chicagoan's position as a professional spokesman for aeronautical enthusiasts. Thurston, who served as Chanute's vice-chairman for the Buffalo meeting, had established a policy of inviting practicing engineers to speak to the Sibley students on current problems of professional interest. He issued such an invitation to Chanute early in 1889. The Chicagoan was anxious to deliver an address on of aeronautics, but prior to the Paris conference was unwilling to broach the possibility to Thurston in spite of their previous association. He felt that the educator might think the topic unfit for presentation before such an inexperienced and impressionable audience, particularly after their shared disaster of 1886.

Chanute's response to the invitation, therefore, was a guarded attempt to discover the strength of Thurston's belief in the flying machine. He wrote, "I trust that you will not think me a lunatic if I say that I have had in mind for years to devote part of my leisure to the opening up of an inquiry as to whether man can ever hope to fly through the air!!!"[19] As he hoped, Thurston had retained his own enthusiasm for the subject, and was most willing to expose his students to Chanute's thoughts on aeronautics. When finally presented in 1890, the talk on "aerial navigation" was well received by students and faculty alike. Unlike his earlier speeches, the Sibley talk was published both in technical periodicals and in pamphlet form.[20]

One of the most important results of Chanute's emergence as

a believer in flight was the fact that other engineers who held similar views were also encouraged to come forward. Forney; A. M. Wellington, an engineering journalist; C. H. Hastings, a well-known midwestern engineer; and Thurston publicly stated their agreement with the Chicagoan. Thurston's espousal of the cause was to be particularly influential, for two of the major members of the developing American aeronautical community, A. F. Zahm and Charles Matthews Manly, were both students at Sibley during this period.

Chanute's success in Paris, Toronto, and Ithaca had relieved his inhibitions about discussing the possibility of flight. After 1890, he began to describe the potential of the flying machine to the readers of both technical journals and popular periodicals. The articles that he produced on this subject were to make his name synonymous with aeronautics within the tiny group of experimenters whose respect and admiration he had already earned and in the mind of the general public as well.

Most influential were the articles published in Forney's *Railroad and Engineering Journal:* "Progress in Flying Machines." The series appeared in twenty-seven installments beginning in October 1891, and were reprinted as a single volume by Forney in 1894.

Chanute never doubted his purpose in writing the articles. In a letter requesting information from Wenham, he remarked, "My general idea is to pass in review what has hitherto been experimented, with a view to accounting for the failures, clearing away the rubbish, and pointing out some of the elements of success, if I can."[21] In essence, *Progress in Flying Machines* was intended not only to survey the history of aeronautics in detail but to indicate those avenues that would prove most fruitful and those areas in which further efforts would be wasted. Chanute also took the opportunity to present a lengthy discussion of the theoretical base from which he believed the flying machine would develop. Eighty years after the original publication, *Progress in Flying Machines* remains one of the most comprehensive and reliable histories of pre-Wright aeronautics available.

The appeal of Chanute's articles was immediately apparent. His already voluminous correspondence increased. From the growing stack of letters that passed across his desk, the Chica-

goan began to select for special encouragement those correspondents whom he felt could contribute the most to the solution of the flying-machine problem. The increase in subscriptions to the *Railroad and Engineering Journal* was another
indication of the popularity of Chanute's articles. Pleased with
his success, the author remarked to Forney, "I am, at last, one
of those literary fellers who can earn his bread with his pen."[22]
Forney responded that the increased circulation had convinced
him that there was a market for a journal devoted strictly to
developments in aviation. Chanute was eager to assist in such a
venture and offered to make a lengthy list of potential subscribers available. In addition, he agreed to allow Forney to publish
the reports to be offered at the upcoming International Conference on Aerial Navigation in the new paper in order to alleviate
the difficulty of finding materials for the initial issues.

The new journal, *Aeronautics,* launched in 1893, was the first
American periodical devoted to this subject. *Aeronautics* was not
the success Forney had envisioned, however. In 1894, when the
losses on *Aeronautics* grew too large, Forney simply stopped
publication. An aeronautical department was reinstituted in the
American Railroad and Engineering Journal. Although he was
disappointed in the failure of the full publication, Chanute remarked that the new section was still of greater value than
European aeronautical journals.

Octave Chanute could look on the decade following Lancaster's Buffalo speech with some satisfaction. His initial goals had
been accomplished.

As a result of his effort, S. P. Langley had launched the first
serious U.S. effort to understand the physics of flight. More
important, a growing number of practical, experienced American technologists were at last joining their European colleagues
in taking a real interest in the flying machine.

At the outset of this period aeronautics in the United States
had been the province of cranks and dreamers. Now, after ten
years of effort on Chanute's part, the stage was set for Americans to capture world leadership in the flying-machine movement.

5

A Meeting in Chicago

For most of the student engineers in the audience, Octave Chanute's Cornell lecture must have seemed venturesome indeed. Not so for Albert Francis Zahm, a twenty-eight-year-old Sibley College graduate student who was disappointed by what he regarded as Chanute's basic conservatism. "Mr. Chanute began his remarks with a hesitancy amounting almost to reluctance," Zahm would later recall, "seeming to entreat the young men not to believe that the study of such a subject [as aeronautics] was a more than probable indication of failing mental vigor."[1] Al Zahm's patronizing attitude was born of an enthusiasm for the bright dream of flight that left little room for the older man's caution.

Zahm was born in New Lexington, Perry County, Ohio, on June 5, 1862, the eighth of fourteen children. He received his A.B. from Notre Dame in 1883 and remained there to work on an M.S. in physics. His growing interest in applied science then led him to enroll at Cornell's Sibley College, where he pursued a second master's in engineering under Robert Thurston. Zahm completed his education at the Johns Hopkins University, winning the Ph.D. in physics in 1898.[2]

Zahm first became interested in aeronautics after entering Notre Dame in 1878. While still an undergraduate, he built a series of model airplanes and several full-scale machines. He suspended one of the latter from the ceiling of the college museum on a 50-foot rope. The tethered craft was powered by bicycle pedals that drove a tractor propeller. Zahm or one of several other volunteers would climb aboard and operate the craft to test the efficiency of the propulsion system, the amount of lift provided by the wings, and the action of the control system. A second machine dating from this early period was a hang glider about which little is known. Many years later Zahm was able to recall few details.

> It was a rectangular sail with strong parallel bars joining the front and rear spars. To the rear extensions of these bars various types of tail could be attached for trail. The operator, with bars under his armpits, would run forward, leap from a long bench and glide to the ground.[3]

He abandoned these experiments upon entering graduate school, devoting the rest of his career to the scientific investigation of aerodynamics. In view of his superior methodology and the extent to which his studies, particularly in the area of skin friction, proved useful, Zahm deserves to be regarded as America's first well-trained aeronautical engineer. Between 1894 and 1905 he was to serve as a constant source of scientific information on aerodynamics.

Zahm's first encounter with Chanute on the occasion of the Sibley College speech in 1890 led to a correspondence between the two men that began in the spring of 1891, when the young experimenter wrote Chanute to bring him up to date on his own work in the field. By December of that year a steady stream of letters was passing back and forth.

Chanute seemed very pleased to have discovered someone with whom he could discourse at length on the physical and mathematical underpinnings of flight. The two men were particularly interested in discovering ways in which a sense of unity could be instilled among aeronautical experimenters. In

May 1892, Zahm suggested the possibility of calling a meeting of engineers and scientists interested in a serious discussion of the problems of flight. The upcoming World's Columbian Exposition seemed to offer the ideal forum.

Since the triumphant opening of London's Crystal Palace in 1851, the nineteenth century had been punctuated by a series of great international fairs. Vienna, New York, Philadelphia, Paris, each in turn had mounted a stunning exposition of the scientific, mechanical, and artistic wonders of the age. In honor of the four-hundredth anniversary of the discovery of America, Chicago planned a fête that would dwarf its predecessors.

A great "white city," a collection of neoclassical buildings, broad avenues, and canals, rose from 686 acres of reclaimed marshland fronting Lake Michigan. From the top of the enormous wheel that would immortalize the name of its designer, George Ferris, to the midway den where Little Egypt captured the hearts of a generation of American males, the fair was a wonder, an expression of the exuberant spirit that marked the city and the nation.

The planners of the exposition borrowed the idea of hosting a series of "congresses" from earlier European fairs. The Paris Exposition of 1889–1890 in which Chanute had taken part was a particularly useful example.

Charles Carrol Bonney had first suggested the continuation of the Paris tradition in a letter to a Chicago newspaper in September 1889. Bonney reasoned that "The crowning glory of the World's Fair should not be the exhibit, . . . however magnificent that display may be. Something higher and nobler is demanded by the enlightened and progressive spirit of the present age."[4] International conferences drawing scientists, artists, writers, philosophers, educators, religious leaders, and engineers were to fulfill the call to a "higher purpose." Charles Bonney was named director of the World's Congress Auxiliary, the organization that was to promote the meetings and to prepare interesting agendas for visiting scholars.

Albert Zahm had followed the growth of the congress idea in the Chicago papers. It seemed to him that such a conference on aeronautics might substantially increase interest in the subject. And there was precedent for such a gathering. The Aeronautical Society of Great Britain's Exhibition of 1868 had been the first attempt to attract an international audience of flying-machine experimenters. Chanute had attended the Second International Congress of Aeronauts and Aviators in Paris in 1889. Zahm envisioned a meeting that would surpass both of these, establishing a baseline of solid, trustworthy technical data from which all flying-machine work could proceed. In addition, such a gathering of reputable technologists and scientists would draw favorable public attention to aeronautics. Although Chanute was intrigued by Zahm's proposal, he had serious reservations, fearing that the event might attract "an invasion of cranks." In spite of his disappointment, Zahm persevered, visiting Bonney and gaining the support of the World's Congress Auxiliary for the scheme. He was immediately named acting secretary but refused to consider accepting a formal position of leadership in the hope that Chanute would eventually be drawn into the venture.[5]

Zahm returned to Notre Dame, where he was teaching, to launch a vigorous letter-writing campaign designed to create fundamental professional support for the conference and to convince Chanute of the potential benefit to be derived from participation. The response was immediate and very favorable. Leading technical journalists were enthusiastic. Forney and Hawthorne Hill of the *Engineering Journal* promised to cooperate in providing publicity for the event. The editor of the *Scientific American* remarked that the conference seemed "very desirable, . . . and doubtless would yield very interesting and important results."[6] A. M. Wellington, editor of the *Engineering News,* and James Means, a good friend of Chanute's who was to become a major figure in the American aeronautical community, also agreed to participate. Thurston was among the important engineering figures who applauded Zahm's efforts and promised to deliver a paper.

Throughout the summer of 1892, Chanute remained unconvinced of the wisdom of the conference, but he did agree to seek the approval of others planning similar engineering meetings under the auspices of the World's Columbian Exposition. As late as September 10, 1892, the Chicagoan voiced his doubt that "we want to promote an aeronautical congress at all."[7] But the growing number of letters that he was receiving urging his participation gradually forced him to change his mind.

During a meeting with Zahm on October 18, Chanute finally agreed to become local chairman and to oversee the general arrangements, providing the planners could avoid "publicity and cranks . . . by all possible means."[8]

Bonney confirmed the appointment of Chanute and Zahm to key positions and offered to pay all expenses involved in printing and distributing the necessary announcements, invitations, and other circulars. In addition, he suggested that the World's Congress Auxilliary might be willing to publish the papers offered at the conference. A thirteen-man committee composed of interested engineers and scientists and of others representing the interests of the World's Columbian Exposition was approved. Chanute was to head this body that would set the agenda and approve papers submitted for reading. B. J. Arnold, a General Electric consulting engineer, accepted his appointment to the group with the comment that he would be pleased to "be of any service to aerial navigation." H. S. Carhart of the University of Illinois; W. H. Rumley, president of the Rumley Manufacturing Company of La Porte, Indiana; Elisha Gray, the Western Electric engineer who had gained notoriety as Alexander Graham Bell's opponent in the telephone patent suit; and S. W. Stratton, a professional physicist later employed by the Bureau of Standards, were among the prominent technical professionals who accepted invitations to serve on the committee.[9]

The first task of the committee was to approve a proposed agenda. Zahm, who had prepared the draft of this circular, called for papers to be presented in three separate areas. The first of these would include the scientific principles underlying aviation. The questions of lift, air resistance, propeller efficiency, aeronautical motors, materials for aircraft construction, the design of airframes for strength and lightness, and the study of air currents were all to be covered during this first session, which Chanute would chair.

The second section of papers would deal with heavier-than-air machines and would include topics such as experiments and observations of bird flight, explanations of soaring and aspiration, suggestions for stabilizing an airplane, and the design of kites. Thurston agreed to preside over the reading and discussion of these offerings. In addition, Thurston prepared a paper of his own on the strength of materials to be used in the construction of a flying machine.

The final area of concentration was to encompass all lighter-than-air craft.

The committee quickly approved the list of topics, and Chanute began to contact those experts in each field who might be willing to prepare and read papers. Langley, G. E. Curtiss and J. E. Watkins of the Smithsonian; A. Goupil, a French experimenter; and such recognized authorities and friends as Maxim, Mouillard, Wenham, Moy, and Hargrave were among those solicited for contributions. In addition, a call for papers went out through technical journals, accompanied by a statement of principles to guide those who wished to participate in the meeting. The emphasis was to be on papers describing experiments actually performed or scientific inquiries aimed at solving the basic problems of flight. No attention was to be given to designs or proposals for flying machines. Chanute, still anxious to avoid providing a platform for aeronautical cranks, feared that if the doors were thrown open to the presentation of such schemes, the whole enterprise would quickly take on the aspect of a circus.

The final dates of the meeting and the creation of a timetable and selection of the site had been accomplished by the spring of 1893. All of those participating in the International Conference on Aerial Navigation were to attend the opening session on scientific principles on the afternoon of August 1, 1893. Concurrent meetings of the other two sections were scheduled for the afternoons of the next three days. Speakers were to be limited to fifteen minutes each, with a discussion period following each presentation. Stenographers were to be present to record the proceedings, and adjacent rooms were made available for the display of materials related to the subjects under discussion. Bonney arranged for all sessions to be held in the World's Congress Art Hall, Lake Front Park, at the foot of Adams Street.

Papers were initially slow in appearing. As late as the spring of 1893 a worried Chanute reported to Zahm, "I am afraid we have not papers enough and while I am not willing to accept poor ones, I think we should hunt up more contributions."[10] A sufficient number of offerings began to arrive as the opening date of the meeting drew nearer, however. Forty papers, covering all of the areas of interest as initially outlined by Chanute and Zahm, were approved for final presentation.

In the end, the European response was particularly gratifying. In addition to those formally invited to prepare reports, such stellar figures as Lilienthal, F. W. Breary, C. A. Parsons, R. Baden-Powell, and Gaston Tissandier expressed interest and sent papers.

American scientists and engineers responded in similar fashion when informed of the meeting and its goals. John Holland, inventor of the submarine and an avid flying-machine enthusiast; Thomas Edison; F. A. Pratt, the pioneer machine-tool manufacturer; Professor Mayer of Stevens Institute; George Hoadley of Swarthmore; George Swain of MIT; and J. B. Walker of the *Cosmopolitan* were among the leading American technologists who offered wholehearted support for the effort. C. F. Meyers, S. A. King, and other balloonists agreed to assist in arranging presentations on progress in balloons and airships.

Langley was one of the few well-known American experts who was not anxious to participate, possibly because he was unwilling to make public the results of his ongoing experiments with powered models. He finally agreed to offer "Internal Work of the Wind" for discussion. Lancaster was almost alone in absolutely refusing to attend or send a paper. Zahm speculated that "the abuse once heaped on him" at Buffalo was responsible for his disinclination to take part.[11]

The congress also served to attract new enthusiasts into the group. Chanute discovered, for example, that a number of Boston-based meteorologists were keen to offer papers emphasizing the relationship between the kites that they had developed to carry instrument packages aloft and the general question of aerodynamics. S. P. Fergusson, A. L. Rotch, W. A. Eddy, C. H. Marvin, H. Helm Clayton, and H. A. Hazen had pioneered in the design of these large and efficient craft and had much to teach those who sought to build man-carrying aircraft. While none of them undertook the construction of a flying machine, these meteorologists came to consider themselves members of the community of aeronautical enthusiasts. After 1893 they were to remain in close touch with Langley, Chanute, Means, and other leaders of the group. They published widely on the subject of aeronautics in both technical journals and popular magazines and were to influence a number of airplane designs, including the successful 1903 Wright machine.

Chanute also saw the conference as a means of introducing one of his own protégés, Edward Chalmers Huffaker, to the world at large. Huffaker, who was to remain an important member of both the Chanute and Langley camps of the American aeronautical community, was born on July 19, 1856, at Seclusion Bend, near Nashville, Tennessee.

At age twenty young Huffaker entered Emery and Henry College, graduating four years later with the college's Bryant prize for excellence in mathematics and the natural sciences. Huffaker then continued his work at the University of Virginia, where he earned an M.S. in physics. His ability was so apparent that the Johns Hopkins University offered him a full scholarship with which to pursue a Ph.D. He refused, remarking that he was "sick of school and such."[12] Huffaker returned to Chucky City, Tennessee, where he taught school for a short time before accepting a much more lucrative position as civil engineer for a number of railroads laying track through the area.

His interest in flight resulted from two articles published by Langley and Maxim in the *Century Magazine* in 1892. He later recalled: "I was led by these same articles to undertake certain experiments with small gliding models, which were patterned pretty closely after the soaring birds."[13]

Huffaker had written Chanute in 1892, offering his observations of the great birds that glided effortlessly over the Tennessee hills. Chanute, who had long been interested in the soaring birds he had observed while vacationing in Florida and Southern California, was intrigued by Huffaker's comments and added the young engineer's name to his growing list of correspondents.

In March 1893 he stopped off for a visit with Huffaker and was treated to a demonstration of small flying models reminiscent of Lancaster's effigies. Chanute was impressed, and immediately invited his young friend to present a paper to the Chicago conference.

Huffaker's paper on soaring flight outlined a few of his own observations and described the small gliders that were designed to demonstrate how the birds remained in the air for long periods of time with a minimum expenditure of power. A typical "artificial bird" featured a cedar spar 3 feet long and roughly 1 inch square that served as the leading edge of the wing. Umbrella ribs, bent to match the curvature of the bird's wing, were placed on either end of the spar. A violin string connected these tips, and the finished wing was than covered with black satin. An oak block 5 inches long and 2 inches square served as the fuselage. Two semicircular pieces of white pine were glued into a cruciform and attached to the rear of the machine to serve as a fixed tail surface. The glider was test-flown and weighted with lead slugs as necessary to balance it.[14]

Huffaker's description of the performance of his models was much more reasonable than Lancaster's had been. He attributed their action both to the air moving over the cambered wing and to the action of ascending currents. The paper was well received when presented at the conference, primarily because Huffaker's education and experience in technology marked him as an acceptable figure and because he could discuss actual experiments with model flying machines as opposed to the theoretical bias of most of the others who offered papers.

John Joseph Montgomery (1858–1911).

John Joseph Montgomery, the most intriguing of the new-comers to put in an appearance at the Chicago conference, came as something of a surprise, even to Chanute. Short, stocky, and balding, this thirty-five-year-old Californian had once been described as looking and talking like an "old professor." His "philosophical walk," a long stride with a peculiar spring at the end, had been the subject of mimicry since his days as a senior at San Francisco's Saint Ignatius College.[15]

Concerned about his health, Montgomery's family had urged him to vacation in Chicago, where he could visit the exposition and attend a few of the associated scientific meetings. Discovering that one of these meetings would deal with aeronautics, he immediately proceeded to the headquarters established by Chanute and Zahm on the fairgrounds, where he introduced himself to the astonished pair as the only successful glider pilot in America.

Almost nine decades after his emergence in Chicago, John Montgomery remains one of the most enigmatic and controversial figures in the history of American aeronautics. Monuments to his daring dot the landscape of his native Southern California, where he is a folk hero. Hollywood has paid him the ultimate tribute of a full-length film biography and a prominent position in a Disney short subject.

Yet opinions as to the importance of his contributions vary from that of Arthur D. Spearman, his worshipful biographer, who characterized Montgomery as the "father of basic flying," to that of C. H. Gibbs-Smith, the English aeronautical historian who viewed him as "the first serious, but not significant, American pioneer." Marvin W. McFarland, editor of the Wright papers, remarked that Montgomery "occupies a place in the aviation literature that ill accords with his real importance, which is negligible," while Victor Lougheed, Montgomery's business partner, observed that "It is a fact of quite inescapable significance that recent activity and present success in aeronautics do date most definitely from the Montgomery machine."[16] It is doubtful that such widely differing educated views can be found toward any other aeronautical pioneer. The source of this disparity is to be found in the welter of conflicting accounts that have long shrouded Montgomery's early work.

He was born on February 15, 1858, in Yuba City, California, a descendant of Virginia and Maryland pioneers who had arrived in the New World during the 1680s. His father, Zachariah Montgomery, a lawyer and journalist, was active in California politics and, in 1885, was named assistant United States attorney general.

John Montgomery's interest in flight was of long standing. His mother recalled that as a baby he would lie on the floor with his arms outstretched imitating the birds in flight. As a teenager he had spent a great deal of time studying the birds, even capturing a buzzard which he kept chained in order to observe the creature's undoubtedly pathetic attempts to fly.

His first encounter with a flying machine came in 1869, when his father took him to see an exhibition of Frederick Marriott's

Avitor in San Francisco. Marriott, an associate of Stringfellow and Henson, had maintained his interest in aviation after emigrating to the United States. The *Avitor* was a large-scale model of a proposed navigable balloon being shown to the public in an effort to raise funds with which to construct a man-carrying craft. Margaret Montgomery, the inventor's sister, remembered that after his return from the exhibition he had constructed an 8-inch model of the *Avitor*, complete with wheeled undercarriage.[17]

Montgomery attended the Notre Dame Academy and Saint Joseph's Academy and received additional tutoring at home that prepared him to enter Santa Clara College in 1874, where he became interested in physics. In 1875, Montgomery transferred to San Francisco's Saint Ignatius College, earning a B.Sc. in 1879 and an M.S. in physics in 1880.

Following graduation, Montgomery returned to the family ranch near San Diego, where he prepared a small laboratory in a barn loft so that he might continue his experiments in electricity, magnetism, and mechanics while learning to manage the family business. But with the gulls constantly wheeling overhead, Montgomery found his boyhood interest in flight returning.

When his first aeronautical project, a series of flying models featuring flat wings constructed in 1881–1882, proved unsatisfactory, he decided to throw "aside all the theories that involved the plane surface . . . [and] follow the construction of the bird's wing in the making of my airships."[18]

Confident that he alone had uncovered the secret of flight in the arched or cambered wing, Montgomery set to work on the first of his man-carrying machines. Early in 1883 he constructed two full-scale flying machines, one single- and one tandem-wing ornithopter, both of which were failures. Partial success, and eventual fame, came with his next craft, a fixed-wing glider built and flown in 1884.

John Montgomery was not the first man to venture aloft in a glider. History is full of tales of isolated individuals who down through the centuries made short glides on primitively fashioned wings. But these stories usually contain little more than a kernel of truth shrouded in legendary accretions. They offered few details that might prove useful to would-be aviators.

Sir George Cayley was the first influential advocate of the glider as the most productive approach to powered flight. More important, he demonstrated that unpowered flight was possible, building three gliders that made short hops with human passengers. By the 1860s Louis Mouillard had made at least two brief forays into the air with hang gliders, while Jean Marie Le Bris, a French ship captain had gone aloft in his large *Albatros* glider, suffering a broken leg in the process. The high aspect ratio multiplane illustrated in Francis Wenham's classic paper of 1868 on aerial locomotion had also attracted the attention of aeronautical experimenters to the glider.

But few were venturesome enough to follow the lead of these pioneers. Of all the approaches to flight, gliding was the most dangerous. To leap into space strapped into a set of frail home-made wings required ultimate devotion to the cause. And once aloft, however briefly, the experience could be terrifying. One has only to recall Mouillard's comment after his first accidental flight of only 138 feet to understand why so few inventors took up gliding. "Goodness," he remarked, "how frightened I had been."[19]

It is quite probable that John Montgomery was as unaware of these earlier gliding experiments as he had been of the studies of cambered surfaces that had been conducted since the eighteenth century. Throughout his career, Montgomery remained confident of his own genius. He had little interest in the work of others, and conducted his own experiments in almost obsessive secrecy. As a result, the details of his early work with gliders remain buried in a mass of shifting, conflicting testimony. Uncertainty surrounds some of the most basic questions.

Chanute provided the earliest and most trustworthy account of Montgomery's first glider in *Progress in Flying Machines.* The report was based on long conversations with Montgomery in Chanute's Chicago residence during the exposition.[20] Some years previously, Montgomery had constructed a monoplane glider with a 20-foot wingspan, a 4 1/2-foot chord and a surface area of 90 square feet. A seat for the pilot was suspended in a central frame, which also carried a horizontal tail that could be raised or lowered by pulleys. The apparatus weighed 40 pounds, which, added to Montgomery's 130 pounds, brought the total flying weight up to 170 pounds.

On the morning in question, Montgomery had taken his glider to Wheeler Hill near the rim of Otay Mesa south of San Diego, close to the spot where the Otay River empties into the lower end of San Diego Harbor. Climbing onto the seat, he grasped the two central bars of the frame and stood facing into a steady sea breeze, which was blowing 8 to 12 miles per hour. He gave a slight jump with no forward run and found himself skimming down the 10-degree slope with his feet barely off the ground. He described the sensation as "firm yet yielding and soft support." He was able to direct his course by shifting his weight to either side. The flight lasted only a few seconds, during which time Montgomery covered 100 feet.

Exhilarated, with "no apprehension of disaster," the young experimenter carried his machine back to the crest. As he rose into position for a second flight, the glider began to twist and sway in the wind. One wing tip became tangled in a bush and "quick as a flash, the operator was tossed some 8 or 10 feet into the air, over-turned, and thrown down headlong." Montgomery was not seriously injured, but his machine, after only one flight, was broken beyond repair.

Two more gliders followed. The first bore a rough resemblance to the original, but was a bit larger, with a surface area of 132 square feet and a total weight of 45 pounds. A diagonal section of the trailing edge of each wing, from the forward tip to the wingroot at the rear, was held to the rest of the wing by springs, but was free to swing down, when struck by a gust. As Chanute understood it, this was an attempt to damp gusts of the sort that had destroyed the first glider. Montgomery inexplicably returned to plane-surface wings for this craft so that, in spite of repeated trials, it refused to leave the ground.

In constructing his third glider he abandoned the gust damping diagonals and returned to cambered surfaces. The wings had a 24-foot span and an average chord of 6 feet, "with the cross-section and front sinuosity . . . of a soaring buzzard. They were so built and braced as to allow rotation in a socket at the front of the frames which supported the seat." As with the previous two machines, a hinged semicircular tail was attached to the rear of the frame. Hand levers enabled the pilot to alter the angle at which either wing met the airstream. Unfortunately, Montgomery was unable to test the new control system, for, like its predecessor, the 50-pound glider could not be coaxed into the air.

All of these machines had been constructed of standard materials. A frame, wings, and tail of ash or spruce, braced with steel wire and covered with waxed cloth in the early versions and waxed silk for the final machines.

According to the Chanute account, Montgomery had one slight taste of success, a single 100-foot glide followed by near disaster. Both subsequent machines were incapable of flight. Confused and uncertain, Montgomery abandoned gliding to "make a careful and complete study of the principles involved."[21] Using a whirling arm similar to but much smaller than Langley's and a wooden water tank in which the flow of suspended particles around a fixed airfoil could be studied, he struggled to understand the physics of flight.

Montgomery felt certain that he was establishing a theoretical foundation for a successful airplane. "I have performed hundreds of experiments," he remarked in a letter to his sister Margaret in November 1885, "and have discovered some important facts and laws. I have had many failures and discouragements, but have become convinced more than ever of the correctness of my ideas and plans." In fact, Montgomery was sure that he had unlocked the secrets of flight. "I have performed a few simple experiments which I would not perform before a scientist for any consideration, for the solution of the problem is very much like that of "standing an egg on its end." In fact, the solution is almost so simple as to be ridiculous."[22]

Within a year he had changed his mind about revealing his theory. Perhaps he had heard rumors of Lancaster's upcoming presentation in Buffalo, perhaps he was afraid that his "ridiculously simple" solution to the problem of flight would be uncovered by another investigator. In any event, he informed his brother James, a Georgetown University law student, that he had decided to present a paper to the American Association for the Advancement of Science and requested information regarding the rules of the organization.[23] But Montgomery's penchant for secrecy was to overpower his desire for recognition. The Californian backed off, and his early work remained entirely unknown outisde his immediate circle of friends and relatives for another seven years.

Montgomery's decade-long silence came to an end in Chicago in 1893. Over the years, additional details would be added to flesh out the bare-bones account that Chanute received at the conference and published in *Progress in Flying Machines.* At the same time, major alterations began to creep into Chanute's original report.

It is important to note that the brief account of Montgomery's early gliding experiences carried in Chanute's book stood uncorrected for over a decade. Montgomery read the proofs of this section and made no major revisions. The two men carried on steady correspondence for two years after their meeting in Chicago and resumed contact after 1905, when Montgomery began making headlines with balloon-launched–glider exhibitions. While he had frequent opportunity to do so, from 1893 to 1905 Montgomery failed to make any corrections in Chanute's account of the Otay Mesa glide.

Nevertheless, in the excitement surrounding his 1905 activity, some startling changes were made in the long-standing account of the 1884 work. In one 1905 pamphlet, for example, the length of the single flight was suddenly doubled to 200 feet.[24] By 1909, when Montgomery published his first account of the early glides, the distance grew to from 300 to 600 feet. Other early flights of just under 100 yards were now recalled for the first time.[25]

The publication of two books, *Vehicles of the Air* (1909) and *Designing Aeroplanes for Amateurs* (1911) by Victor Lougheed, was to become a major factor in the creation of the Montgomery legend. Lougheed regarded the Californian as a forgotten aeronautical genius, and saw the origin of all lateral control systems in the final unsuccessful gliders tested at Otay Mesa.

The first of these, in which the trailing edge was hinged and fitted with springs, was now reported to have been later fitted with two successive pilot-operated mechanisms that transformed the "gust dampers" into "steering air brakes" similar to the "annularies" of the Chanute-Mouillard glider. Lougheed argued that this mechanism as well as the final, unsuccessful variable incidence machine represented an attempt to provide control in roll. In fact, there is no evidence to indicate that anything more than the automatic gust damping or steering air brakes suggested by the Chanute account of 1894 was ever intended. In any case, as both machines were incapable of flying, Montgomery was unable to pursue his notions of control. None of the aeronautical pioneers who struggled with the problems of control during the years after 1884 was in the least influenced by Montgomery.

Lougheed's public-relations effort prepared the ground for even more sweeping claims. By 1910 Montgomery himself had settled on the final distance that would be claimed for the flight, "about 600 feet," a 500-percent increase over the length originally given to Chanute.[26]

And so over the years the original single glide similar to those achieved by Cayley, Mouillard, Household, and others grew to many flights of extraordinary length. The impulse to "update" the original account to keep pace with the advance in aeronautics had apparently proved irresistable.

The confusion surrounding the basic facts of the 1884 glide grew even more perplexing as a result of two unsuccessful patent suits brought by Montgomery's heirs against the Wright-Martin Company and the United States in 1917. Claiming that Montgomery's early work antedated and formed the basis for the Wright brother's success, the inventor's family trotted forth a series of witnesses who claimed to have been present at the original flights.

Charles Burroughs who, as a fourteen-year-old boy, had lived on the ranch next to Fruitlands, the Montgomery home, recalled "a number of flights" ranging from "200 to 300 feet." Montgomery's brother James was a bit more explicit. He was positive the date had been 1883, not 1884, and insisted that there had been a number of flights, the best of which covered 600 feet.[27]

The Montgomery legend took on its final dimensions as journalists discovered the story during the 1930s and 1940s, producing a spate of articles based on interviews with James Montgomery and other surviving members of the family. Chanute's original account was now scarcely recognizable. James, a septuagenarian, was at last able to put an exact date to the flight, August 28, 1883. In these new accounts, the older brother plays a conspicuous role in the proceedings, pulling the glider into the air with a 40-foot rope tied to the nose of the craft. Many flights were made that day, he recalled. The best of these glides had covered exactly 603 feet, a distance which James stepped off with the assistance of an obliging journalist. Altitudes of 35 to 40 feet had been commonplace. The day of triumph had come to an end only when James allowed the rope to become tangled in John's legs, bringing the glider violently to earth.[28]

The process of enshrinement was complete by the mid-twentieth century as filmmakers, monument builders, and the anonymous bureaucrats responsible for naming schools, airfields, and freeways enthusiastically endorsed John Montgomery as the man who "opened for all mankind the great highway of the sky."[29] The reality, that balding fellow with the "philosophical walk" who met with Octave Chanute in Chicago, was lost in the shadow of the larger-than-life mythic figure created by the legend makers.

But in 1893 the legend making still lay in the future. Montgomery, after years of effort in total isolation, relished his first contact with the great men of American science and technology whom he met in Chicago. His enthusiasm was apparent in letters to his family. "It's a grand thing," he wrote, "to be among the leading scientists of the world, being introduced to them as a young man who, cut off from all scientific association, has for years through pure love of science devoted himself to scientific investigation in its most advanced stages."[30]

Certainly Chanute and Zahm had been most impressed. While time was too short to invite Montgomery to deliver a full paper to the conference, they did ask him to serve as a commentator for several speakers, notably Huffaker. Chanute hoped that the Californian would take the opportunity to describe his gliders, but Montgomery, preferring the role of theorist to that of experimenter, asked if he might offer an abstract outlining his understanding of the physics of flight instead. Chanute was reluctant, remembering the reaction to Lancaster's theoretical presentation at Buffalo, but finally acceded to the request.

As scheduled, the first meeting of the conference took place on the afternoon of August 1, 1893. Bonney offered an opening address, after which Chanute gave a short introductory talk. The proceedings continued for some three hours, a time period that Zahm pronounced "all too short."[31] Roughly 100 persons were present, and reporters were "in constant attendance."

With Thurston in the chair on the second day, unspecified trouble developed. "Cranks ruled for a moment," but order was quickly restored. The most useful activity on Tuesday was an informal gathering following the presentation of the papers. On this occasion participants discussed the possibility of founding an aeronautical society, establishing a journal, and raising funds to guarantee publication of the conference proceedings.

A more ambitious proposal was offered during a second such unofficial gathering after the session on August 3. Chanute, seeking to take advantage of the enthusiasm of the moment, offered to become one of twenty subscribers, each of whom would donate one thousand dollars toward the construction of a flying machine that the group would select as most promising. Arrangements were made to continue the discussion after the final meeting on August 4. At that time an R. D. Raney of Detroit urged that serious consideration be given to Chanute's plan. He argued that European enthusiasts had long concentrated on perfecting navigable balloons, and that Americans should, therefore, neglect this field in favor of developing a heavier-than-air machine. C. D. Mosher, a prominent New York engine designer, pointed out that recent advances in power-plant technology had made light, powerful aeronautical motors a reality. Although Zahm reported that the members were enthusiastic, the brave talk came to nothing. Chanute was unable to find a single individual to participate in the fund-raising scheme with him.[32]

While the Chicago conference failed to produce a formal aeronautical society or increased funding to support experimenters, Chanute and Zahm could only regard the venture as a success. With the exception of Lawrence Hargrave's first description of the box kite and a passing mention of John Montgomery's glider, little new information was made available. The presentations, on the whole, were scarcely more than cautiously optimistic. They were selected for reading precisely because they emphasized a serious mathematical approach to the solution of key problems in aerodynamics rather than dramatic breakthroughs. Chanute and Zahm had been careful to restrict participation to recognized men with formal training in science and engineering. The papers by men like Thurston; A. M. Wellington; C. E. Duryea, a prominent civil engineer; C. H. Hastings, a well-known Chicago engineer and an associate of Chanute; and Professor De Volson Wood of the Stevens Institute of Technology may not have been exciting, but they were evidence that professional leaders could interest themselves in the flying-machine problem without suffering ridicule. Even prominent government officials like Langley and H. A. Hazen of the Weather Bureau had participated. Chanute had succeeded in demonstrating to his peers and to the public that serious, responsible men believed in the possibility of flight and were willing to work toward eventual success.

The columns of the *Pittsburgh Dispatch* indicated the real achievement of the Chicago meeting:

> The Chicago Conference undoubtably marks a new era in aeronautics. It brought together many scientists and engineers who have been engaged seriously upon the problem of flight. The subject, it was shown, is one for the study of men of broad knowledge, and accurate training, and is no longer to be considered the hobby of mere cranks.[33]

Nor was this important point lost in the technical press. A reporter for the *Engineering News,* commented: "A notable evidence of the importance which the question of aerial navigation is assuming in the minds of many able men is that it should be deemed either desirable or possible to hold a 'World Congress' of three days devoted exclusively to it."[34]

The proceedings of the International Conference on Aerial Navigation were published in Forney's new journal, *Aeronautics*. Although the World's Congress Auxiliary found itself financially unable to support the publication of the papers as a single volume, a sufficient number of subscriptions were collected to induce Forney to issue a limited printing of the collected presentations. As Zahm had hoped, the published proceedings of the conference served as a bench mark, indicating the state of aeronautics in the summer of 1893.

The meeting had been a success for many of the individuals involved as well. Zahm had become, and would remain, a recognized aeronautical authority. For Chanute the meeting terminated almost twenty years of preparation and marked the beginning a period of intense involvement in flying-machine work that would continue until his death in 1910. Huffaker left the meeting to begin an extended period of full-time involvement in aeronautics that would place him in the heart of both the Chanute and Langley camps and eventually carry him to an isolated fishing village on the Outer Banks for an eventful season as Chanute's representative in the camp of Wilbur and Orville Wright.

Of the major participants, only John Montgomery was unaffected by the conference. As Chanute had feared, the Californian's observations on the physics of flight met a cool reception. After his return home, Montgomery remarked to his friend James Leonard, "They laughed at all I proposed."[35]

He could find some comfort in Chanute's continued interest in his experiments, and in the extended description of his gliders in *Progress in Flying Machines*, which appeared in 1894. As he informed his sister Jane, "Some of my work is beginning to tell. A work on flying has been published and my experiments have been described; and three men mentioned as giving the most reliable data, viz: Maxim, Lilienthal and Montgomery."[36]

But Montgomery was still dissatisfied. He regarded the experiments of 1884–1886 a failure, but believed that his subsequent laboratory studies were of extraordinary value. He was now eager to publish the results of this work.

At the exposition Chanute had asked Montgomery to prepare
a short, clear statement of his aeronautical theory. He did so,
evidently believing that Chanute would arrange for immediate
publication. Some months later Montgomery queried his Chicago friend as to why the article had not appeared. Chanute's
answer is another indication of the general reaction of knowledgeable enthusiasts toward Montgomery's theoretical work.

> The article is now in my hands, and I fear that its publication
> would do you no credit, inasmuch as you have confused pressures
> with energy, statics with dynamics, and reached erroneous con-
> clusions. Neither have you done yourself justice in the presenta-
> tion of your experiments. They are given as evidences of a theory
> which can be seen to be erroneous, i.e., that gravity is a motive
> power capable of overcoming itself in the air, while we know it
> does not on land or on water. The proper way in my judgement,
> would be to present the experiments by themselves, as curious
> facts, and to draw whatever inferences you want to advance, in
> foot notes, or in a second part of the essay.[37]

Chanute agreed to send the paper to the editor of the *Scientific
American,* but he emphasized that "I shall be much surprised if
that paper accepts it." In August 1895, having had the same
article rejected by both this journal and the *Railroad and Engineering Journal,* Montgomery wrote another rather caustic letter
to Chanute. The Chicagoan again attempted to point out the
author's theoretical shortcomings.

> I regret to infer from the conclusion of your letter that you feel
> a little sore because your paper has, as you express it, been "de-
> nied publication." I regret it both because I feel certain that
> neither of the publishers to which it was offered had the slightest
> motive to suppress anything which you advanced. . . . I fear it will
> not be received with commendation by the men who are compe-
> tent to discuss it.[38]

Unable to publish his psuedoscientific speculations, and unwilling to return to active experimentation, Montgomery gradually lost interest in flight. He began a teaching career, first at

his own alma mater, Saint Ignatius College, then at Santa Clara College, where he was to remain until his death in 1911. His position during this period is clouded at best. He was listed in various catalogues with titles ranging from electrician to professor.

The tragedy of Montgomery's early career as an aeronautical innovator is apparent. He rejected the opportunity to pioneer the art of gliding in order to embark on studies of little value to active experimenters and for which he was ill prepared. He viewed himself as a scientist, a man for whom theory was the route to success. By 1895 he had come to believe that if his scientific speculations were rejected, there was little point in soiling his hands with further experimentation. As we shall see, he was to recognize his error after 1903, when it was too late to regain his position of leadership, although he would die in the attempt.

With the conclusion of the third International Conference on Aerial Navigation, aeronautics in America entered a new phase. The ground had been prepared for serious experimenters. New faces were to enter the field as the flying machine at last approached respectability.

6

Boston:
The Third Circle

Samuel Cabot was impressed by what he had heard of the proceedings in Chicago. He was also quick to note the similarities between his own career and that of Octave Chanute. Like Chanute, he was an engineer specializing in the production of wood preservatives, the owner of a Chesea, Massachusetts, firm that manufactured coal tar, creosote, tar paper, lamp black, disinfectants, and insulating material. Both men had followed the classic pattern for late nineteenth-century engineers, making a successful transition from a career as a working technologist to a position of business leadership. But the most striking similarity between them was the fact that both had been bitten by the flying-machine bug.

Cabot's latent interest in flight was awakened by the favorable publicity surrounding the International Conference on Aerial Navigation. Having read and been impressed by Chanute's Cornell lecture, the Bostonian had, while vacationing on Cape Cod in August 1893, conducted some "interesting experiments on levitation produced by human muscles with various wings, using a large beam in the open air."[1]

In addition, he had convinced the Boston Charitable Mechan-

ics Association, a local philanthropic group to which he be-
longed, to sponsor "an exhibition in their immense hall . . . of
all apparatus, motors, light engines, boilers, explosive engines,
et al., which would in any way be of use in aeronautical matters." Cabot himself had donated some prize money for the
venture, which, he hoped, would be "a scientific stimulus to
invention."

Cabot first wrote Chanute in August 1893, requesting advice
as to how the Boston exhibition should be conducted. Chanute
responded discouragingly, suggesting that there was not enough
creditable aeronautical equipment in the United States to justify
such an exhibition. Cabot took the advice but continued his
correspondence with Chanute, describing his own experiments,
which included work with clockwork-powered ornithopters,
kites, and the construction of a primitive wind tunnel and other
devices designed to measure the lift provided by various test
surfaces.

Chanute recognized that Boston was the home of a number of
aeronautical enthusiasts and frequently asked Cabot to investigate some of the area men whose work had come to his attention.
One such request was to prove particularly influential. On January 30, 1894, Chanute inquired about James Means, who had
recently printed a pamphlet, "Manflight." Means was also seeking "to get up a party to offer a prize for soaring machines,"
according to Chanute's sources. As usual, Cabot replied
promptly, informing Chanute that Means, whom he had never
met, was "a manufacturer of boots who has been very successful,
and who has interested himself very deeply in the study of
Aeronautics."[2]

Cabot did meet Means, and in the years to come, these two
men would form the nucleus of a third major center of aeronautical activity in the United States. A formal organization, the
Boston Aeronautical Society, would be created as a result of
their work. The members of this group, many of whom were
men of considerable wealth, would function as agents of cross-
fertilization, encouraging and publicizing the aeronautical
efforts of others, while struggling to get into the air in machines
of their own design.

James Means was to become the most important figure in the Boston group, and a major force for cohesion in the total community of U.S. aeronautical enthusiasts. His importance as a publicist, correspondent, financial supporter, and intermediary in the activities of the group placed him in a role second only to that of Langley and Chanute.

Born in Dorchester, Massachusetts, in 1853, Means had attended the Massachusetts Institute of Technology but learned the shoe-manufacturing business in an uncle's plant in Brookfield, Massachusetts. In 1878, then age twenty-five, he borrowed $5,000 from his grandmother and established his own shoe factory in Brockton. The young manufacturer was phenomenally successful. Recognizing the importance of capturing the mass market, he established a low-profit margin and sold his James Means Shoes in volume at $2.50 to $3.00 a pair through national retail outlets.

By 1893 he had amassed a sizable fortune and withdrew from business, determined to spend his most productive years pursuing goals that he believed to be more important than the accumulation of money.

After his retirement from business, many of his friends must have assumed that the energetic Bostonian would devote his full energies to politics, an activity that had always fascinated him. But Means had other plans. His imagination had been captured by the image of the soaring bird. His long-standing latent interest in flight was reawakened early in the 1880s, when an issue of the *Annual Report* of the Aeronautical Society of Great Britain and J. B. Pettigrew's article on "Flight" in the ninth edition of the *Encyclopaedia Britannica* caught his eye. A period of critical reading in the aeronautical literature was followed in 1889 by the publication of Means's first article on the subject. Entitled "Manflight," the piece originally appeared in the *Boston Transcript* and was published as a pamphlet later in the year. The author listed the various types of possible flying machines, including balloons, ornithopters, fixed-wing craft, helicopters, and designs that combined the different features of all the others. At this early date, Means preferred the helicopter and included a rough sketch of such a machine, featuring one vertical "fan" and another mounted on the nose of the "car" for forward motion. A rudder for steering was placed on the tail of the craft.

When "Manflight" was reissued in 1891, Means modified this scheme by doing away with the nose propeller and making the vertical shaft rotate forward for the straight flight. A "rudder" was added to each side of the machine to act as a steering air brake.[3]

Mean's vision of the practical flying machine was radically altered by the publication of Langley's *Experiments in Aerodynamics*. Writing in *Frank Leslie's Weekly* in 1893, Means now argued that three problems remained to be solved before an airplane could be flown: to demonstrate scientifically the possibility of winged flight; to develop a suitable aeronautical motor; to discover a means of controlling the motion of the craft. He argued that Langley had already solved the first, while engineers were hard at work developing light but powerful engines. Only the difficulty of flight control remained to be overcome. Means noted that full-scale machines with which to investigate various types of control mechanisms would be costly and suggested, therefore, that initial experiments be carried out with small flying models.[4]

In another article published in the *Boston Transcript*, on July 17, 1893, Means offered to encourage the construction of flying models by donating $100 to a prize fund, provided that an additional $900 be subscribed by interested readers. The total would be awarded to the most successful model submitted to a board of competent judges.

He also included detailed plans for a small glider that he had designed as "an instrument for making scientific experiments."[5] In order to launch such models from high altitudes, Means attached them to kites with a slow burning fuse that would automatically release the gliders once they were well aloft. In this manner, the Bostonian was led not only to develop his gliding models but also to take an interest in kite theory and construction. However, James Means's real contribution to the study of "manflight" did not result from these experiments.

As early as 1892, the Boston enthusiast had emerged as a major publicist of the flying-machine movement. His earliest articles were sometimes published under the pseudonym "John Meade," but by 1893 he had become publicly known as a defender of the faith. In addition to publishing his own thoughts on the subject, Means bombarded major newspapers and national magazines with suggestions as to how they might serve science and boost their circulation as well. Accordingly, he wrote to the editor of the *New York Herald:* "You will see . . . that this branch of science *must have* a newspaper organ—will the *Herald* be that organ?"[6]

He suggested that Forney sponsor a contest with $100 prize to anyone sending in the most efficient model glider. He described a similar scheme to other large metropolitan dailies, carefully pointing out the potential for good photo stories. Means even approached a known enthusiast, John Brisben Walker, the editor of *Cosmopolitan,* with the idea of awarding a cash prize to the first man to construct a successful Lilienthal glider in America. This could be followed by a flying competition at some future date when others had built similar machines.[7]

During the same period, Means was widening his circle of aeronautical acquaintances. Langley, Chanute, Huffaker, Zahm, and other members of the emerging experimental community were all aware of the Bostonian's activity by late 1893. Chanute's reaction to this eager newcomer was typical. Though the Chicagoan initially regarded him as naïve and a bit brash, he soon recognized the value of Means's talent as an organizer and publicist.

By the spring of 1894, Means had decided how he might be of most assistance in hurrying the advent of the flying machine. In November of that year, he described his plan to Israel Lancaster:

With a view to further awakening a general interest in this important matter I am now making a compilation of aeronautical articles which I shall soon print in a book of 100 to 200 pages. This will probably be done at a loss, as the demand for such a book is, I think, not likely to be large. But if it does anything to increase the number of experimenters I shall be satisfied.[8]

Means felt that senseless rivalry, jealousy, and uncertainty as to what other experimenters were doing had become a serious obstacle to progress in the field. He hoped to alleviate this situation by publishing an *Aeronautical Annual*.

The first issue of the *Aeronautical Annual*, the journal that was to make its editor one of the best-known men in the flying-machine fraternity, appeared in 1895. Means had contacted leaders in the field all over the world requesting contributions, but the material received was so sparse that he decided to republish historically important works on aviation. Leonardo da Vinci, Thomas Walker, Sir George Cayley, F. H. Wenham, and Benjamin Franklin were all represented. A series of short notes on current work in progress was also included. The major problem, of course, was that Means began the series in 1895, just prior to the success of Langley and Chanute and at a time when both men and all of their co-workers were trying to avoid calling undue attention to their work.

The 1896 edition of the *Aeronautical Annual* came much closer to fulfilling the goals that Means had set in founding the series. This time, major pieces by Lilienthal, Maxim, Chanute, and A. M. Herring, an associate of Chanute, were presented. In addition, C. H. Lamson, J. B. Millett, A. L. Rotch, W. H. Pickering, and S. P. Fergusson provided shorter articles dealing, for the most part, with kites.

The third and final volume of the *Annual* appeared in 1897. It was the richest of the three, containing articles that have become classics. Langley, Chanute, and A. M. Herring presented the results of their successful experiments of 1896. In addition, Pilcher and Huffaker also offered accounts of their experiments.

The series had thus far been a great success, and the editor had every intention of continuing the work. He hoped to devote almost all of the next volume to European developments and made a trip to Europe during the fall and winter of 1897 to gather material. Means discovered, however, that having covered the experiments of most of the major figures, he had little more to say. He was also a bit worried about the continued financial loss that he was suffering on the publication. While the *Annual* had been extremely popular, so many had been distributed free that the revenues obtained could not cover the printing costs. Thus, by late 1897, he had decided to push the date of the next volume back to 1899. Eventually this date passed and it became apparent that the *Aeronautical Annual* was a thing of the past. A final volume, entitled the *Epitome of the Aeronautical Annual,* did appear in 1910, but it was for the most part a collection of the most popular pieces carried in the earlier issues.

There can be little doubt that Means's efforts had a substantial impact. His personal scrapbooks were filled with newspaper clippings lauding the *Annuals.* The presence of this collection of aeronautical literature in libraries around the nation provided a ready source of original accounts of flying-machine experiments for Americans, including the Wright brothers.

In addition to editing the most influential aeronautical magazine of the period, James Means was also an unsuccessful lobbyist for national legislation in support of flying-machine experiments, but his involvement in the organization of the Boston Aeronautical Society was to have far greater public impact.[9]

By 1895 Means and Cabot had been joined by other prominent Bostonians interested in the problems of flight. A. A. Merrill, a local bank teller, was one of the most enthusiastic aeronautical amateurs in the area. Having cooperated with Cabot and an MIT student in conducting early wind-tunnel research, Merrill emerged as one of the leaders of the Boston Aeronautical Society.

W. H. Pickering, a Harvard professor of astronomy, was, for example, with Samuel Langley, one of few American scientists with a serious interest in flight. His interest in aeronautics dated back to 1877, when he had begun experiments to determine the lift produced by "helicopter" fans of various sizes. He continued this work for almost twenty years and by 1895 was testing "fans" as large as 21 feet in diameter. Much later, in 1903, Pickering constructed an interesting engine test rig. He described the craft in an article published in 1908:

> two fans were mounted side by side on a light steel framework, power being transmitted to them through long steel rods, furnished at both ends with universal joints. The power was gener-

ated by two small electric motors and transmitted to the rods by balanced pulleys. On starting the fans, the machine rose rapidly in the air through a height of three feet, which was as far as the cord holding it to the floor would permit it to go.[10]

The astronomer then placed a roll of steel wire and a white rabbit in the car of the helicopter. Once again it rose from the floor of the workshop. He eventually discovered that the craft could lift a load of about 4.5 pounds. He proudly claimed to have been the first man to fly a living creature in a machine. It should be noted, of course, that Pickering's helicopter had absolutely no stability. If it had been released from its tether, or been allowed to ascend much more than 3 feet, it would immediately have fallen off on one side and crashed.

David Todd, director of the observatory at Amherst, was another astronomer associated with the Boston group. Todd had visited Langley at the Smithsonian on a scientific errand in 1890, but came away far more impressed by the aerodromic work. Returning to Amherst, he "devoted a good deal of attention to aerial experimentation for the next few years." He constructed a "multitude" of model airplanes of various shapes and sizes, turning the "College Tower" into a flying field. These studies were abandoned in about 1898, because "it seemed invention was at hand." Positive that Langley was about to achieve success, Todd began to concentrate on developing a landing system for flying machines. Once this problem was solved to his satisfaction, he decided to return to the design of the machine itself. While the astronomer did not describe his proposed craft in detail, he did remark that it differed radically from the Langley aerodromes, "which always seemed to me to have salient defects, or deficiencies of a sort to handicap, if not actually preclude, successful flight."[11] Todd's craft was never constructed, and after 1901 he turned to the investigation of hydroplane boats and propellor efficiency.

The Boston-based, kite-flying meteorologists who had participated in Chanute's Chicago conference in 1893 were also to become active members of the local aeronautical circle. Abbot Lawrence Rotch was the guiding spirit of this group. A graduate of MIT, he had established a weather observatory in 1885 atop the Great Blue Hill, a prominent landmark rising 635 feet above sea level some 10 miles south of Boston, near Milton, Massachusetts. Rotch employed a number of extraordinary men at the new establishment, three of whom, Charles H. Marvin and H. Helm Clayton—both meteorologists—and S. P. Fergusson, a mechanic, were to become particularly interested in the problems of flight.

Aerology, the study of the upper atmosphere, was the primary concern of the staff at Blue Hill. Initial research was conducted with a variety of self-recording meteorographs designed and constructed by Fergusson. These were sent aloft on balloons, following European practice.

The appearance of William A. Eddy on the scene in 1894 was to alter this procedure, however. Eddy, a journalist living in Bayonne, New Jersey, had a long-standing interest in aeronautics. He had undertaken experiments with kites early in the 1890s to solve some of the problems of heavier-than-air flight. By 1894, he had developed a tailless Malay kite that demonstrated great stability and could readily lift light loads.

Initially, these kites were used to carry small model airplanes aloft. Samuel Langley visited Eddy's workshop in March 1894 and took measurements of the kite and model gliders. It is not clear whether Rotch first came into contact with the New Jersey experimenter through Langley or as a result of one of the many newspaper articles covering Eddy's activity that were published during late winter and early spring 1894.

Kites had long been used to obtain weather soundings, but not until Eddy's improved design was linked to the self-recording instruments developed at Blue Hill was the real potential of the kite as a scientific tool realized. The earliest application of this new system was attempted in August 1891, when Eddy sent up a 1 3/4-pound Fergusson instrument package 1,500 feet. Tandem kites were soon being used regularly at the observatory.

In perfecting these devices, Rotch, Marvin, and Fergusson were drawn into a more serious investigation of the mechanics of flight. They noted, for example, that when a line broke, the weight of the meteorograph was usually sufficient to balance the kite so that it glided smoothly back to earth. During the course of an expanded program of reading, study, and investigation, they came into contact with Means, Cabot, and other interested Bostonians as well as with Chanute, Langley, and the members of the aeronautical community. In addition, they were able to interest General H. A. Hazen of the U.S. Army Signal Service in the virtues of kites as a means of gathering data for weather forecasts. When Hazen joined the U.S. Weather Bureau, he and Cleveland Abbe, pioneer American meteorologist and an old friend of Langley, also became involved in aeronautical studies aimed at improving kite design. S. A. Potter of Washington, D.C., was a particularly important kite experimenter employed by the Weather Bureau under Hazen.[12]

These meteorologists were quick to perceive the superiority of the box kite introduced by Lawrence Hargrave at the Chicago conference. By October 1896, these devices had almost completely replaced the Eddy design, and altitudes of up to 1 2/3 miles were soon attained at Blue Hill.

Rotch, Marvin, Fergusson, Hazen, and other meteorologists were soon taking part in major aeronautical conferences like that held in Chicago in 1893, by which time they were clearly regarded as members of the American aeronautical community. Influential experimenters came to view the meteorologists as an important source of information on kite performance that could be applied to the design of airplanes as well. It was primarily for this reason that outside funds were frequently made available for atmospheric studies conducted with kites. The Hodgkins Fund grant that Langley approved for Rotch in 1897 is a case in point.

The public certainly regarded the meteorologists as men contributing to the solution of manned flight. Frequent newspaper articles appearing during the 1890s featured headlines such as "Kites and Flying Ships" or "William Eddy and Aerial Navigation." By 1896, newspapers were frequently ignoring the fact that scientists remained interested in kites because of their utility in lofting instruments. Most editors preferred to emphasize the meteorologists and their kites "as a step toward the solution of the problem of navigating the air."[13]

The Boston meteorologists also drew several independent inventors into the larger community of U.S. aeronautical enthusiasts. Rotch and his associates at Blue Hill, for example, took a special interest in the "aerocurve kites" developed by Charles H. Lamson of Portland, Maine. Lamson was a jeweler by training but had turned to the manufacture of luggage carriers and other bicycle accessories. He had experimented with a variety of kite types for many years prior to his public success of 1896. Almost all of these were influenced by Hargrave's box kites. Constructed in a variety of sizes, Lamson's kites usually consisted of a forward section composed of two biplane wings. Four pairs of vertical braces tied these two surfaces into a single unit. A "keel" or uncovered frame of wooden stringers connected the forward section to the rear surfaces. The tail assemblies varied among the many types that Lamson constructed. In the large man-lifting vehicles, the rear wings were exactly the same as the forward wings. The smaller kites used to lift meteorological instruments at Blue Hill and U.S. Weather Bureau stations usually carried much smaller superposed triangular sails.

Lamson's interest in kites had always been aimed at the eventual production of a manned glider. In 1895, he had obtained a set of Lilienthal glider plans in Germany and had constructed

A meteorological kite flying under the clouds.

a duplicate of the German master's standard glider. Disappointed by the lack of stability exhibited by this machine, he decided to enlarge one of his kites to man-carrying dimensions.

Lamson's first large kite was unveiled before a crowd of 15,000 spectators in Portland, Maine, on August 23, 1896. Weighing over 100 pounds and measuring 30 feet in length, the monster had a wing span of 28 feet. The upper surfaces in the front and rear were separated from the lower wings by 7 feet. A 150-pound dummy was attached to the frame separating the two wing pairs. A fifteen-man crew carried the giant kite to the launching point. The craft rose rapidly to an altitude of 600 feet when the tow rope snapped. Even Lamson seemed surprised when his creation glided smoothly to earth of its own volition, landing so lightly that no damage was done to the kite. The inventor told the newsmen present that he had demonstrated that "the time is very close at hand when people will be sailing through the air. I think that time will be here inside of three years."[14]

During winter 1896–1897 Lamson constructed a second man-carrying kite. The new craft had a wingspread of 26 feet and was roughly 26 feet long. The wing area totaled 600 square feet. The frame was constructed of straight-grained American spruce. The first flight was made from Falmouth Farside on May 19, 1896. On this occasion the kite was sent to an altitude of 1,000

C. H. Lamson.

feet. While being reeled back in, the line parted and the craft glided back to the ground, sustaining slight damage to one wing tip.[15]

On June 2, Lamson himself made an ascent to 50 feet that was witnessed by Rotch, Fergusson, and Clayton. Fred Bickford, one of Lamson's assistants, then made a flight to 300 feet.[16]

One of the most memorable flights of the Lamson man-lifter took place on July 11, 1897, when Grace M. Gould, a reporter for the *New York Journal*, went aloft. Her account of the terrors of the air remains a classic.

Our heroine was at first a bit nonplused by the "unkitelike" appearance of the craft. Expecting a typical shield-shaped kite, she found instead "something that looked like the rigging of a schooner yacht, without any hull." Lamson and his assistants led the reporter into the midst of the fluttering muslin and pointed to the board swingseat slung in front of the bicycle wheels used to maneuver the craft on the ground. "Now," said the chief operator, you don't want to be scared, and you don't want to be rattled. You're in no danger as long as you keep your head, and you don't fall."

With this comforting assurance ringing in her ears, Miss Gould and her kite were tipped back, were turned into the wind, and began to climb into the air. Brushing the hair from her eyes, she began to relax and enjoy the ride.

> The big, birdlike thing to which I clung was soaring up and settling down and travelling over the field like a gull trying to cross a windstorm. I would not have been at all surprised to have seen the big wings flap.
>
> There was a big red barn at the edge of the field, with lightning rods sticking up from it, and for a second I had a horrible fear that I would be swept over that and bruised against the lightning rods. Then I remembered that the nonchalant men who had hold of the end of the cord were not going to let me out into any such collision.
>
> I swayed a good deal, and I bounced some, as if the ropes had been rubber bands, but after the first five minutes my heart quit

getting up into my throat and I really felt quite superior. Then my wayward feet touched something, and my swing seat was on the ground. My flight was over."[17]

Miss Gould, probably the first woman ever to fly in a heavier-than-air machine, was enthusiastic. When Lamson asked how she had liked the trip, she replied, "Better than a bicycle, a merry-go-round, and a shoot-the-chute all combined, but I did want to fly over the barn!"

The Blue Hill experimenters were impressed with Lamson's work and remained in Maine for some time selecting smaller versions of his kite for use with their self-recording instruments. By 1895, Lamson was corresponding regularly with Octave Chanute, Samuel Langley, and other leading aeronautical authorities.

A core of independent aeronautical experimenters had developed in the Boston area by 1894. These men, under the leadership of Means, Cabot, Merrill, Pickering, and Rotch, banded together to form the Boston Aeronautical Society on March 19, 1895. The leaders of the new organization were determined that their society would be more active than similar groups that had been established in Europe. Members would, of course, gather to present papers and discuss the scientific and technical aspects of the problems, but the emphasis was to be placed on experimentation. Means underlined this goal in preparing the constitution of the Boston Aeronautical Society. He included a statement that the society was to "encourage experimenters and study with aerial machines and to advance the science of aerodynamics."[18]

The membership was limited to twenty. Meetings were to be held every month. In accordance with the desire of the group to become involved in active experimentation, plans were made to establish a testing site in the Boston area. They hoped to find a farm with a barn to be used both as a workshop and storehouse. It was also suggested that a "revolving slope" designed by Merrill be constructed for glider flights. A balloon would be provided so that relatively large models could be released at high altitudes. Finally, a skilled mechanic would be hired to oversee work on the machines designed by the members and to conduct his own experiments as well.

Such an ambitious program would be expensive, and the creation of an experimental fund became the first order of business. Means took charge of the matter and throughout the summer and fall of 1895 sent letters soliciting contributions to a number of wealthy men, including J. R. De Laniar, J. M. Sears, Augustus Hemingway, Albert Pope, and John Jacob Astor. Each of these requests was carefully framed to appeal to the particular interests of the man involved. For example, Means suggested to Pope, the Hartford bicycle and automobile manufacturer, that "your experience as a pioneer in the development of *one* mode of human locomotion might lead you to take an interest in *another* mode."[19]

Means and J. B. Millett, a publisher and kite enthusiast, paid visits to many of the prospective donors. A small fund was gradually established as a result of these efforts and the contributions of the members. Means himself turned the meager profits of the second issue of the *Aeronautical Annual* over to the society and provided $100 in prize money for a kite contest. Cabot sponsored a photo contest with cash awards going to those who produced the most revealing pictures of birds in flight. An enthusiastic and well-connected amateur, Miss Octavia Chanute, won the contest.

Joint flying trials were planned for summer 1895, but as a number of members hoped to conduct private experiments during this period, the group flight tests were postponed until October. These were canceled entirely when it became apparent that no one had built a glider. Interest then shifted to the possibility of purchasing a Lilienthal glider or an American copy of the German craft.

During March 1896 Means and Millett had decided that they would temporarily set aside their plans to purchase and fly a Lilienthal glider in favor of persuading the German master himself to make a personal-appearance tour in the United States. The two men cabled Lilienthal on March 20, offering to guarantee expenses if he would spend several months in Boston giving talks, making exhibition flights, and instructing

Americans in the art of gliding. The Boston Aeronautical Society would make all arrangements and place a generous proportion of the profits derived from the venture in its experimental fund.

Once again Means attempted to draw others into the venture. He asked John Brisben Walker to consider partial sponsorship of the Lilienthal tour in return for exclusive interviews that would be granted to the *Cosmopolitan*. Means and Millett informed General Adolphus Greely of the prospect of the foreign glider expert's visit and suggested that Sergeant Ivy Baldwin, a noted Army balloonist, be detached to the Boston Aeronautical Society so that he could be instructed in the operation of a Lilienthal machine.

The grandiose plans collapsed, however, when Lilienthal rejected their offer. Business commitments, he said, would preclude a visit to America during the summer of 1896. He was interested, however, and might be willing to come the following year. Lilienthal's death and the newspaper coverage of the *New York Journal*'s Lilienthal glider convinced the Boston Aeronautical Society that it should look elsewhere for publicity.[20]

The group finally decided to hold their first open field trials for flying machines near Boston during the fall of 1896. Experimenters all over the nation and the world were informed that major cash prizes would be awarded in a variety of categories. Three kite contests would also be sponsored. Many experimenters like Hargrave became very enthusiastic about the event and sent kites to be entered and flown in absentia.

The deterioration of personal relationships between key members of the Boston Aeronautical Society was to destroy much of the promise of the organization. Means, Merrill, and Pickering had been appointed to the committee planning the autumn flying meet. Initial meetings were held, and Means believed that all of the rules had been firmly established. Pickering and Merrill met a second time without Means's knowledge, however, and arbitrarily changed the regulations for the contest. Without informing the editor, the two men published a revised circular and distributed it to those who had originally expressed an interest in entering.

The result was total confusion. Hargrave, in particular, seriously questioned the good faith of the sponsors of the event. Chanute expressed his disappointment as well. Means was incensed that his two colleagues had seen fit to change the rules behind his back and remarked that he believed their action to have been "ill considered." He penned an angry letter to Merrill pointing out that the unauthorized rule change had "placed the Society in a ridiculous position."[21]

Pickering and Merrill viewed the situation as a tempest in a teapot, an attitude that only made Means more angry. Exasperated over what he viewed as the frivolous approach of the other members, he resigned from the Boston Aeronautical Society on December 18, 1896. Continuing squabbles suggest, however, that the ill feeling between Means and other members was not totally the result of this single episode. Merrill, for example, believed that the editor had attempted to "buy" honors in the group with generous contributions to the prize fund. Means replied that this had not been his intention at all. He was also offended when Merrill intimated that the editor had not paid a promised $150 to the kite prize fund. In the midst of these bitter recriminations the planned competition collapsed. A final notice was circulated informing potential contestants that insufficient entries were responsible for the cancellation.[22]

James Means and the members of the Boston Aeronautical Society followed separate paths after this point. Means remained a major figure in aeronautical journalism, a confidant of Chanute, Herring, and others, and a personal friend of Samuel Langley. He would continue to be an intimate observer of and commentator on the aeronautical scene, but his days as the center of enthusiasm in the Northeast had passed.

The Boston Aeronautical Society continued to function for some time following Means's departure, but the group's activities were subdued. No longer was word of their proposed contests carried by newspapers across the United States. Nevertheless, the organization was able to achieve one of its original goals by hiring a full-time professional mechanic, Gustave Weisskopf, to oversee the construction of a society flying machine.

Weisskopf, a German, had approached James Means in 1895

with tales of long flights made in a glider that he had constructed while a seaman in Brazil. Weisskopf, or Whitehead as he came to call himself with increasing frequency, must have made a favorable impression on the other members of the Boston Aeronautical Society as well, for he was soon employed as that group's first professional mechanic. Means's friend Millett was certainly won over and may, in fact, have been the man who actually hired Whitehead for the society.

Few contemporary accounts of the German's work in Boston are available, but letters passing between Cabot and Chanute make it clear that a flying machine was under construction. By May 1897 Cabot was expressing his disappointment to Chanute.

> Weisskopf so far has made a conspicuous failure with his apparatus, and I fear that he is a pure romancer with a supreme mastery of the art of lying. I feel, however, that it is perhaps a little premature to make a final condemnation of him.[23]

Nevertheless, Chanute once again exhibited his generosity by donating $50 to the expenses involved in constructing and testing the "Weisskopf apparatus." This was in addition to the $100 he had contributed to the Boston Aeronautical Society's prize fund for a kite essay contest.

No good description of Whitehead's 1897 Boston machine remains. Many years later, however, A. P. Horn, who had assisted the German during this period, recalled the gliders.

> We made one of bamboo guyed with pinao wire and covered with fine woven cloth, a seat was suspended between the wings to support the operator, working two smaller wings for propulsion.[24]

Horn commented that they had also constructed a machine "after the pattern of Lilienthal," whom Whitehead claimed to have known. It is apparent tht the first of these two craft was not a true glider, but included smaller wings intended either to be flapped or used as oars for propulsion.

Whitehead, who weighed 200 pounds at the time, made attempts to fly with the two machines, but he remained firmly earthbound. As Cabot remarked:

> I have had occasion, since last writing you, to modify my views about Weisskopf's failure so far. He very foolishly attempted his experiments in a place which would have been dangerous had he got a flight . . . he was condemned to disappointment from the beginning.[25]

Whitehead left Boston in the spring of 1897 when the initial funds supporting his work were exhausted. Cabot hoped eventually to rehire him, but Whitehead's subsequent moves to Buffalo and Pittsburgh made this impossible. After his departure, the German was to remain apart from the mainstream of the aeronautical community, too independent and eccentric to ally himself with an established figure or group again.

Chanute, Langley, Means, and the other leaders of the flying-machine movement rapidly lost what little interest they had in Whitehead's activity after his departure from Boston. He emerged occasionally, as in 1902 when Langley dispatched an assistant to Atlantic City where the German was exhibiting a strange flying machine, and again in 1904 when Chanute noted that Whitehead was exhibiting an aeronautical motor at the St. Louis World's Fair.

For the most part, however, Whitehead's later work drew almost no attention from knowledgeable authorities. The occasional brief newspaper story or article in an obscure mechanic's magazine suggesting that Whitehead had been very busy during the years 1897–1902 was completely discounted.

These accounts lay buried for more than three decades, until the 1930s, when an enterprising journalist launched a vigorous campaign to resurrect what became known as "The Lost Flights of Gustave Whitehead." As a result of this effort Whitehead became the most frequently mentioned of several candidates said to have preceded the Wrights into the air.[26] This campaign to establish Whitehead's aeronautical primacy was conducted by determined partisans who drew on the fading memories of aged men and women to buttress their hero's shaky case.

As with John Montgomery, the facts of Gustave Whitehead's aeronautical career have become so confused that any attempt to arrive at the truth of the matter requires the most careful scrutiny of the original sources.

Whitehead's extraordinary flight claims begin after his move to Pittsburgh. Louis Darvarich, who assisted Whitehead during this period, claimed years later that the two had developed a successful steam-powered flying machine in spring 1899. According to Darvarich, this craft carried them to an altitude of 25 feet. The flights came to an end, he continued, when the machine, with both men aboard, crashed into a three-story building in April or May 1899.[27]

There is not a shred of evidence to support this story. No photos of the machine either in the air or on the ground were taken. No news stories were written to chronicle what should have captured front pages across the nation. No mention of treatment for the supposed injuries has been discovered in Pittsburgh police department, fire department, or hospital records. It is difficult to believe that any student of the case could give any credence to the Pittsburgh story.

By 1900 Whitehead had settled in Bridgeport, Connecticut. Newspaper accounts of the period suggest that he supported his growing family by working as a coal-wagon driver and a night watchman. But he had not lost interest in aeronautics.

As late as 1968 a one-time Whitehead co-worker would allege that flights of up to 200 feet were made in a machine constructed within a year of his arrival in Bridgeport. Once again, there is no evidence to substantiate the fading recollections of an old man struggling to recall events that had occurred a lifetime before.[28]

One of Whitehead's most oft-repeated claims relates to a flight of 1 1/2 miles said to have been made on August 14, 1901, in a machine referred to as No. 21. The earliest description of this craft appeared in a *Scientific American* article of June 8, 1901, written by Stanley Yale Beach, son of the publisher of the journal. Beach's detailed account, the first available of any Whitehead machine, described a monoplane "built after the model of a bird or a bat." It was constructed of wood, steel, and canvas.

A 10-horsepower engine powered the four wheels on which the craft manuevered on the ground while a 20-horsepower calcium-carbide or acetylene power plant drove the twin propellers that would move No. 21 through the air. The foldable wings and triangular birdlike tail totaled 450 square feet of surface area.[29]

The Beach article attracted wide attention. Only ten days after its appearance, the *New York Herald* followed with a well-illustrated piece: "Connecticut Night Watchman Thinks He Has Found Out How to Fly." It was a sympathetic portrait of the young German, who now claimed to have built a grand total of fifty-six flying machines to date. Why the machine in question was numbered only 21 was not explained. More important, Whitehead informed the reporter in an offhanded manner that No. 21 had already made a flight of 1/2 mile.[30]

On August 18, 1901, a local paper, the *Bridgeport Sunday Herald,* carried what purported to be an eyewitness account of a much

Gustave Whitehead, his daughter, and No. 21.

longer flight in No. 21. According to the reporter, Richard How-
ell, the trial had taken place shortly after midnight on August
14 in a large field near Fairfield, Connecticut. The manned ascent was preceded by an unmanned test flight in which the craft
was described as looking, "for all the world like a great white
goose raising from the feeding ground in the early morning
dawn."[31]

The machine was then returned to the starting point, where
Whitehead removed the 230 pounds of sand ballast and climbed
into the cockpit. As a small band of assistants watched in amaze-
ment, the craft darted down a slope and into the air. Avoiding
a clump of trees, the pilot kept his machine aloft for 1/2 mile
before cutting power and gliding to a landing. Later, in 1902, the
inventor would amend the total distance flown on August 14 to
1 1/2 miles. Whitehead was reported to be pleased with the performance, and remarked that he would enter into a partnership
with W. D. Custead of Waco, Texas, to "perfect a machine that
will come nearer to the point of success than any other machine
thus far made."[32]

This sounds very convincing, but even a quick look beneath
the surface reveals some serious flaws in the account. First, as
to the machine itself. Whitehead's No. 21 as described in the
news stories, was an incredibly complex machine with two engines, folding wings, a low undercarriage, and no apparent system for balancing the craft in roll. News photos that appeared
at the time of the alleged flight show an incomplete craft missing
the engine of which the inventor seemed so proud.

Charles Manly, Langley's chief aeronautical assistant after
1898, reinforced these doubts. Manly received trustworthy accounts of the craft when it was exhibited at Young's Pier in
Atlantic City in September 1901. He remarked that, in his knowledgeable opinion, "the man is a fraud insofar as he claims to
have flown in the machine, since I understand that the whole
construction is so flimsy that I doubt whether the framework
would hold together."[33]

Still, we are left with the compelling *Bridgeport Sunday Herald*
eyewitness account of an actual flight. And what a story! The
dream of the ages had apparently been realized in Bridgeport

and the *Herald* had a golden opportunity to scoop the world. Surely this deserved banner headlines on the front page.

Yet the account appeared, not on page 1, but in the feature section. Headed "Flying," the story was not illustrated with the photos that any alert editor could have had taken during the four days between the flight and the appearance of the article, but by a drawing of four witches seated on brooms. The by-line and other accouterments of a straight news story are also missing.

Even more telling is the fact that not one of the four Bridgeport dailies carried an account of the supposed flight either before or after the *Sunday Herald* story. Nor did this or any other paper choose to follow up the extraordinary account. Other eastern dailies would almost certainly have been interested in further information, for at least two had picked up the original account. Strange treatment indeed for the story of the century.

This was, after all, the age of the enterprising reporter. Two years later Wilbur and Orville Wright flew only 852 feet, not in Bridgeport, a relative metropolis, but four miles from Kitty Hawk, a tiny, isolated village on the Outer Banks. The brothers took every precaution to insure the secrecy of their work, yet a reporter in distant Norfolk, Virginia, picked up the story and prepared an inaccurate wire-service account that appeared in several papers. The reaction was immediate, forcing the Wrights to hold a press conference after their return to Dayton. The contrasting languor of the Bridgeport editors is remarkable if, in fact, the story was ever regarded by local citizens as anything other than a hoax or a bit of overimaginative journalism.

Once again, Whitehead's supporters, operating decades after the fact, were able to collect assorted affidavits from aged citizens who claimed to recall the events of August 14, 1901. As might be expected, these documents are so confusing and contradictory that they cannot be accepted as evidence for the flight. It is important to note that an independent investigator, canvassing Whitehead's old Bridgeport neighborhood in 1936 could find no one who had ever heard of the alleged flights. One of those questioned, the brother of an old Whitehead assistant, could not recall any family discussion of the event.[34]

The most persuasive evidence against the Whitehead flight is to be found in the text of the *Sunday Herald* article, however. The reporter named only two witnesses, James Dickie and Andrew Cellic. When interviewed in 1937, Dickie remarked that No. 21 had never flown. Nor had he ever heard of Cellic. He remarked, "I believe the entire story of the *Herald* was imaginary, and grew out of the comments of Whitehead discussing what he hoped to get from his plane. I was not present and did not witness any airplane flight on August 14, 1901. I do not remember or recall ever hearing of a flight with this particular plane or any other that Whitehead ever built." The evidence against the alleged flight of August 14, 1901, is overwhelming.[35]

But the 1901 claims were only the beginning. In two letters published in the *American Inventor* for April 1, 1902, Whitehead described two more flights on January 17, 1902, in a new machine, No. 22. One flight had covered 2 miles, the other 7 miles over Long Island Sound.

Whitehead remarked that the craft took four months to be constructed by fourteen men at a cost of $1,700. He claimed that it was powered by a 40-horsepower five-cylinder kerosene motor that operated at 800 rpm and weighed 120 pounds. The fuselage, built of steel tubing braced with piano wire, was 16 1/2 feet long, 3 1/2 feet wide, and covered with aluminum sheeting. The ribs were made of steel tubing and the wings covered with 450 square feet of silk. Two contrarotating propellers, each 6 feet in diameter, were provided. A 12-foot tail, which, like the wings, could be folded against the fuselage, brought up the rear.

Like No. 21, the new machine would run along the ground on four automobile wheels, but was intended to land in the water. The first of the alleged flights of January 17 covered 2 miles, after which Whitehead settled into the water and was towed back to the starting point. During the second flight Whitehead claimed to have climbed to 200 feet and cruised in a circle for 7 miles "at a frightful speed." After a safe landing, he placed his machine in storage until spring.[36]

If true, Whitehead's achievement was extraordinary indeed. Flights of 2 and 7 miles at an altitude of 200 feet with circles thrown in for good measure would certainly indicate that the problem of flight had been solved.

But there is no more reason to believe this account than those of the earlier flights. There are no photos of the machine in flight, no trustworthy corroboration from contemporary witnesses, no inquiring reporters attempting to probe for the truth of the story. Only a bold assertion by the inventor.

Moreover, there is strong circumstantial evidence arrayed against Whitehead. His financial supporters, the men who should have been best informed as to the German's achievements, refused to accept his claims. Stanley Yale Beach, author of the original *Scientific American* story, had convinced his father to underwrite Whitehead's work. Beach remained associated with the German for many years and had every reason to hope for a flight, yet his recollection is clear. "I do not believe that any of his machines ever left the ground . . . in spite of the assertions of many people who think they saw them fly. I think I was in a better position during the nine years that I was giving Whitehead money to develop his ideas, to know what his machines could do, than persons who were employed by him for a short period of time or those who have remained silent for thirty-five years about what would have been an historic achievement in aviation."[37]

The experience of Herman Linde, who had supported Whitehead since his arrival in Connecticut, was also less than satisfactory. On April 5, 1902, the Bridgeport *Evening Farmer* reported that the two men were experiencing financial difficulties apparently resulting from Whitehead's having overdrawn one of Linde's accounts. Certainly it was a strange situation for a man who claimed to have flown 7 miles only three months earlier. Even the members of Whitehead's family could not recall his having mentioned the long flights of 1901–1902.[38]

Whitehead's subsequent behavior is inexplicable if we accept the truth of his early flight claims. He continued to build flying machines, but completely abandoned the design that had supposedly proved so successful, working instead on a glider patterned after a triplane constructed by Octave Chanute.[39]

The question is obvious. If Whitehead had flown in 1901–1902, why did he not work to improve his basic design? Why, in fact, did he turn his back on machines for which he made such extravagant claims to construct rude copies of gliders designed by men who had never flown more than a few hundred feet? Why did he not repeat his 7-mile flight, or even the 200-foot flight, in public?

The best efforts of Whitehead's supporters have failed to provide any of the answers. Gustave Whitehead was not a neglected aeronautical genius who flew before the Wrights. Nor did his work prove to be of value to other experimenters. Rather the story is one of press agentry and wishful thinking triumphant.

Means, Cabot, Merrill, Lamson, and other members of the Boston circle were much less controversial than Whitehead, yet they were to have greater impact. While they made few technical contributions, they were almost without peer as publicists in the service of aeronautics. In spite of the demise of their formal organization, they would remain closely involved with the work of the most active aeronautical research centers until the final success was achieved.

7

S. P. Langley: The Scientist as Engineer

On November 22, 1886, Samuel Langley received an intriguing offer from Spencer Fullerton Baird, aging secretary of the Smithsonian Institution. Baird informed Langley that the institution's board of regents had recently created two new assistant secretarial posts. George Browne Goode, a long-time Smithsonian staff member, would take command of museum programs. Would Langley be interested in a similar position of responsibility over international exchanges, the library, and publications?

Langley was indeed interested. During his two decades in Pittsburgh he had felt isolated, cut off from close association with those who shared his interests and enthusiasms. Within a year of his arrival at Allegheny he had complained to Cleveland Abbe, a Cincinnati colleague, that "here there is no one to talk to."[1] "Astronomy has only one disciple in this community," he lamented in 1869. "I should enjoy a visit and a little sight of some one interested in what interests me."[2] He remarked to his friend C. S. Pierce, philosopher and mathematician, that he was "out in the cold" and far removed "from the companionship a student of science wants."[3] For years he had complained of the low state of culture in Pittsburgh, pointing to a general disinterest in science and the arts.

In addition, there was the question of prestige. By 1887 Langley had become a leader of American science. He held honorary degrees from some of the great universities of the world, including Oxford, Cambridge, Harvard, Yale, Princeton, Michigan, and Wisconsin. International scientific societies had showered him with awards. In 1886 he received the Henry Draper medal from his fellows of the National Academy of Sciences. The Janssen medal of the Institute of France, the Medal of the French Astronomical Society, and the Rumford medals of both the Royal Society of Great Britain and the American Academy of Arts and Sciences attested to his distinguished reputation.

Nor was Langley's fame restricted to scientific circles. Even Andrew Carnegie expressed a desire to meet the astronomer, explaining that "it is my weakness to be companion to great men."[4]

Langley saw these accolades as evidence of the fact that he had outgrown the Allegheny Observatory. The Smithsonian offer fit

Samuel Langley with relatives in Rome.

his requirements for a more prestigious and highly visible post. A promise that he would eventually take Baird's place sealed the decision.

Initially, Langley planned to split his time, spending seven months a year on research, three months on his new administrative duties in Washington, with two summer months being devoted to travel and study, but Baird's death the following summer made this impossible. As promised, in November 1887 Langley was named the third secretary of the Smithsonian Institution.

He found the Washington social and intellectual climate all he had hoped. Here at last, safely ensconced within a tight circle of elite friends and associates who wielded power and influence in the nation's capital, he found the admiration and respect he had so missed in Pittsburgh.

Langley roomed at the Cosmos Club, a favorite gathering place for the American scientific, political, and artistic elite. At his first official dinner, three Supreme Court justices and three United States senators echoed a toast offered by the chief justice of the United States in his honor. Henry Adams, intellectual arbiter of the day, was one of many who regarded Langley as his guide through the mysteries of science. The new secretary had arrived at last.[5]

Now Langley was free to pursue his own scientific interests. The days of begging for meager research support were over. As head of the Smithsonian, Langley commanded the single largest source of research funding in America. He was encouraged by the regents to draw on these accounts to support his own work.

Langley was to use this position of stewardship wisely, shaping the course of the institution for decades to come. The Smithsonian Astrophysical Observatory, the National Zoo, and an increased emphasis on public education through museum programs are a legacy of Langley's tenure in office.

But throughout these years aeronautics was the secretary's major interest. Gradually, between 1887 and 1903, he transformed the Smithsonian carpentry and machine shops into a research and development facility aimed at the production of a successful flying machine.

Much to his delight, Langley discovered that his new circle of
Washington associates included a significant number of men
who were interested in aeronautics. Alexander Graham Bell, for
example, had already conducted experiments with small model
aircraft propelled by black-powder rockets. As a result of Langley's regular attendance at the Wednesday-evening discussion
sessions that Bell hosted at his home, the two men became fast
friends. Bell was to remain one of Langley's staunchist supporters. After 1903, he undertook his own flying-machine work, culminating in the establishment of the Aerial Experiment Association in 1907.

Other members of Bell's informal discussion group became
even more actively involved in Langley's aeronautical effort.
Charles D. Walcott of the U.S. Coast Survey and Carl Barus of
the Bureau of Standards were to play key roles. General H. A.
Hazen, chief of the U.S. Signal Service, was one of several influential military leaders who followed Langley's progress with
interest. Even Edward Everett Hale, the venerable chaplain of
the U.S. Senate and the author of a science-fiction tale involving
a manned orbiting satellite, listened with interest as Langley
outlined his plans for a flying machine.[6]

Albert F. Zahm was also to join the circle of Washington aeronautical enthusiasts grouped around Langley. Zahm
had remained in close touch with Chanute following the International Conference on 'Aerial Navigation, but he was
not involved in the gliding experiments conducted by the
Chicago circle after 1894. He refused an opportunity to become U.S. consul in Barcelona, choosing instead to enter the
Johns Hopkins University, to work toward a Ph.D. in physics,
which was granted in 1895. His dissertation, a study of the
air resistance encountered by projectiles moving at high
speeds, established his reputation in the American scientific
community.

Zahm then returned to Notre Dame to resume his duties as
an instructor of physics and mathematics. Soon after his arrival
in South Bend, he received a call from the Right Reverend John
J. Keane, rector of the Catholic University of America in Washington, D.C., who found Zahm "enthusiastically building model

airplanes and studying the principles of flight." Impressed by the young man's credentials, Father Keane offered him a position as head of Catholic University's department of physics and mechanics. Zahm accepted immediately, reporting to his new post in August 1895.

Over the next five years, with the financial assistance of Hugo Mattulath, a wealthy experimenter, Zahm constructed the first well-equipped aerodynamic research laboratory in America at the Catholic University. Complete with a 40-foot wind tunnel producing air speeds of up to 25 miles per hour, the facility was unfortunately wasted on preliminary studies for an enormous flying machine projected by the eccentric Mattulath.[7]

During the 1890s Bell, Walcott, Barus, Zahm, and others formed a subset of the larger Washington intellectual community. Convinced that Langley and his associates at the Smithsonian were the most likely candidates for success with a powered flying machine, these men used their influence with Congress, federal agencies, the press, and the nation's scientists and engineers to support and defend the Smithsonian aeronautical program.

Langley could not have hoped for better circumstances under which to continue his aeronautical work. Certain that his experiments at Allegheny had established powered flight as a possibility, he now commanded the money and support necessary to provide a convincing demonstration for skeptics like Lord Kelvin, who had questioned the validity of *Experiments in Aerodynamics.*

The rubber-powered model airplanes designed and built at Allegheny and the Smithsonian were the first attempt to provide a practical illustration of the theoretical principles that he had evolved. When these craft proved less than successful, the secretary argued that the fault lay in the fact that the rubber strands did not produce sufficient power. The answer, Langley reasoned, was to build a model flying machine large enough to support the weight of a more powerful engine. This seemed the cheapest and simplest means of cementing his own position as an aeronautical pioneer. After all, he argued:

It is to be remembered that the mechanical difficulties of artificial flight have been so great that, so far as is known, never, at any time in the history of the world has any such mechanism, however activated, sustained itself in the air for more than a few seconds, never for instance, a single half minute.[8]

The secretary was determined to make such a flight.

While Langley was confident that he could achieve his goal, he recognized his limitations. His training and experience as an architect and astronomer had done little to prepare him to solve the difficult technical problems that he knew would be encountered. Langley realized that he required the services of mechanical specialists who could translate his computations, rough sketches, and theoretical suggestions into a piece of operating machinery.

Langley chose his initial team with care. Carl Barus, physicist and hydrographic expert employed by the Geological Survey and the United States Weather Bureau who joined the Smithsonian staff as a physicist in 1893, filled the gaps in Langley's knowledge of physics and mechanics and served as a liaison between the secretary and his machinists. He was so important a figure during the early development of the steam aerodromes that a *Chicago Tribune* reporter, writing in 1893, identified his as the man "who knows all of the airplane."[9] John Elfreth Watkins, curator of the mechanical collections of the Smithsonian Institution, served as the secretary's "volunteer" expert and chief technical adviser in steam-engine design. Machinist L. C. Maltby assisted in the design of the engines and oversaw the metalwork in the museum shop, while George E. Curtiss performed general aerodromic work and served as liaison with Chanute and other aeronautical authorities.

A number of other employees, notably carpenter R. L. Reed, were pressed into full-time service in the design and construction of the flying machines. Better-known and more experienced aeronautical enthusiasts were to enter and leave Langley's employ between 1890 and 1903, but most of this original cadre would remain throughout the entire period.

The secretary realized that he was facing a more difficult

problem than he had encountered during the course of the experiments in aerodynamics. He was no longer simply trying to obtain valid scientific data, but was building a large, heavy machine that would fly. Langley felt that the new technology that he was developing deserved a new name. In December 1890 he contacted a philologist for suggestions on applicable terms drawn from classical languages.

The scholar responded with three possibilities, all from the Greek. These included "aerobater," one who walks through the air; "anemodromic," or wind-drawn; and "aerodromoi," or air runner. Unfortunately, Langley preferred the third phrase, and from this date all of his flying machines were to be known as "aerodromes," representatives of the new science of aerodromics. As any student of Greek could have told him, "aerodrome," properly translated, is a place where the machines fly, not the machines themselves.

Langley's earlier experiments at the Allegheny Observatory had indicated that power for a flying machine would not present a major stumbling block. He realized, at least on a theoretical level, that the most important unanswered questions lay in the area of control and stability. He provided an unequivocal statement of this belief in a *Cosmopolitan* article published in 1893.

> I repeat then (for this is a fundamentally important fact), that it is not so much the power, as the skill to guide it, which we lack. It is already demonstrated that the power is actually here, in certain recent engines; but the "learning to guide it," however brief the process, is attended with such risk as to make the first who try to learn objects of deserved interest and a solicitude we should only bestow on those risking their lives not out of foolhardiness, but for a useful end.[10]

The studies that preceded the publication of *Internal Work of the Wind* had convinced Langley that upper-air gusts were so unpredictable and violent that inherent stability would be an absolute requirement, particularly in the case of his large models that would not have a pilot on board to control the movement of the craft. By 1898, when he began work on a full-scale manned aerodrome, he had come to believe that human reactions were too slow to deal with the rapid changes in wind speed and direction that would be encountered in flight. The secretary was correct in identifying stability and attitude control as the central problem remaining to be solved. Unfortunately, the practical difficulties of producing a small but powerful engine and a lightweight airframe were to draw him so far afield that by 1903 no serious attempts had been made to develop a reasonable guidance system.

Langley drew on a variety of Washington resources to finance the construction of the aerodromes. As early as 1874 he had found support for his solar research in the Bache Fund of the National Academy of Sciences. By 1889, he had been awarded a number of additional Bache grants in excess of $1,500, some of which were applied to the aerodromes.[11]

The Hodgkins Fund was a more important source of funding. Thomas George Hodgkins, an Englishman living in Setauket, Long Island, had bequeathed $200,000 to the Smithsonian in 1891, stipulating that one-half be used in "the investigation of the properties of atmospheric air."

In 1892, when Hodgkins died, $50,000 was added, which was used to support tuberculosis and air-pollution studies as well as such varied aeronautical research as E. J. Marey's photographs of birds in motion, a number of meteorological projects including W. A. Eddy's kite experiments, the publication of aeronautical manuscripts, and, in 1919, Robert H. Goddard's early rocket work. The regents allowed Langley to draw freely from this account for the construction of the aerodromes.[12]

In addition to such formal support, Langley's position as the head of the Smithsonian Institution permitted him to call on the services of a staff that boasted expertise in a variety of vital areas. While it was necessary to use the grant funds for complicated machine work and the necessary metal stock, all of the carpentry, much of the simple machining, most of the raw materials, and the required salaries would be carried on the Smithsonian accounts.

Langley's first serious step was to survey possible power plants. Although confident that he had demonstrated the amount of power required, he still faced the practical problem of selecting a suitable engine from among several available alternatives. All aeronautical experimenters of the period were naturally attracted to the internal combustion engines recently developed in Europe, but the secretary felt that the problems of scale precluded his use of such a motor. While the necessary power was certainly available in a gasoline engine, existing methods would not permit the construction of a sufficiently lightweight hydrocarbon power plant. Plans for such a motor were therefore set aside to await the construction of a full-scale flying machine capable of supporting the extra weight. Electric motors could not be considered in the absence of lightweight batteries, and hot-water engines were out of the question because of the necessity for heavy tankage. A gunpowder motor was considered but rejected because of its unreliability and danger.

Liquid carbonic acid yields an even flow of carbon-dioxide gas that can be used to operate a standard steam engine. Such a power plant would not require a complex and heavy system of boilers, condensers, and separators, but there were disadvantages to be considered as well. The rapid expansion of the gas made serious inroads into the latent heat of the liquid. Lumps of solid acid were often introduced into the system, blocking the pipes leading from the reservoir to the engine. Finally, such motors were plagued by freezing pipes and valves.

Simple compressed air engines could not supply sufficient power for a long enough period of time to keep Langley's large models in the air. This left only the steam engine. Although steam required some excess weight unnecessary with other power systems, the technology had been thoroughly explored. The existing body of knowledge on the construction of lightweight steam engines, coupled with the practical experience of his own staff in this field, convinced the secretary that steam offered the most reasonable chance of success.[13]

By November 1891, with the preliminaries complete, Langley ordered the construction of his first powered aerodrome, identified as No. o. Those involved in the design of this first machine were working completely in the dark. While some of the data from the more successful rubber-powered models could be applied, almost nothing was known of the correct hull form, wing design, the most effective means to build a very light, strong airframe, or even the most efficient size and weight.[14]

A few basics were apparent. The most important realization had come during October 1890, when Langley finally rejected the plane surface in favor of cambered wings. Two large rubber-powered models, numbered 30 and 31, were used to test a variety of wing configurations. The decision to use tandem wings or a large surface forward and a slightly smaller one aft was based on the meager data gathered in this manner. This configuration was to characterize all subsequent Langley aerodromes.

Langley had also begun a series of experiments with a gyroscopically controlled guidance system during late 1890. As the problems with the airframe and engine multiplied, however, this work was abandoned.

A memo from Langley to John Watkins, dated April 30, 1891, marked the beginning of serious work on the steam engine for No. 0. At the secretary's request, Watkins prepared initial drawings and designed the lightweight "beehive" boiler, to be constructed of copper tubing arranged in a series of coils. The engine, actually built by Maltby, weighed 4 pounds and produced the required 1 horsepower at a steam pressure of 60 pounds per square inch. A less successful engine, yielding only about .044 horsepower, had been constructed by B. L. Rinehart, a Smithsonian mechanic, and was also considered as a possible power plant.[15]

No. 0 was a larger craft than those that followed. In this case, the secretary, who was still arguing for the necessity of a gyroscopic autopilot device that was never completed, felt that the machine should be as large as possible in order to guarantee a spectacular flight. Additional tests conducted on a whirling arm in the Smithsonian's West Shed were used to determine the power-weight ratio that would serve as a reasonable limiting factor on the size of the craft.

The hull was shaped like a mackerel, the form Langley believed to be "most advantageous so far as the resistance of the air was concerned." When complete, the tapered body was symmetrical, 5 feet long and 10 inches in diameter. A long bowsprit in front and another at the stern carried the tandem wings. The surfaces at the front of the craft measured 50 square feet, while those at the rear totaled 25 square feet. The slightly cambered wings were constructed of aluminum covered with black silk. Twin pusher propellers 80 centimeters in diameter would move No. 0 through the air. A single gear box drove separate shafts set at an angle of 25 degrees. Initial computations called for the propellers to be run at speeds of from 400 to 500 rpm, but neither the Rinehart nor the Maltby engine was ever able to turn this rapidly.[16]

The Smithsonian staff completed work on their first model in the spring of 1892, but Langley abandoned the hopelessly overweight, underpowered, and structurally weak craft without a flight trial. The two spars projecting from the front and rear proved too thin to bear the weight of the hull and engine. The flimsy wings deformed in the slightest breeze. In the course of construction so many changes and additions had occurred that the estimated weight of 27 pounds 11 ounces had swollen to an actual weight of 44 pounds 8 ounces. Langley recorded his disappointment in his private notebook: "The year [1891] ended with the feeling on the writer's part that great labor had been incurred, and very little information had been gained."[17]

Langley first outlined his plans for a second machine, to be called No. 1, in a letter to John Watkins written in May 1892. A more complete description of this craft and initial plans for a third machine, No. 2, followed on June 13. By September 29 the secretary had ordered work to begin on yet another model, No. 3, designed for use with a carbonic-acid gas motor. The desire to gain broad experience with a variety of different aerodromes and engines was the only apparent reason for constructing so many machines at one time.[18]

With work under way on the aerodromes, Langley faced the problem of how and where he would fly his craft. These were not small models that could be hand launched into the wind from any convenient field. Moreover, the aerodrome would have to achieve flying speed very quickly in order to conserve the limited capacity of the boiler and reservoir for as long a flight as possible. Finally, Langley was concerned about bringing his craft safely to earth.

He concluded that the aerodromes should be catapulted into the air over a large body of water. The launching mechanism would hold the craft steady and release it for flight at precisely the right moment.

The Smithsonian staff tested a series of potential launchers at the National Zoo. By the time flying trials began, they had developed a catapult featuring a long arm with a track on which the aerodrome would sit.

The launch system evolved during long years of fruitless testing. By 1896, when the first successful flights were made, a complex, sophisticated overhead catapult was employed. Nine helical springs operating under tension through a two-sheave pulley that multiplied their movement by four, propelled a small four-wheeled launching car down a 20-foot track. The aerodrome, suspended from three points beneath the launch car, was automatically pitched forward and released as it approached the end of the rail.

Langley had first considered placing the launch mechanism on top of a tower built on the shore so that the machine could make full use of a long fall toward the water to build up flying speed. By the fall of 1892 he had rejected this notion in favor of a boat.

That November he purchased a houseboat measuring 12 feet by 30 feet. The "scow," as the secretary termed it, drew only 1 foot of water. A 19 foot by 10 foot shack on its deck rose 16 feet above the water, providing the necessary high ground from which to launch the aerodromes. The houseboat had two rooms, containing light shop facilities where aerodromes could be assembled, stored, and repaired. The boat was refurbished in Georgetown, after which the U.S. Coast and Geodetic Survey offered to tow it at no charge to the Smithsonian. Having devised a means of launching his craft, Langley had still to select a site. During the late summer of 1892 the staff surveyed the length of the Potomac in search of a quiet backwater where the river was wide enough to permit flights of reasonable length to be made entirely over the water.

They finally settled on Chopawamsic Island, a small triangular spit near the west bank of the Potomac, not far from the Quantico Station of the Washington and Richmond Railroad Company, some 30 miles south of Washington. For the next four years, each spring the houseboat would be towed downriver to an anchorage between the island and the west shore of the river. With the exception of a single narrow channel, the Potomac was so shallow in this area that there would be little trouble in recovering the aerodromes from the water after a flight.

By mid-November 1892, the Smithsonian staff was rapidly completing work on Nos. 1 and 2. Both aerodromes, like their predecessor, were tandem wing machines in which the forward surfaces were larger than the rear wings. A central rod running from bow to stern supported the wings, tail and hull and provided what little structural strength the new craft possessed.

No. 1 was roughly two-thirds the size of the first aerodrome, but much sturdier. Twin shafts set at a 25-degree angle carried the pusher propellers. Maltby constructed the engine, which operated on either steam or carbon dioxide. With the engine running at a pressure of 45 pounds per square inch, the propellers revolved at 653 revolutions per minute, enough to lift only about one-eighth the weight of the machine.[19]

Langley recognized that No. 1 was an underpowered failure. The central rod made it impossible to develop an efficient arrangement for the engine and boiler. More important, the workmen had found it impossible to hold the weight of the craft to original estimates. Determined to avoid this problem in the future, the secretary issued balance scales to each man and insisted on a strict record of weight and trim.

Aerodrome No. 2 was smaller than No. 1. Built entirely of wood, the machine was powered by twin propellers set on parallel shafts driven through a single gear box. When tested on a pendulum in the laboratory, No. 2 was able to lift roughly one-fifth of its 1,800-gram weight. While this was an improvement over the previous models, the power was still insufficient for sustained flight. Moreover, Langley judged No. 2 to be "in every way too weak." His devotion to weight-saving techniques had resulted in a machine that was too light and flimsy to hold together in the air.[20]

The well-funded Smithsonian effort had thus far produced three large models so inadequate that they were scrapped without flight trials. The experience to date clearly illustrated Langley's general approach to innovation in technology and set a pattern for all future aerodromic work. Charles Greeley Abbot, Langley's friend and colleague, realized that the secretary's methodology was a carry-over from his scientific experience.

> Whether from natural disposition or from a deliberate conviction that time could be saved thereby, or both, his method of attack upon a new experimental problem was to make rough trials at once, to improve the method as experience dictated, and at length reach the final dispositions as the result of correcting this or that detail after trial, rather than by first spending long and careful study over every detail before reducing any part of the work to practice.[21]

Translated into the terms of the aerodromic work, this meant that Langley seesawed back and forth between models that were first too heavy, then too light. He was searching for an ideal— the lightest possible model capable of flight with a steam engine on board. It was a classic case of "cut and try" engineering, an exercise in empiricism.

Machine No. 3 incorporated all of the lessons in engine and airframe construction learned during the work on the earlier craft. A new type of burner, called an aeolipile, produced much higher temperatures than the standard alcohol-fueled burners used previously. As a result, the two-cylinder engine was able to lift 35 percent of the total 2,050 gram load. Still not enough power for flight, but encouraging nevertheless.[22]

The design of No. 4 began in mid-December 1892. The usual problems of weight plagued construction, but by March 11, 1893, the secretary pronounced the craft complete. The area of the front and rear wings totaled 14 square feet. The machine weighed 4,750 grams completely fueled and carrying sufficient water for a two-minute flight. The usual double-tube helical-coil copper boiler was fired by a fully developed burner. A success-

ful force pump fed water to the boiler while a separator protected the pipes from melting and encrustation. The great advantage achieved in the new power system was that pressures
as high as 70 to 100 pounds per square inch were now possible.
No. 4 was first tested on the pendulum in mid-October, at which
time it lifted 40 percent of its dead weight. Theoretically, this
meant that Langley's new machine should just be able to maintain itself in the air.[23]

After three years of effort, the secretary was ready to begin
his first real flight tests. On November 16, 1893, the crew tran-
sported No. 4 downriver to the houseboat. At 7:30 the next
morning Langley, Barus, Reed, and Maltby stepped off the train
at the Quantico station only to discover that their problems had
just begun. As Langley explained, "Here was met for the first
time the difficulty of managing such an aerodrome in the open
air before launching." The light morning breeze blew No. 4
about so severley on the launcher that it was apparent no flight
could be made.[24]

In all, nine trips were made to Quantico between November
16 and the end of the year, all of them unsuccessful. The basic
problem remained the same. A barely perceptible breeze of 3 or
4 miles per hour was enough to prevent a launch.

The magnitude of the problem became fully apparent early in
1894. Bell accompanied Langley to the houseboat on January 8
and experienced the frustration so familiar to the crew at Quantico. Problems were first encountered in lightning and maintaining the alcohol burners. Once this difficulty had been overcome, the wind had fallen and a flight was attempted with a new
launcher the secretary had designed for use on this occasion.

The problems uncovered during the attempts to develop a
workable release for the old "starter" had led him to wonder
whether such a catapult was really necessary. This time the
aerodrome would be held on an arm 25 feet over the water and
simply dropped in the hope that it would attain flying speed
before it struck the surface. The machine dropped straight into
the river with the propellers turning at 600 revolutions per
minute. It was obvious that this method would not succeed
unless the aircraft could be released into a 25- to 30-mile head-

wind. It seemed simpler to return to the development of the traditional design.[25]

Further trials were suspended until the spring, as Dr. Barus took command of all efforts to prepare No. 4 and 5 for flights from a new launcher in the fall.

No. 5 was largely complete by early October. The new craft weighed 30 pounds, including an engine and boiler totaling 7 pounds. A split midrod that would accommodate the power plant replaced the old single rod that had created so many problems. Each of the four wings was constructed of spruce ribs and pine spars covered with white silk and measured 2 meters long and 805 millimeters wide. A hickory spring allowed the cruciform tail to give when struck by wind gusts to restore equilibrium. The two sets of wings were attached the fuselage at a dihedral, or angle to the body, of about 20 degrees, creating a measure of lateral stability. A movable copper float on the underside of the machine controlled the position of the center of gravity.[26]

The engine for No. 5 also differed from the earlier two-cylinder models. The new single-cylinder power plant developed about 1 horsepower in normal operation and featured a burner fueled by gasoline rather than alcohol in an effort to further increase the available heat.

No. 4 was rebuilt during this same period. A new engine, operating at a pressure of 90 pounds per square inch, drove the 70-centimeter propellers at 700 revolutions per minute. New wings covered with goldbeater's skin carried 28 square feet of lifting surface. Efforts to reduce the weight of the craft were carried to such an unfortunate extreme that the new frame "was scarcely able to support itself in the shop." After strengthening, "new No. 4" was judged ready for preliminary flights.[27]

The first opportunity for a trial came on October 7. Reed, Maltby, and Barus had spent several days fitting the new launcher on the houseboat and generally preparing both machines for flight. A number of "dummy" models were thrown from the new catapult, which seemed to be operating perfectly. The first attempt on October 7 was with the "new No. 4," fitted with its new large wings. Although the catapult functioned flawlessly, the model, operating at full power, traveled no farther than had the unpowered dummies. Observers noted that during its fall to the water the wing tips had been forced upward at an unnatural angle and the surface of the wings had taken on a "pocketed" appearance, indicating structural weakness.

Though there was little daylight left, it was decided to attempt a quick launch of No. 5. The wings were guyed at a dihedral angle of 20 degrees and the center of gravity adjusted. The model climbed away from the houseboat at an angle of 60 degrees, stalled, and fell backward into the water after only three seconds, yet Langley was elated. "On the whole this was nearer a "flight" than anything yet reached and I felt that I had learned something most important from the failures, such as the need of more efficient guying of the tips."[28]

Over the next two months, the crew conducted a series of flight tests with the two aerodromes. The final catapult design was demonstrated repeatedly, but unquestionable flights of significant duration continued to elude Langley.

By late November, winter weather forced a retreat to the Smithsonian shops until spring. This period of forced retirement from the test site was put to good use. The staff conducted its first serious experiments to gauge the strength of the wings and to assist in devising a means of maintaining the proper angle and curvature of the lifting surfaces. They inverted No. 4 and 5 in the shop and spread sand over the underside of the wings to represent the combination of air pressure and the weight of the hull supported in flight. In both cases "The flexure of the wings under these circumstances was beyond all anticipation and was amply sufficient to explain why the aerodrome did not fly." Difficulties encountered in guying the wings to correct this condition led to extensive revisions, including the extension of the hull of No. 5.[29]

No. 4, so completely rebuilt earlier that it was now officially known as "new No. 4," was radically altered again during winter 1895. This time so little remained of the original model that Langley and his staff felt justified in renaming the craft No. 6. They faced a new season of flying trials with two aerodromes that represented the culmination of a five-year effort.

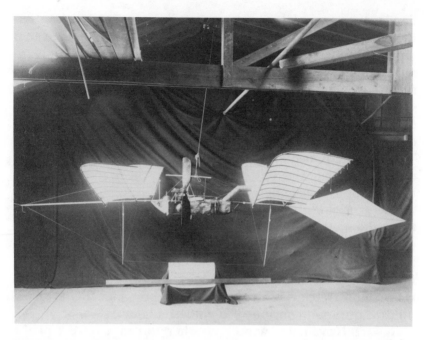

Aerodrome No. 6 had yet to reach its final configuration in this photo of December 4, 1895.

Two new staff members were hired to aid in the revision of the aerodromes and to participate in the upcoming test flights. The first of these men, E. C. Huffaker, came to the Smithsonian primarily as a result of the efforts of Octave Chanute. Langley and Chanute had enjoyed a long period of friendship and mutual support dating from the Buffalo meeting of the AAS in 1886. It was, therefore, with great interest that Langley read Chanute's letter of November 24, 1894. The Chicagoan reported his experience with Huffaker, offering a sketch of the young man's background and remarking that "He is making a fair living . . . but told me he would greatly prefer more scientific work." Langley was interested and requested that Chanute write him privately as to Huffaker's "moral qualities."[30]

Chanute informed the secretary that Huffaker had "made a good moral impression on me." Moreover, he was held in high esteem by the county people around Bristol, Tennessee, and, as "a Southern man . . . I believe personal relations with him would be pleasant."[31]

Langley hired Huffaker in December 1894, setting him to work calculating more efficient wing forms for Nos. 5 and 6 with the whirling table. He was also involved in the construction and trial of a final series of rubber-powered models used to flight test alternative wing configurations during the winter and spring of 1894–1895.

The secretary developed such respect for his new employee's talents that he was willing to overlook Huffaker's disregard for the social graces.

Accustomed to inspecting Smithsonian facilities clad in a morning coat and striped pants, Langley walked past Huffaker's office one morning only to find him sitting without coat or tie, his feet propped up on the desk. A tin-can spittoon nailed to the wall had obviously been put to good use. The prim, exasperated secretary turned to his friend Cyrus Adler, the Smithsonian librarian, and remarked that he supposed so valuable a man as Huffaker would have to be accepted "as God made him."[32]

Through his contacts with the larger aeronautical circle, Langley also found a man to superintend the coming flight tests. Langley and James Means, both native Bostonians, had known one another for some time. When they met at the wedding of mutual friends in the spring of 1895, Means spoke in glowing terms of a young New Yorker, Augustus Moore Herring, whom he had recently met. Langley had, in fact, seen a description of Herring's work in a Chanute article appearing in the *American Engineer and Railroad Journal* for January 1895, and was pleased to hear Mean's confirmation of Herring's talent.

Born in Sommersville, Georgia, in 1865, Herring was the son of a wealthy cotton broker. When the family moved to New York, Herring, age eighteen, entered the Stevens Institute of Technology to study mechanical engineering. He seems to have become interested in flight as early as 1880, when his father presented him with a toy helicopter. During his four years at Stevens he constructed several unsuccessful gliders, a task that claimed more of his time than did his formal studies. He was to have graduated in the class of 1888, and, in fact, his name does appear on the active role until June of that year. He did not graduate, however, and for many years thereafter claimed that his thesis on the subject of flight had been rejected as too visionary. Records at the Stevens Institute tell quite a different story. Faculty minutes on Herring's case indicate that he was unable to complete the work in mathematics, analytical chemistry, and drafting. The undergraduate thesis, which he simply did not submit, did not deal with aeronautics, but was a design study for a marine steam engine.[33]

Having left school, Herring had some initial success in building a reputation as a consulting engineer. But when his business was destroyed in the panic of 1893, the young engineer was reduced to serving as a chainman on the New York Central Railroad.

Herring returned to aeronautics during the summer of 1894, when, inspired by Lilienthal's early flights, he built two gliders loosely patterned after those of the German master. Chanute had first discovered the New Yorker's activities in a Rochester newspaper article of February 1, 1892, describing these craft. Letters passed between the two men, and the Chicagoan soon realized that he had found a new disciple.[34]

When his attempts to help Herring find a better job proved unsuccessful, Chanute hired him in December 1894 to build a series of gliders that would be jointly developed. A number of models were built and tested and the work was just getting seriously under way when Langley, as yet unaware of Chanute's connection with Herring, traveled to New York to meet this promising newcomer on May 13, 1895. Herring showed the scientist his successful Lilienthal glider, and Langley took copious notes on the techniques that the glider enthusiast had developed for constructing light airframes and wings. In addition, the secretary plied Herring with questions relating to possible improvements in balancing and controlling Nos. 5 and 6. He was so pleased with the response that he offered Herring full-time employment as an overseer of the work in aerodromics for $150 a month, considerably more than Chanute was paying. One week later, on May 20, 1894, Herring came to Washington to accept the position and almost immediately realized that major problems were in the offing. Only five days after accepting his new job, he wrote Chanute. It was obvious that the pressure that the secretary had applied on Frank Very during the early years at Allegheny was still a fact of life for Smithsonian workers:

> Even in a few days work under him I could forsee a possibility that he and I might not be able to agree—The chief thing is the way he will give orders to me to design a certain piece of apparatus—to weigh so much, and to have approximately a certain form—then the drawing is given to a workman to execute—while I do something else—in the meantime changes occur to him which he orders made in the first piece of apparatus, a new drawing for which is made by someone else—irrespective of the calculations I have previously made of strength and sizes of material used—these changes are sometimes made without my knowledge and as I am pressed for time I have no opportunity to make calculations of strain under the new conditions—it is evident though that I will be held more responsible for any defects; this under similar conditions is more than any other respectable engineer ought to be willing to submit to.

Herring was shocked at Huffaker's state of mind.

> I might say that as exemplified by his treatment of Huffaker and the other workmen he [Langley] is extremely impatient—poor Huffaker has been considerably worried—so much so that I believe he is on the verge of nervous prostration—he cannot multiply two numbers together without making a mistake.[35]

In fact, Herring had discovered the darker side of Samuel Langley's nature. What a friend would characterize as "an eagerness to push on in scientific pursuits which amounted at times to impatience,"[36] the secretary's subordinates viewed less kindly. At best, Langley was a difficult man to work for. He was an impatient, demanding perfectionist who insisted on absolute obedience.

Craftsmanship was never enough for the secretary. Each finished aerodrome was a work of the machinist's art. Countless hours had to be spent in fitting and polishing dozens of individual components to jewellike perfection.

In addition, Langley had for years refused to delegate author-ity. While he appointed work supervisors, he insisted on person-ally inspecting the "wastebooks" in which each man was re-quired to log his daily activity in minute detail. Nor, as Very had discovered, was Langley particularly given to treating his em-ployees with kid gloves.

Washington gossips spread tales of Langley's imperious atti-tude. As one columnist noted, "It is well known that the profes-sor "has a way with him" of making his royal personality felt in his big brownstone building." He was also accused of taking credit for other men's work. A few of his peculiarities, notably his unwillingness to allow a subordinate to precede him down a hall or up a flight of stairs, became matters of jest among the staff.[37]

Langley, the Boston Brahmin, and Herring, the Georgia pa-trician, were destined to clash.

The trials of the 1895 season began on the morning of May 9, with Alexander Graham Bell acting as official timekeeper. No. 5 was launched three times that day. The best of the flights, which lasted six seconds, led Langley to comment that "This was the nearest approximation to horizontal flight of any at-tempts and was at a rate of between 30 and 40 miles an hour."[38]

Herring traveled to Quantico for the first time on June 7. When two attempted launches ended in failure, it was decided to allow Herring to retreat to the shop with both aerodromes for the entire summer in the hope that greater progress could be exhibited in flights that fall or early winter.

Herring did make major improvements in the aerodromes. By fall 1895, they had assumed the classic configuration that was to be continued in the full-size machine. Both front and rear wings were now the same size, and the elastic tail surface, a cruciform placed on a spring to give in a wind gust to maintain balance, had become a permanent feature. As Herring had predicted, however, his personal relations with the secretary were rapidly approaching an impasse.

On June 25, he wrote Chanute that he was still very unhappy with working conditions at the institution. Langley demanded to sign all drawings before they were turned over to the work-men. Herring feared that this "is likely to give them the impression that though I am in charge of work the Secretary does not trust me and is calculated to lessen their respect for my authority." He remarked that "I would not care to . . . [continue] if I could better myself elsewhere."[39]

In a complaint reminiscent of Very's earlier objections, he recounted a particularly galling episode that occurred early in September, following Langley's return from Europe.

Mr. Langley came home last Saturday [and] he seemed very much pleased with a great deal of the work but was loud in his condemnation of several changes that were made, and several more that were not. It turned out in investigation that we had probably had difference of opinion on all the points at issue but I had followed his instructions as closely as possible—the funny part was that he was not pleased with just those particular changes and was with everything else that had not been under discussion. His greatest fault is excessive impatience and an extreme hurrying of the workmen so that they become "rattled" and do poor work.[40]

One of Herring's objections was the secretary's refusal to recognize his contributions to the effort. In November, for example, he complained to Chanute that "My relations here are not entirely congenial. . . . One of the disagreeable features is Mr. Langley's inability to distinguish between the ideas of other people and his own. Whether this is intentional or not I can't say—the effect is the same."[41]

The growing disaffection was mutual. The secretary had decided that Herring had done little or nothing to improve Nos. 5 and 6. Impatient as always, he concluded that Herring was no longer of any service to him.

Late in November 1895 Langley called Herring into his office to inform him that he could accept no further delays. Nos. 5 and 6 must be prepared for flight immediately. The secretary recorded the outcome of the meeting in his private wastebook. "Mr. Herring having been told that No. 6 must be taken into the field within a week, resigned his position on some irrelevant excuse. . . . It seemed to me that he was aware that his wings, on which so much time and money have been spent, were so constructed, so unfit, as to be evident failures before trial."[42]

Herring reported his change of status in a letter to Chanute. "I have had an interview with Mr. Langley which has culminated in my determination to resign. . . . I intend telegraphing you of my intention to resign before making any application for other work in case you wish to have me continue your soaring machine work."

On November 28, the Chicagoan telegraphed his young friend, "Can employ you for a time come when ready." Thus, Herring returned to Chanute's employ and immediately began work on the gliders that were to enjoy success in the air over the sand hills bordering Lake Michigan the following summer.

At the Smithsonian, work continued on Nos. 5 and 6 following Herring's departure. R. L. Reed was placed in general charge of the remaining work on the aerodromes, which included the construction of new sets of wings for both craft and an extra rudder, a new boiler, and three spare propellers for aerodrome 5.

The secretary was particularly proud of the engines that powered the two aerodromes. After six years of effort the Smithsonian team could point to "unprecedented results." The engine of No. 5, for example, delivered 1 full horsepower, yet its 26 moving parts weighed only 26 ounces. Langley admitted, however, that these motors were very specialized devices.

It is proper . . . to remind the reader that these engines were designed for altogether special conditions, viz: to be not only of extraordinary lightness, but to run for a brief period with a maximum of power, to be gained under any conditions of sacrifice. . . . The results attained in weight, then, have not been reached so much by employing novel devices as by using very high speeds, dispensing with the jacketing, and building and rebuilding the engines until experience had shown the very minimum weight in each part which would serve the purpose, and doing this throughout with the most careful workmanship.[43]

In May 1896, Reed and Maltby once more went down the Potomac to prepare for yet another season of test flights. Langley and Alexander Graham Bell arrived on the afternoon of May 6. No. 6 was prepared for launch, but a guy wire caught on a piece of the catapult and the left wing was broken off before the machine left the track. Since No. 5 was prepared for flight, the secretary moved to a vantage point on the shore. Huffaker and an assistant were to launch the aircraft, after which they would be charged with providing an accurate record of the time of the flight. Dr. Bell was posted on the starboard side of the houseboat with a camera. All was ready by 3:05 P.M. Langley recorded this sequence of events in his private wastebook.

The aerodrome with 150 [pounds] of steam pressure, and [?] revolutions per minute, left the track, at a height of 20 [feet] above the water, moved northward against the gentle wind, falling slightly (3 or 4 feet) at first then moving . . . forward and slightly upward,

Workmen on the houseboat prepare to launch No. 5.

with an inclination of the midrod to the horizon of about 10°, which remained remarkably constant throughout the flight. It commenced turning to the right, and moved around with great steadiness in curves . . . passing almost over Mr. Bell, making two complete turns . . . slowly ascending with great smoothness and uniformity of motion and with a notable constancy of the angle of the midrod to the horizon. Near the later part of its course, it reached a height which is estimated differently as at 70, 80 and 100 feet. Here after about 1.20 [1 minute, 20 seconds] the wheels ceased turning, evidently from lack of steam, and the machine settled forward, slowly changing the angle of the aerodrome to a slight inclination downward, and finally touched the water, to the south of the House Boat.[44]

The aerodrome entered the water 142 yards astern of the launcher. It was estimated to have covered a total of 3,300 feet during the course of its curved flight. The propeller counter had registered 1,166 revolutions. It had traveled at a speed of 33 1/2 feet per second, or 20 to 25 miles an hour. One wing had been considerably "kinked" as a result of air pressures encountered during its flight. Langley felt that this deformation had caused the constant circling that had marked its course through the air.

By 5:10 P.M., No. 5 was dry, and the canted wing had been reguyed. As on the first occasion, the craft completed three circles and rose to an altitude of about 60 feet. The propeller stopped revolving at the peak altitude, and the machine glided slowly to the water. It was later found to have traveled some 2,300 feet.

The two flights of May 6, 1896, marked the end of an epoch in the history of flight. For the first time a large flying model with a self-contained power plant had remained in the air for a length of time sufficient to demonstrate that it had unquestionably flown. Alexander Graham Bell was ecstatic.[45]

Langley had achieved his goal, but he was not eager to make a public statement of success until he was certain he could guarantee a repetition of the flight at will. Bell, however, believed that the news should be released immediately. On the

The launch of No. 5.

evening of the flight Bell sent a memorandum to the secretary on this subject:

> I am quite aware that you are not desirous of publication until you have obtained more complete success in obtaining horizontal flight under an automatic direction but it seems to me that what I have been privileged to see today marks such a great progress on everything ever before done in this way that the news of it should be made public, and I am happy to give my own testimony on the results of two trials, which I witnessed today by your invitation hoping that you will kindly consent to making it known.

The inventor continued with a detailed account of the flights.

For the first trial the apparatus, chiefly constructed of steel and driven by a steam engine, was launched at a height of about 20 feet from the water. Under the impulse of its engines alone, it advanced against the wind, and while drifting little and slowly ascending, it described a curve of about one hundred metres in diameter and having been driven in its course for about a minute and a half from the time of departure and at a height in the air which I estimate at 81 feet, the revolutions of the screws ceased, for want of steam. . . . The second trial repeated in nearly every respect the action of the first and . . . with identical results.[46]

The secretary accepted Bell's advice. Langley had obviously invited his friend to attend the trials over the years in the hope that he would witness the final success. An eyewitness account of a flight written by the internationally known inventor of the telephone would convince Lord Kelvin and all of those who had questioned the validity of the Langley law and other findings presented in *Experiments in Aerodynamics*. Once such testimony was in hand, the secretary lost no time in circulating Bell's letter to key popular and technical journals in the United States and Europe. The resulting impact on both public and professional attitudes toward flight was enormous.

Before the secretary left on his annual European tour that spring, he ordered No. 6 to be prepared for trials in the fall. By November 27, 1896, aerodrome No. 6, which had begun its career as No. 4 four years earlier, was ready for its final trial. As usual, Reed and Maltby traveled to Quantico on the early train to prepare the houseboat for the activities of the day. Langley arrived at 12:13, accompanied by Frank G. Carpenter, a newspaper reporter, and Mr. Emerson, a Smithsonian employee, who was to operate the camera. High winds prevented a launch until 4:25, when the machine was finally released with a steam pressure of 125 pounds per square inch in the boiler. The model remained in the air for 6 1/4 seconds, covering approximately 180 yards. This flight, that would once have been regarded as a triumph, was a disappointment after the performance of No. 5. The problem lay in a faulty synchronizing gear that had permitted one propeller to turn faster than the other, causing the craft to bank into the river.

The next day, Saturday, November 28, seemed most inauspi-

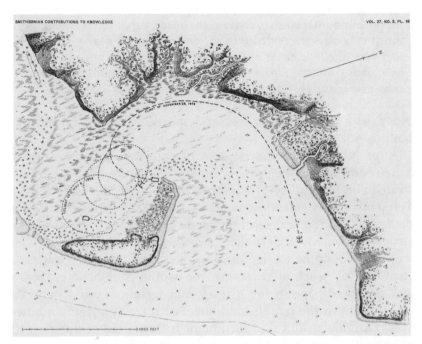

SMITHSONIAN CONTRIBUTIONS TO KNOWLEDGE　　　　　　VOL. 27, NO. 3, PL. 18

The flights of Nos. 5 and 6. The small wedge-shaped area is Chopawamsic Island.

cious. But a period of relative calm followed the wind and rain of the morning, and by 4:20 No. 6 once again stood on the launcher. The condition of the craft was exactly as it had been the day before, but the float had been repositioned to bring the nose of the model up in the air. The aerodrome was provisioned for a two-minute flight. The earlier rains had soaked the craft, bringing its weight up to as much as 12 kilos. One minute forty-five seconds later the secretary had another successful flight to report.

> The aerodrome went horizontally directly into the teeth of a gentle southern wind, slowly turning to the right, occupying a horizontal course, and appearing to approach dangerously near a wood on the west shore. It continued turning until, catching the breeze in the *rear*, it moved more rapidly dipped and rose but once (and this slightly) and continued its *remarkably* horizontal flight, not being (except for a moment) more than two yards out

of the horizontal course, about eight or ten yards above the water until it finally descended into the bay at a point nearly in a line between the houseboat and the hotel at Quantico, and . . . about 150 yards from the north shore. It was taken out quite uninjured and another flight might have been tried had daylight lasted.

No. 6 had traveled 4,200 feet at a speed of about 30 miles per hour.[47]

After No. 6, there was no question but that Samuel Langley had accomplished the goal set in 1886. Not only had he demonstrated the possibility of constructing a large, heavier-than-air flying machine by means of a series of physical experiments, but he had solved the technical problems by constructing two very large unmanned models that had unquestionably flown. The secretary's judgments had been proved valid. Had he chosen to abandon his work at this point he would still have earned a well-deserved page in the history of aviation. Having spent so many years in the search for a successful flying machine, however, Langley would find it difficult to resist the temptation to enlarge his models and attempt a manned flight in a full-scale machine.

8

Lilienthal and the Americans

Early Sunday morning, August 2, 1896, Robert W. Wood, a correspondent for the *Boston Transcript*, met Otto Lilienthal on the platform of Berlin's Lehrter Station. Lilienthal, dressed in a flannel work shirt, knickerbockers with thickly padded knees, heavy brogans, and a knitted cap, arrived just before dawn, accompanied by his fourteen-year-old son and a mechanic from his machine shop. He was the image of an athlete, compactly built, broad-shouldered, barrel-chested, with a head of curly red hair, a full beard and mustache, and a ready smile that had etched deep lines around his eyes.[1]

Together, the four men boarded a train headed out of Berlin toward the Rhinow Mountains, a range of high, barren hills 100 miles to the north. This excursion was a weekly ritual for Lilienthal, who repaired to the seclusion of Rhinow each Sunday to continue a series of manned glider flights that had brought him world fame since 1891.

It is not too surprising to find Lilienthal accompanied by an American reporter on this occasion for nowhere had his work found a more receptive audience than in the United States. As a result of the efforts of Chanute, Langley, Means, and others,

Otto Lilienthal (1848–1896).

his name was familiar to American newspaper readers. Accounts of his daring exploits provided a rich source of feature material that captured the imagination of the public. Wood was only the latest in a string of reporters dispatched to satisfy American curiosity about the "flying man."

Two hours after departing Berlin the small party reached Neustadt, where they were met by a farm wagon in which they rode the final 20 miles to the small village of Rhinow.

Following a brief lunch at the local inn, Lilienthal retrieved the glider to be flown that day from the barn where it was stored. The group then drove 3 miles to the test site.

Wood found himself entering a long range of steep hills rising abruptly from the surrounding fields. Ranging in height from 100 to 300 feet, the slopes were carpeted with thick grass and moss. The hills were conical, offering an opportunity to fly into the wind regardless of the direction from which it came.

Lilienthal first supervised the unpacking and assembly of the glider, a biplane with a 20-foot wing span and a 6-foot gap between the upper and lower surfaces. Wood was enthralled by the sight of the completed machine laying before him on the grass.

So perfectly was the machine fitted together that it was impossible to find a single loose cord or brace, and the cloth was everywhere under such tension that the whole machine rang like a drum when rapped with the knuckles. As it lay on the grass in the bright sunshine, with its twenty four square yards of snow white cloth spread before you, you felt as if the flying age was really commencing. Here was a flying machine, not constructed by a crank, to be seen at a county fair at ten cents a head, or to furnish material for encyclopedia articles on aerial navigation, but by an engineer of ability . . . a machine not made to look at, but to fly with.

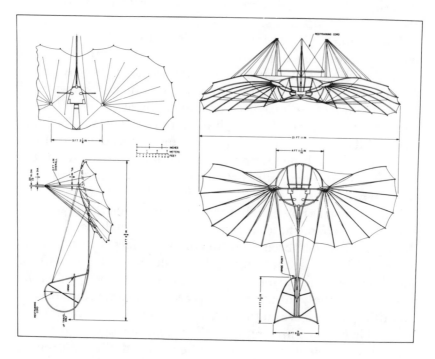

A standard Lilienthal glider, 1894.

While Wood positioned his camera, the other three men carried the glider to the crest of a nearby hill. Lilienthal crawled beneath the craft, worked his arms into a set of cuffs that would give him leverage on the machine, grasped a bar near the forward edge of the wings, and stood "like an athlete waiting for the starting pistol." As the wind freshened, he took three steps down the slope and was immediately lifted into the air. Flying straight out from the summit, he passed over Wood's head at an altitude of 50 feet, "the wind playing wild tunes on the tense cordage of the machine."

A sudden gust caught the left wing tip lifting it and sending the machine on a broad, sweeping turn from which Lilienthal recovered with a powerful throw of his legs. Having recovered his balance, Lilienthal swooped low over the fields at the base of the hill, "kicking at the tops of the haystacks as he passed over them." Now very close to the ground, he kicked forward to raise the leading edge of the wing, brought his craft to a dead stop in the air and dropped easily to earth.

The young reporter found it difficult to contain his excitement. "I have seen high dives and parachute jumps from balloons," he remarked, "but I have never witnessed anything that strung the nerves to such a pitch of excitement, or awakened such a feeling of enthusiasm and admiration as the wild fearless rush of Otto Lilienthal through the air. The spectacle of a man supported on huge white wings, moving high above you at race horse speed, combined with the weird hum of the wind through the cords of the machine, produces an impression never to be forgotten."

When a brief shower fell a few minutes after the first flight, Lilienthal, Wood, the two assistants, and a small band of children who had gathered from neighboring farms to watch the antics of "Die weise Flidermaus" found shelter under the wings of the glider. As crickets bounced around on the fabric, Lilienthal remarked to the youngsters that the insects sometimes became unwilling passengers on the gliders. On these occasions he could hear their frantic chirping over the sound of the rushing wind.

As the rain blew over, flights were resumed, the children falling over one another as they ran downhill in pursuit of the glider.

Toward the end of the afternoon, having witnessed ten flights, Wood could no longer resist asking if he might try his own hand with the glider. Lilienthal agreed and ordered the machine taken only a dozen yards or so up the slope. Wood then positioned himself in the frame and lifted the machine.

He discovered that simply standing in place, attempting to balance the glider was so difficult as to give him a feeling of "utter helplessness." Wood now studied the machine in which he was about to risk his life.

As you stand in the frame your elbows are at your side, the forearms are horizontal, and your hands grasp one of the horizontal cross-braces. The weight of the machine rests in the angle of the elbow joints. In the air, when you are supported by the wings, your weight is carried on the vertical upper arms and by pads which come under the shoulders, the legs and lower part of the body swinging free below.

On a signal from Lilienthal, Wood ran down the hill into the wind. He found the weight of the machine reduced with each step, until, suddenly, he was airborne.

Lilienthal in the air.

I was sliding down the aerial incline a foot or two from the ground. The apparatus dipped from side to side a great deal. ... The feeling is most delightful and wholly indescribable. The body being supported from above, with no weight or strain on the legs, the feeling is as if gravitation had been annihilated, although the truth of the matter is that it hangs from the machine in a rather awkward and wearying position.

Wood's day in the Rhinow hills had resulted in the finest firsthand account in English of Lilienthal's personality and technique. But there were to be no more opportunities for the follow-up interviews the reporter planned. The following Sunday, August 9, 1896, Otto Lilienthal stalled and fell from an altitude of 50 feet while flying a standard monoplane glider. He died the next day in a Berlin hospital.

At the time of his death, Otto Lilienthal was forty-eight, having been born in the Pomeranian village of Anklam on May 24, 1848. As boys, Otto and his younger brother Gustav were fascinated by the storks native to the region. In later years Gustav recalled that a fairy tale in which a tired willow wren is given a ride on the back of a stork and receives a lesson on the art of flying with fewer wing beats had particularly "impressed us with the possibility if attaining such [flight] by simple means." The boys' "susceptible minds" were also influenced by the romantic accounts of balloon flights during the period.

They constructed their first flying machine, a small fixed-wing glider that proved unsuccessful, at age thirteen and fourteen. Over the next seventeen years they were to build other craft, most of them ornithopters, with the meager sums they were able to save while attending technical schools. By 1880 Otto was an established engineer, the owner of a firm producing engines, boilers, marine signals, and mining equipment. But he had not forgotten his youthful passion for flight.[2]

By 1879, now a mature, experienced engineer, Otto Lilienthal, had finally come to the conclusion that a successful flying machine would require the solution of a number of key problems that could best be attacked individually. He expressed a genuine understanding of this situation in 1889.

Formerly men sought to construct flying machines in a complete form, at once capable of solving the problem, but gradually the conviction came that our physical and technical knowledge and our practical experience were by far insufficient to overcome a mechanical task of such magnitude without more preliminaries.[3]

There would be no more ornithopters based on guesswork and intuition. His major emphasis was now on the serious study of the principles of flight. Lilienthal established a workshop and experimental area in the home he constructed in the Berlin suburb of Gross-Lichterfelde in 1878. It was here that the engineer conducted his classic studies of air pressure and lift.

As a result of these imaginative laboratory experiments, he provided a final demonstration of the superiority of the curved or cambered wing section. Lilienthal invariably preferred the simplest cambered wing—the arc of a circle. He determined that a camber of 1 in 12 was ideal. That is, the chord, a straight line drawn from the leading to the trailing edge of the wing, should be 12 times as long as the distance from the chord to the bottom of the wing at the midpoint, where the arch was highest.

Lilienthal also studied the problem of air resistance and speculated on the movement of the center of pressure on the wing at various angles of incidence. In addition, he devised an air-pressure table that enabled an experimenter to calculate the wing area required to support a given weight at a particular speed.

Lilienthal's laboratory test program differed significantly from earlier work, notably Langley's *Experiments in Aerodynamics*. The German engineer was not interested in a theoretical study of the physics of flight. Rather, he sought to solve the most practical and immediately pressing engineering problems that stood in the way of a successful flying machine.

Langley turned to the laboratory to prove the possibility of flight, then resorted to the crudest cut-and-try approach to engineering his flying machines. Lilienthal, on the other hand, ignored theory, concentrating all of his energies on such central issues as the proper size and shape for a wing. It was a classic illustration of the difference in attitude between the scientist and engineer.

Lilienthal published the results of his work in *Der Vogelflug als Grundlage der Fliegekunst,* which appeared in Berlin in 1889. *Vogelflug* and other articles Lilienthal published prior to his death in 1896 provided absolutely essential information on which all subsequent serious glider experimenters would rely.

But the laboratory tests and resulting publications were only the necessary preliminaries. Lilienthal had now obtained sufficient data to begin serious work with full-scale gliders.

Between 1891 and 1896 he completed nearly 2,000 flights in sixteen separate glider types. Most of these were simple monoplanes with stabilizing surfaces on the rear of the machine. Ribs and other covered portions of the craft were usually constructed of split willow. The wings, which resembled "the outspread pinions of a soaring bird," averaged between 10 and 20 square meters in area and were covered with cotton-twill shirting doped with a special colloidal solution in order to create as airtight a surface as possible.

The normal glide ratio of these machines averaged 8 feet of forward flight for every foot of vertical fall. In all Lilienthal gliders the pilot hung vertically in an elliptical section between the wings. Control was provided by the movements of his body. While Lilienthal recognized the inadequacy of this method of control and gave some thought to alternative systems, he did not develop and test them.[4]

During this period Lilienthal began to experiment with slightly different glider forms, including biplanes and craft with folding wings for easy storage. A *New York Herald* correspondent who visited him in 1894 witnessed a flight with a folding-wing glider.

> The operator so adjusts the apparatus to his person that when in the air he will be seated upon a narrow support near the front, and, with the wings folded behind him, makes a short run from some elevated point, always against the wind, and when he has attained sufficient velocity, launches himself into the air by a spring or a jump, at the same time spreading the wings, which are

at once extended to their full breadth by atmospheric action, whereupon he sails majestically along like a giant sea-gull.[5]

The biplane was designed to increase the available wing area without extending the span to extreme lengths, which would upset it in crosswinds. Like the folding-wing apparatus, the double-surface glider was less successful than the normal machines. The need to add extra surface to an already successful glider or to introduce the luxury of easy storage not only added extra weight, but decreased the strength of the original. In the case of the biplane, stability was also sacrificed. Lilienthal clearly recognized the deficiencies of these experiments, and returned to his standard design.

The German master attempted to build powered airplanes twice during his career. The first, constructed in 1893, carried a 2-horsepower carbonic-acid gas motor that drove ornithoptering wing tips. Lilienthal realized the impossibility of flying it, for no trials were attempted. A second powered flyer, built in the spring of 1895, was almost like the first, with the exception of the fact that it spread 20 meters of wing surface. Unsuccessful flight tests were conducted with this airplane.

Lilienthal's approach to the propulsion problem was curious —and instructive. His insistence on the use of flapping wing tips in preference to a conventional propeller is an indication of the extent to which he was captivated by bird flight.

The very fact that Lilienthal saw the powered hang glider as a necessary intermediate step toward a genuine airplane is significant. He believed that the problems of flight would be overcome through a slow, steady process of evolution. One step would follow naturally after another, from laboratory studies to a primitive glider to a more sophisticated glider to a simple powered machine to a genuine airplane capable of sustained flights under the control of the pilot. No intellectual leaps or technical breakthroughs were required—only persistence and courage. It would remain for two young men from Dayton, Ohio, to prove him wrong.

With the benefit of hindsight, it is apparent that Lilienthal was pointing the way to success. It was much more difficult for his contemporaries, absorbed in their own divergent approaches to flight, to recognize Lilienthal's prescience.

Strangely, his work did not strike a particularly responsive chord among European experimenters. While Lilienthal's efforts were fully chronicled in newspapers and magazines in Great Britain and on the Continent, a groundswell of enthusiastic imitators failed to appear. Several Lilienthal gliders were purchased by scattered experimenters like the Irish physicist George Francis Fitzgerald and the Russian Nikolai Zukovsky, but few flights were made with these machines. More important, with the exception of Percy Pilcher, no European was able to use the basic Lilienthal pattern as a stepping stone to an improved machine.

An explanation for this reluctance to carry Lilienthal's work forward is to be found in the fact that major European flying-machine experimenters were well into their own research programs when Lilienthal burst upon the scene with his gliders in 1891. Many of these men were already encumbered by fixed ideas that prevented a clear vision of what the German had accomplished. Thus, for Maxim, Lilienthal would remain little more than "a flying squirrel," while French pioneer Gaston Tissandier characterized Lilienthal's flights as "a simple fall, deadened or lessened by plane surfaces." Such established figures found it extremely difficult to admit that Lilienthal might be anything more than a "mere parachutist."[6]

But Americans, who had scarcely begun practical flying experiments by 1891, found Lilienthal's work a revelation. Fledgling aviators who had been inspired by Chanute, Langley, and others lost little time in emulating the German gliding master.

Chanute and Langley share the credit for introducing Lilienthal to their countrymen. George E. Curtiss, one of Langley's most talented subordinates and the man responsible for keeping the Smithsonian staff up to date on developments in European aeronautics, was one of the first Americans to note Lilienthal's early published reports of his gliding experiments. Curtiss not only brought this material to Langley's attention, but he sent translations to Chanute along with a selection of photographs showing Lilienthal gliding through the air.

Langley, then in the early stages of the struggle to launch one if his aerodromes on a substantial aerial journey, was sufficiently intrigued to arrange the publication one of Lilienthal's articles in the Smithsonian *Annual Report.* Chanute was far more enthusiastic. As readers of *Progress in Flying Machines* were aware, he had long believed that the manned glider offered the surest route toward a successful powered airplane. Significantly, the men in whose work he took the greatest interest were gliding pioneers like Mouillard and Montgomery. But no one had impressed him more than Lilienthal.

Chanute covered the German's work in detail in the articles for Forney. When *Progress in Flying Machines* appeared as a single volume, the emphasis was even clearer, underscored by the inclusion of a special appendix covering Lilienthal's latest experiments.

James Means was also an early Lilienthal supporter, featuring several pieces by the German experimenter in the *Aeronautical Annual.*

Lilienthal's fame spread quickly beyond the confines of the aeronautical community. Mass-circulation magazines like *McClure's* commissioned him to prepare special articles. Big-city newspaper editors, who had turned from hard news to comics and human-interest stories in an effort to expand their readership, found Lilienthal to be an inexhaustable fount of feature material.

Recent advances in photographic and printing technologies played an important role in building American interest in Lilienthal. The many articles that appeared were illustrated by startling images of a man soaring in space, swooping effortlessly downhill while earthbound spectators watched in awe. And these articles were immediately available to the smallest local weekly, thanks to the telegraph and the wire service.

All of these factors combined with a growing interest in flight to transform Lilienthal into one of the first mass-media heros. The reading public knew that an article with a heading like "The Flying Man," "The Winged Prussian," or "The German Darius Green" could only concern the latest exploits of Otto Lilienthal. He was the man who could fly. Not very far or very fast or very high, it was true, but fly nevertheless.

The leaders of the aeronautical movement in America were quick to build direct contacts with Lilienthal. Chanute opened his personal correspondence with the German in 1893. In addition to serving as Lilienthal's chief English-language publicist, he worked to interest Captain William Glassford, chief signal officer of the U.S. Army, in purchasing a Lilienthal machine for testing. In addition, Chanute, like Means and his Boston colleagues, attempted to attract Lilienthal to America for glider demonstrations. Chanute also offered help in popularizing gliding as a sport in an effort to increase the sale of Lilienthal machines in the United States.

While Chanute was never to meet Lilienthal, other Americans journeyed to Germany to do so. Samuel Langley, for example, visited Lilienthal's Berlin workshop in the summer of 1895.

Since Lilienthal spoke no English or French and Langley no German, the two men were forced to resort to gestures to bridge the language gap. Langley was disappointed by a large monoplane under construction in the shop. The wood, he remarked, was "very crooked and irregular," while the machine as a whole was too "heavy and clumsy" to meet Langley's exacting standards.

Lilienthal also displayed an engine for one of his proposed powered hang gliders to his American guest. It weighed 3 1/2 kilos, had a 150-cubic-inch displacement, and carried a cylinder of compressed gas sufficient for a two-minute flight.

That afternoon Lilienthal treated Langley to a gliding demonstration from the artificial hill at the nearby brick works. Langley, impressed with the performance, concluded that, in spite of his earlier criticism of the glider in the shop, "handsome is as handsome does."[7]

Samuel Cabot spent a day and a half with Lilienthal the following summer. Like Langley, he witnessed a long series of flights and came away with the feeling that Lilienthal was "one of the most interesting men I ever met."[8]

While the elder statesmen of aeronautics thought, wrote, visited, and dreamed, a generation of young American engineers built and flew copies of Lilienthal machines. In Boston, Samuel

Cabot and A. A. Merrill constructed crude replicas of Lilienthal monoplanes, based on available photos and descriptions. Gustave Whitehead's claim to have worked with Lilienthal was a major factor leading to his employment with the Boston Aeronautical Society.

At least one experimenter affiliated with the New England circle, C. H. Lamson, went even further. Ordering a full set of plans from Lilienthal, he built and flew an exact replica of a standard Lilienthal glider before moving on to his work with man-lifting kites.

William Randolph Hearst is the only American known to have purchased an original Lilienthal glider. Hearst, recognizing the growing public interest in Lilienthal, hoped to headline reports of the glider test flights in an effort to boost the circulation of the *New York Journal.*

Purchased in late April 1896, the glider was initially flown near Bayonne, New Jersey. Harry B. Bodine, a young man with "a local reputation in many kinds of sports," was selected to pilot the craft. Frank Ver Beck, a local artist, was also given an opportunity to fly the machine.

C. H. Lamson flies his Lilienthal glider in 1895.

The 1894 Lilienthal glider purchased by William Randolph Hearst appeared the worse for wear when exhibited in a 1906 New York aeroshow.

The first trials were made with the glider being flown as a kite, but Bodine's self-confidence soon led him to try free flights. By April 27, after only a few days' practice, the *Journal* was bragging of glides of up to 75 yards. Trials were moved to the estate of J. Harper Bonnell, on Staten Island, early in May. The paper's readers were regaled with tales of stalls, spins, and spectacular flights for the next several months, after which these efforts were eclipsed by the reports of success on the Potomac and over the Indiana Dunes as well as the death of Lilienthal himself later in the year.[9]

Nor was this enthusiasm for Lilienthal restricted to individuals. The first glider club in America was born as a result of the wave of Lilienthal-inspired publicity that swept the nation. Its founder was Charles Proteus Steinmetz, the "wizard of Schenectady."

Steinmetz was one of the first of the professionally trained applied scientists whose work in the new industrial research laboratories was to bring the fruits of modern science to the American consumer. His work with alternating currents, electric motors, arc lamps, induction regulators, and high-voltage power systems marked him as one of the finest theoretical engineers in America. Steinmetz and his "man-made lightning" became a symbol of man's growing dominion over nature.

Like so many other technical professionals during the last decade of the nineteenth century, Steinmetz became fascinated by the possibility of heavier-than-air flight. As a young émigré, he eagerly followed newspaper and journal accounts of Lilienthal's exploits. Discovering that a number of his co-workers shared his enthusiasm, Steinmetz organized the first glider society in America, possibly in the world. Established in 1894 as the Mohawk Aerial Navigation Company, Ltd., the early membership consisted for the most part of General Electric employees. Steinmetz served as president and member of the council.

Most of these men joined with lighthearted motives. Steinmetz himself remarked: "The Company was formed to drive dull care away, and also to provide a ready and effective means of transportation outside the limits of Schenectady." The single-page constitution gave the purpose of the group as "the study of air currents at high elevations." Stockholders included anyone showing an interest in flight who was willing to pay the $2 membership fee.

The first man-carrying "kite" constructed by Steinmetz and his band consisted of a five-pole frame stretching 30 feet from tip to tip. It was 15 feet from front to rear and carried 250 square feet of cotton wing. The "wizard" recommended the study of its design "because it embodies most of the points which the designer of a successful kite should avoid." Tests of the glider were held at Rotterdam Junction, a small suburb of Schenectady. A strong wind was blowing as A. H. Armstrong, who had been selected as "Lord High Victim in Chief," climbed between the wings. With volunteers tugging at the craft, it rose a few feet, then crashed to earth. Repeated attempts to launch the machine "only succeeded in still further reducing it to a state of wreck."

Membership was enlarged in order to gather as many $2 con-
tributions as possible to be applied to the construction of a new
glider that was finished on August 1, 1894. The new craft was
smaller than the first, with a 24-foot wing span and an 8-foot
chord. The engineers had by this time abandoned the kite idea.
The second machine was a true glider. A small group of hills
near Hoffman's Ferry, New York, was selected as a test site. The
Mohawk Aerial Navigators discovered that, although they had
made every effort to hold weight to a minimum, their glider was
too heavy to fly. Armstrong was able to make a few short jumps,
but none of these could be dignified by the term "flight."

The third glider was constructed of steel tubing joined by
aluminum castings and guyed with steel wire. Work was begun
on September 1, 1894. When complete, the wing span was 24 feet
and the depth 8 feet. The camber was 1 in 10. This time, leather
straps were provided through which the operator could pass his
arms. The third glider weighed 50 pounds.

On October 28, 1894, the men once again returned to Hoffman's Ferry. The new machine was no more successful than its
predecessors. "Indeed, so self-willed did it [the glider] become,
that it insisted upon bunting its nose into the earth, in spite of
the remonstrance of the operator, and by so doing fractured
several of its ribs." Armstrong, quite naturally, was "somewhat
diffident about asking for more endeavors on its part, and . . .
contented himself with trotting up and down hill and telling
what he could do if he only wanted to."

By 1895, the interest of the membership was beginning to
wane. Steinmetz circulated retouched photos showing the
glider in flight, but even these illustrations of what might be
accomplished could not convince the Mohawk enthusiasts to
return to the workshop. The "wizard of Schenectady" passed
from the aeronautical scene without having made a single flight.
His presence in the field, however, is a further indication of the
interest that the nation's finest applied scientists had taken in
flight.[10]

Of all the American disciples of Lilienthal, Augustus Moore
Herring was the most significant. After leaving the Stevens

Institute of Technology and suffering a business failure in the panic of 1893, Herring held several minor jobs to support himself while working on a series of Lilienthal monoplane gliders. The first two craft were constructed during the summer of 1894. The first of these had 129 square feet of wing area with a 20-foot span. Herring made a number of flights with this frail machine, which weighed only 14 3/4 pounds. The best of these was about 80 feet in length with a fall of 17 feet.

Herring's second Lilienthal copy was much sturdier, "built to withstand any heavy shocks that might occur from my unskillful handling." The glider featured folding wings 132 feet square. It weighed 26 1/2 pounds and made flights in excess of 150 feet from a 17 1/2-foot drop. As in the case of the first glider, this machine had a horizontal tail surface, but no rudder.

The gliders were constructed of clear, straight-grained spruce. The wings were covered on both sides with nansook muslin varnished with shellac. Piano wire guyed the wings to a central pylon. The pilot suspended his body between twin elliptical ropes that formed the wing roots.

Herring's second glider was destroyed in a wind storm in the fall of 1894. That December, a third Lilienthal machine was approaching completion in the shop. The new craft weighed just under 19 pounds. The wings spread 158 square feet, and its surface was treated with varnish.[11]

Herring, like Lilienthal, constructed his airfoil as a perfect circular arc. The original camber of 1 in 16 was altered to 1 in 30 when rebuilt following a crash.

The wings featured a set of movable surfaces on the leading edge. These were intended to function as steering air brakes similar to those employed by Mouillard and Montgomery.

Flying from a small hill near his home, Herring reported flights of up to 45 feet to Chanute. On several occasions he believed he could have flown over 100 feet had he not been forced to land to avoid hitting a boulder, "which spoils an otherwise good hill."

Chanute was particularly interested in Herring's comments on the control of the gliders.

The balancing and guiding of a Lilienthal machine is very much like riding a bicycle or rather learning to without a teacher—but [it is] probably as easy to control after you have mastered the art (which I haven't) as a bicycle is.[12]

Herring believed that at least a year of steady practice would be required to master the machine fully.

Chanute watched the rise in American gliding activity with some apprehension. A conservative, cautious man, he believed, correctly, that his own books, articles, and speeches were in large measure responsible for persuading many of these young aviators to risk their lives in home-built gliders.

By 1895, the first phase of his own aeronautical career was complete. The time had come to move beyond the speeches, conferences, and theoretical studies. If Chanute was to maintain his leadership of American aeronautics, he had no choice but to begin active gliding experiments.

9

Chanute:
The Glider Years

Octave Chanute stepped from a Chicago train onto the platform of the tiny station at Miller, Indiana, on the morning of June 22, 1896. With his fringe of gray hair, neatly trimmed goatee, and mustache, he resembled William Shakespeare. Short, bald, and portly, he scarcely cut an adventurous figure. Yet Chanute had come to this isolated spot to pursue one of the great adventures of all time. He had come to fly, or rather to watch a number of his younger, more agile, and more athletic assistants fly.

Chanute had worked toward this day for over two decades. He had hoped to build and fly gliders from the beginning of his interest in the problems of aviation. As an engineer, he was accustomed to investigating the ramifications of a given project as thoroughly as possible on paper, then carrying it to fruition by transforming theory and computation into operating machinery. It would have been out of character for him to have devoted twenty years of spare-time research to aeronautics without attempting to apply the insights gained to the design and construction of an actual flying machine.

Chanute's first concrete design for an aircraft dates from December 1888, when he described a machine that he felt would combine the advantages of both lighter- and heavier-than-air craft. It would carry a two-man crew at speeds of 30 mph for up to four hours. The angle of inclination of the wings positioned at the side of the gas bag could be altered to climb or descend without valving gas or dropping ballast.[1]

By 1891 Chanute had abandoned the airship and was giving his full attention to his first glider scheme. Based on Mouillard's ideas, the new craft would feature birdlike wings, with leading edges that could be lowered to act as steering air brakes. The finished glider was to be tested hanging between two poles. But the press of business forced the abandonment of the project before construction began.[2]

Chanute had founded a wood-preservation firm in 1890, and for many months thereafter he was so preoccupied with business matters and the increasing pace of his activities as an aeronautical publicist that he could give little thought to the design of a flying machine. It was at this point that Chanute first received news of Lilienthal's success in Germany. These early reports were the decisive factor in turning Chanute, and a great many other Americans, into enthusiasts of active gliding.

The publicity surrounding Lilienthal's effort resulted in a major shift in emphasis within the American aeronautical community. The thrust of the flying-machine movement was redirected from laboratory experiments, publications, speeches, and meetings to active experiments with full-scale gliders. Scores of young men across the nation were determined to sample the thrills of "aerial tobogganing." Numbered in this group were two brothers from Dayton, Ohio, who would take the final steps toward building a successful airplane.

Chanute was to set this process in motion as, inspired by his contact with Mouillard and Lilienthal, he became determined to build and fly gliders himself. In letters to friends he expressed a desire to develop a practical glider. In October 1892, for example, he wrote Wenham.

It is in my mind, that when this is completed I may offer to be one of a little group which can afford to lose their money, to try

certain experiments which I think are needed upon curved surfaces, and to test the value of such proposals by inventors as seem
to express true merit. All of this of course providing that Mr.
Maxim or some other person does not in the meantime wing his
way into the skies, as most of them hope to do at the first trial.[3]

By 1895, his business interests were once again well in hand
and his commitments for speeches and articles had been
fulfilled. With the publication of *Progress in Flying Machines,* the
first phase of his work in aeronautics was successfully completed. The time had come to begin serious work on a flying
machine.

At this moment, Chanute first became aware of A. M. Herring, the young New Yorker experimenting with Lilienthal
gliders. Long letters filled with technical discussions began to
pass between the two men. Chanute was overjoyed to have
found a man who had actually flown in a heavier-than-air machine. He plied his young friend with questions regarding the
performance of his craft.

Late in December 1894, Chanute unveiled his own glider design. He wrote Herring that the craft was intended to carry one
man. It was to be built as a glider, but "it is intended eventually
to add a motor, and two screws, revolving in opposite directions." It was to demonstrate a system of automatic stability that
Chanute had developed. Chanute believed that if the center of
maximum lifting pressure on the wing surfaces could be made
to adjust automatically to shifts in the glider's center of gravity,
"the operator need only intervene when he wants to change
direction, either up or down, or sideways."[4]

Chanute introduced two factors that he felt would insure such
stability. He believed, on the basis of "abundant experiment"
that a great many wings set in tandem would reduce the movement of the center of pressure on each surface. He therefore
suggested that his craft have as many as four pairs of biplane
wings set one behind the other. The second feature that he
developed to insure automatic stability in high winds consisted
of allowing each pair of wings to pivot on the central frame.
Under normal conditions they would be held in position by coil

springs, but when a gust struck the craft the wings could rotate slightly to the front or rear to return the glider to its original attitude. He described the operation of the system to Herring.

> if the speed of the wind increases the wings are blown backward, . . . the aeroplane tips slightly to the front, thus decreasing the angle of incidence, so that the aggregate "lift" is diminished, and as soon as the wind gust is past, the spring pulls the wings forward into their normal adjusted position.[5]

Chanute called for four pairs of tandem biplane wings on each side of the proposed glider, a total of sixteen in all. These were to be attached to the longitudinal girders that formed the fuselage of the machine. A Howe bridge truss was to be used in the construction of the body of the craft to insure maximum strength with minimum weight. The main girders were to be 1 inch square and shellacked or varnished to make them waterproof, "for I should expect most of the experiments to be tried over water."[6]

The wings, constructed of cane or bamboo, were to be as light and narrow as possible. Each of the sixteen surfaces would be 6 feet long, and 2 feet, 2 inches wide at the root. Chanute agreed with Wenham that such an aspect ratio would guarantee swifter flight. In addition, such narrow wings would permit most of the weight of the machine to be carried on the frame rather than by the lifting surfaces. Each wing was to be positioned on the frame with a dihedral angle of about 5 degrees to provide some lateral stability.

The pilot would stand on a narrow running board in the fuselage, controlling the direction of flight "within certain limits" by leaning in the appropriate direction. Handles to control the rotation of the wings were provided. A "horizontal rudder," or elevator, governed altitude.

Some of those to whom Chanute described the craft were less than enthusiastic. Mouillard, for example, remarked that he could see no value in either the biplane or multiple tandem wing configuration.

When Herring expressed interest in the scheme, Chanute commissioned him to test the principles underlying the design with models, after which the two men could proceed with the construction of a full-scale glider. The Chicagoan established credit for the young engineer at a New York bank so that Herring could draw funds for necessary materials. In addition, Chanute provided a stipend of five dollars a day. Herring was to be allowed a great deal of latitude in building the small craft so long as he adhered to the basic design. Early in 1895, Herring began work on two models, the first roughly one-third, the second three-eighths the size of the proposed full-scale craft. Both models were constructed so that four, eight, twelve, or sixteen wings could be tested in tandem biplane sets on the same craft.

Herring drew a number of conclusions from the trials that were conducted over the next few weeks. The successful operation of the wing rocking automatic control system was encouraging. New data on the ratio of wing span to chord and on the proper distance between the upper and lower wings of a biplane also proved invaluable.[7]

As the model tests concluded, Herring and Chanute continued to give serious thought to their next project—the full-scale glider. They saw the need for a wheeled undercarriage, or floats, at the front and rear to cushion landing shocks.

The pilot's position and freedom of movement were also of concern. Herring argued that the operator should be seated on a sliding rest for ease of control. He sketched a glider in which the pilot would be completely enclosed within an open, trussed, triangular frame. The main stringers were located at each of the angles. All the wings were to be attached to these longerons.

After some discussion Chanute and Herring redesigned the fuselage so that it was a square structure in section, the four corner stringers being drawn into a point at either end. The sides, the top, the bottom, and the interior, except for the area where the pilot was seated, were trussed with wire. Herring estimated that the glider would include 130 separate pieces of wood, 274 wires, and from 28 to 100 small pieces of metal, exclu-

sive of nuts and bolts. The New Yorker claimed that the fuselage of the finished craft would weigh 9 pounds and the wings
11 to 12 1/2 pounds. The wire fittings, seat, and tail would raise
the total weight to about 32 pounds.[8]

Before work began on the manned glider, however, Herring accepted the position with Samuel Langley. While Octave
Chanute was careful to mask any bitterness that he may
have felt after Herring's departure, he did express some pique
in a letter to James Means, who had originally recommended
Herring to the secretary. "You did me rather an ill turn,"
he wrote, ". . . but I felt that the Smithsonian Institution
was so much better equipped than myself to accomplish success that I let Mr. Herring go, and stopped my experiments."[9]

While Chanute had temporarily set his own experiments aside, he remained in close touch with Herring and
kept him fully informed of developments in aeronautics. On
June 20, 1895, for example, Chanute described an interesting
scheme being promoted in Denver, where "the people propose
to open a large exposition on the 1st of July 1896, and want to
make experiments in aeronautics a prominent and attractive
feature."[10]

Captain William Glassford, chief U.S. signal officer, suggested
the purchase of a Lilienthal glider, but Chanute counseled that
the promoters support American aeronautics by purchasing
Herring's third Lilienthal copy.

Herring, who had begun to realize that he would not be
allowed to develop his own ideas while in Langley's employ,
thought that Chanute's proposal might offer a means of financing the construction of an airplane of his own design. He wrote
Chanute that his 1894 Lilienthal machine was in no condition to
fly, but if the Denver promoters could furnish $20,000 to $30,000,
he would build the world's first successful man-carrying airplane. He envisioned a steam-powered craft to be produced by
July 1, 1896, at a cost of $27,000. Herring was so sure of himself
that he remarked, "I am willing to stake my reputation on it,
that it will fly with one man."[11]

Chanute was hopeful, but cautious, promising to present

Herring's case to the people of Denver. Essentially, Herring suggested a $25,000 subscription to cover the cost of materials, labor, and $200 a month for himself. In return, he would produce a machine capable of flying several thousand feet.

Captain Glassford and the members of the Denver committee ultimately decided that Herring's plan was far beyond their means and stated their desire to sponsor the flight of a glider "that is complete and ready for use." The amount at their disposal was only $100, and they saw little hope for raising a sum even close to Herring's requirements. His plans dashed, Herring had little choice but to continue with Langley until conditions at the Smithsonian became intolerable or until something more attractive appeared. He was determined to work toward a successful flying machine until the final goal was achieved, whatever the cost.[12]

By the time Langley forced Herring's resignation in December, Chanute had already put two other men to work constructing gliders, but was more than happy to welcome his old assistant back into the fold to oversee the activities. This time Chanute was determined that a finished glider would be produced and flown the following summer. Herring immediately moved to Chicago, where activity was well under way in the shop of William Avery, an experienced carpenter and electrician.

Arriving in Chicago on December 12, 1895, Herring set to work refurbishing his final Lilienthal glider, which would be tested as a control against the new machines being planned. When complete, Herring's Lilienthal machine had a wing span of 20 feet and a chord of 7 feet, 6 inches. The wings carried 168 square feet of surface. The entire machine, minus pilot, weighed 36 pounds. A double rudder was added to the tail to provide stability.[13]

The New Yorker's second task was to construct and fly a "ladder kite," that would provide data to be used in refining a new multiplane design that Chanute had developed. The serious problems of air flow interference that Herring had uncovered in tests with the one-third and three-eighths models of the tan-

A. M. Herring stands with the rebuilt Lilienthal glider flown at the Indiana dunes in 1896. William Avery stands to the right.

dem wing craft in 1894 and 1895 had convinced Chanute that this wing configuration would so reduce the lift of the rear surfaces that a new arrangement should be tried. He now suggested a glider in which the twelve wings would be stacked one on top of the other, rather than placed as biplane sets in tandem fashion. Herring's kite illustrated that this wing form would prove efficient, and work continued on the new multiplane Chanute glider in Avery's shop.

When complete, the new Chanute apparatus carried twelve wings, each 6 feet long with a 3-foot chord. The individual wings measured 14 3/4 square feet and were attached to the fuselage so that they could move to the front or rear. This feature was intended to provide the sort of automatic stability achieved with the earlier models. The total wing area was 177 square feet. The original plan called for eight wings in front, and four following

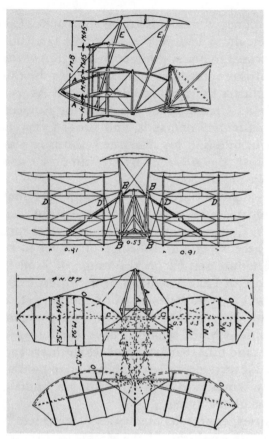

Chanute's 1896 multiplane in its final configuration.

surfaces placed in the rear. The pilot hung by his arms beneath the front eight wings. The lifting surfaces and fuselage were designed so that the twelve wings could be positioned in every possible combination in the front or rear. The finished machine weighed 36 pounds.[14]

Meanwhile, a third machine was being designed by William Paul Butusov, a Russian emigrant who claimed to have constructed and flown a very large manned glider at Eden's Pond, near Mammoth Cave, Kentucky, in 1889. Butusov worked for two years in the area and claimed to have achieved flights lasting up to forty-five minutes and covering many miles.

When his money was exhausted, he approached Chanute, who found it difficult to believe the Russian's tale, but was sufficiently impressed to finance the reconstruction of the Kentucky machine. Butusov agreed to test his craft with the Lilienthal and multiplane gliders prepared by Herring and Avery. In a letter to James Means, Chanute remarked that the Russian "was very modest in his money demands, and proved very faithful and industrious in building his machine." Butusov was, however, unable to finish the *Albatross* by the time of the initial tests during the spring of 1896.[15]

Chanute had given a great deal of thought to suitable areas in which he and his assistants might successfully conduct their tests. Both the California and Florida coasts were considered but abandoned because of the difficulty of travel to such distant locations. Chanute settled on the range of sand hills on the southern shore of Lake Michigan near Miller, Indiana.

The site was only 30 miles east of Chicago, yet, as reporters were later to note, anyone trying to find the camp without explicit directions risked spending days wandering lost through swamps and sand hills that even the local hunters and fishermen hadn't seen. Nevertheless, the combination of gentle slopes, soft sands, steady winds, and isolation made the Indiana dunes an ideal spot for glider flying.

For centuries, enormous quantities of sand had been blown toward the southern shore of Lake Michigan. In spots where the resulting bluffs ringing the lake were pierced by storms, sand had been carried inland, creating a wasteland of shifting dunes that covered the native marsh and forest land to the south. Hardy vegetation was sometimes able to anchor the drifts in place, enabling large prominances like the 190-foot Mount Tom dune, covering more than 100 acres, to grow. Elsewhere the dunes, pushed about by the constant winds, alternately buried and revealed the underlying landscape.

In the closing years of the nineteenth century, the dune country was a land of contrasts. Lying within easy traveling distance by train or boat from Chicago and smaller urban centers, it remained sparsely populated and was, as one observer remarked, "as desolate as the Sahara."

Chanute and his four assistants reached Miller on the morning of June 22, 1896. In addition to Herring, Avery, and Butusov, who had been intimately involved in the design and construction of the gliders, Chicago physician James Rickets, "who had a slack practice and a taste for aviation," accompanied the party. Chanute, a cautious man, had invited Rickets to attend for obvious reasons. The men would be testing experimental gliders in an isolated area miles from the nearest hospital. In the event of a serious accident the doctor's presence could mean the difference between life and death for one of the enthusiasts.[16]

Immediately after their arrival, the men loaded their gear onto a wagon and made the 3-mile trip to the dunes. With the camp established, they then assembled the gliders that would be flown during the opening phase of the flight trials.

Chanute later described the method of flying all of the machines to be tested.

> The method of carrying on these adventures is for the operator to place himself within and under the apparatus, which should, preferably, be light enough to be easily carried on the shoulders or by the hands, and to face the wind on a hillside. The operator should in no wise be attached to the machine. He may be suspended by his arms, or sit upon a seat, or stand on a running board, but he must be able to disengage himself instantly from the machine should anything go wrong, and be able to come down upon his legs in landing.[17]

This method of launching the gliders into the air had been adopted from Herring's experience with his earlier Lilienthal machines.

> Facing dead into the wind, and keeping the front edge of the supporting surfaces depressed, so that the wind shall blow upon their backs and press them downward, the operator first adjusts his apparatus and himself to the veering wind. He has to struggle to obtain a poise, and in a moment of relative steadiness he runs forward a few steps as fast as he may, and launches himself upon the breeze, by raising the front edge of the sustaining surfaces, so as to receive the wind from beneath at a very small angle

(2 to 4 degrees) of incidence. If the surfaces and wind be adequate, he finds himself thoroughly sustained, and then sails forward on a descending or undulating course, under the combined effects of gravity and of the opposing wind. By shifting either his body or his wings, or both, he can direct his descent, either sideways or up or down, within certain limits; he can cause the apparatus to sweep upward so as to clear an obstacle, and he is not infrequently lifted up several feet by a swelling wind. The course of the glide eventually brings the apparatus within a few feet of the ground (6 or 10 feet), when the operator, by throwing his weight backward, or his wings forward if they are moveable [as in the case of the twelve-wing multiplane], causes the front of the supporting surfaces to tilt up to a greater angle of incidence, thus increasing the wind resistance, slowing the forward motion, and enabling him, by a slight oscillation, to drop to the ground as gently as if he had fallen only one or two feet.[18]

Chanute had originally believed that flying hang gliders might be dangerous, but he quickly realized that his fears were unfounded. During the summer and fall of 1896, the tiny group of experimenters repeatedly demonstrated that "a week's practice sufficed for a young, active man to become reasonably expert in these maneuvers." Herring and Avery made most of the glides. Butusov proved much less adept than the two younger men, but was to make occasional flights as well. Chanute, who believed that he was too old to play an active role in the trials, did not attempt to glide, although several photographs do show him strapped into the multiplane glider. In addition, Chanute's son Charles and several reporters, who regularly appeared at the camp, were allowed to try to glide.

Chanute and his assistants had initially brought two gliders to the dunes. The first of these was Herring's rebuilt Lilienthal machine. It was first tested soon after their arrival on June 22. Within two days flights of up to 100 feet were obtained with the glider.

From the outset the craft seemed "cranky" and difficult to balance in the air. When large sections were cut from the wings to alleviate the problem, the control difficulties only increased.

On the morning of June 29, Herring was finally able to stretch a glider to 116 feet. Late that afternoon the Lilienthal glider turned over on landing and was broken beyond repair.

In assessing the performance of the glider Chanute remarked that it was "uncertain in its action," and required "great patience." The primary problem lay in the pilot's need to "shift his weight constantly, like a tight rope dancer without a pole." All things considered, the craft was "a gliding, not a soaring machine," and he was "glad to be rid of it."[19]

The second glider tested was Chanute's multiplane. When first flown on the afternoon of June 24, it was immediately apparent that the superposed wings at the front caused far too much lift, forcing the machine to glide in a nose-up position. In order to test the craft in as safe a manner as possible, 12 pounds of sandbags were tied onto the pilot's position, so that it could be flown as a kite. The men enjoyed some success in balancing the craft in this manner, but late in the afternoon it was blown over and damaged slightly. Chanute commented in his diary that "all are afraid because of its [the multiplane's] novelty." As late as Friday, June 26, Chanute remarked that Herring and Avery were still reluctant to jump with it, "as the wings seemed too frail to sustain a man of, say, 150 lbs. and 25 lbs. of machine." The glider was held stationary in the wind while down was released in front of it to gauge the action of the air currents passing over the surfaces.

On June 27, the Chanute multiplane was rerigged with four planes in front and eight to the rear. Herring made test jumps of up to 27 feet in a wind that varied from 7 to 10 miles per hour. The glider was slightly damaged in one of these tests, but repairs were made in only ten minutes.

Wind gusts blowing off the lake early the following morning caused real problems. Since their arrival the five men and any reporters who wanted to stay the night had been housed in the large tent that had originally been intended to protect the gliders. The experimenters had quickly discovered that the machines could be left outside without damage if weighted with sand. At about 1:00 A.M. on Sunday, June 28, the wind blew the big tent over onto the glider, causing severe damage. Avery fought to put the tent back up in a driving rain, while the others pulled the glider to safety. Once the shelter was erected, it was decided that Avery, the finest workman in the group, would remain on the site to effect repairs while the others returned by train to Chicago for visits with their families.

Avery rebuilt the multiplane once more with one biplane in front and eight surfaces behind. The machine's balance when standing in a wind was still not satisfactory, as there was now too much lift on the tail. The eight wings were then transferred back to the front and the remaining four were used on the rear. The machine now proved much easier to control, both while being carried about on the ground and when in flight.

Both Herring and Avery made glides of over 76 feet against the morning wind with the glider and "pronounced the machine more stable in its present shape than that of Lilienthal." But there was still room for improvement.

Experiments with the remaining Chanute machine continued on Tuesday, June 30, 1896. The twelve-wing craft with the now standard four biplane surfaces in front and two behind was altered by raising the top wing of the front set to determine if this would make the machine easier to control or make a substantial difference in lift. The total weight was under 37 pounds. It was test-flown with a 5-pound sandbag on the leading edge. Manned flights were made with the wings in this configuration on the next day, and the glider proved "as easy to handle as with the top wings lower down." Moreover, it seemed to exhibit greater lift.

In a final effort to improve the balance and flying characteristics of the Chanute multiplane, one of the wing pairs from the tail was placed in the open space between the raised top surface and the wings below them. The multiplane now took on such an insectlike appearance because of the visual confusion of wings forward and aft and the frame and myriad brace wires that it was affectionately dubbed the *Katydid*.

The first manned flights with the reconstituted *Katydid* were made on July 2. It proved steady and manageable in the air. "Scores" of jumps were completed, the longest of which was a 60-foot flight by Herring. The angle of descent had been about 17 1/2 degrees, and the glide ratio roughly 1 in 3 1/2—that is, 3 1/2 feet of forward motion for every 1 foot of fall. Gunnysacks were wrapped around the wires surrounding the pilot to protect him in the event of a crash. The single remaining pair of rear wings was now free to flex up and down to maintain equilibrium, while the ten wings in front could rotate as originally planned to provide automatic stability.

Uncertain winds and an evening storm prevented any flights on the next day, but July 4 was an ideal day for trials. The best jumps in the morning averaged only 55 feet, but the wind picked up during the afternoon and Avery was able to stretch a glide to 78 feet. Herring, always the more successful pilot, claimed a flight of 82 feet, 6 inches. The crew stopped the trials at 2:00 P.M., returned to the camp, and packed. They left Miller on the 6:41 train for Chicago. Their baggage and the gliders followed them on a later express train.

The growing crowd of newsmen and curiosity seekers were a primary reason for bringing the first series of trials to an end. Chanute had not been anxious to draw the attention of the press and had been careful to keep word of the two gliders under construction from becoming public. The small group had sneaked out of Chicago during the early morning hours to avoid attracting attention, but the arrival of this strange band of men at Miller with large packing crates filled with camping gear and pieces of wood, wire, and fabric was a major event in the tiny community. Calls were made to the city, where reporters quickly guessed the purposes of this camping expedition to the shores of Lake Michigan. The first reporter, from the *Chicago Tribune*, arrived on the scene on the evening of June 23.

Once news of the trials leaked out, reporters from a variety of Chicago newspapers and the national wire services made the trek to Miller. Chanute and his companions had soon become national celebrities, and their activities were followed by readers across the United States.

Chanute hoped that the group might be able to continue its work in privacy after a short break. In addition, the frequently altered *Katydid* was much in need of a complete refurbishment. Finally, a few weeks in Chicago would enable Butusov to complete work on his *Albatross* while Herring and Avery constructed a new glider conceived during the first period on the dunes.

During the month that Chanute and his assistants spent back in the Avery workshop in Chicago, the *Katydid* was placed in its final form. The old fuselage frame was retained, but major changes were made in the wings. Four pairs (eight wings) were now stacked one on top of the other. The top set of wings on the original craft was replaced by a single large, kitelike surface centered horizontally over the whole machine. The tail surfaces included a pair of standard wings attached to the frame at the same level as the lowest pair of front wings. In addition, a very large vertical rudder was included. The total area of the front wings was 143.5 square feet, while the rear set totaled 29.5 square feet. When complete, the new *Katydid* weighed 33 1/2 pounds. The wing span was about 16 feet and the craft some 10 feet long. It measured slightly less than 7 feet from the base of the lowest front wing to the top of the overhead kite surface.[20]

Some problems had been encountered with sticking pivots on the original craft. This arrangement was now replaced by one in which all four of the front wings were tied together by rods. Rather than rotating individually, the surfaces now worked in unison. Ball bearings were placed at the level of the lower wings and that of the third set from the bottom, so that the system would operate more smoothly than had previously been the case.

The new glider built during the hiatus in Chicago was the most significant and influential aircraft of the pre-Wright era. Although it would come to be known as the "two-surface machine," the craft was originally built as a triplane.

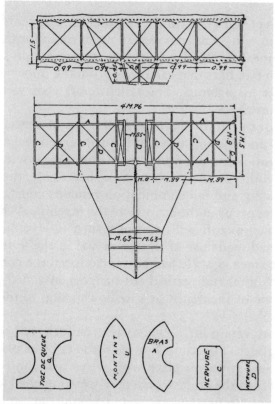

The two-surface glider in the 1897 Herring configuration.

The glider represented a new approach to the problem of inherent stability. The wings of both the models that Herring had built for Chanute in 1895 and the multiplane *Katydid* glider had been free to rock or rotate, varying the position of the center of lifting pressure on the wing in an effort to compensate for gusts. The wings of the new triplane would be rigid, held in place by the familiar Pratt truss that Chanute had used so often in bridge construction. Solid uprights connected the three superposed wings, providing strength in compression, while crossed diagonal wires across the front, back, and sides carried loads in tension. The result was a single rigid box framework.

Each of three wings was covered with varnished silk and had

a span of 16 feet and a cord of 4 feet, 3 inches. The central section of the bottom wing was removed to make room for the pilot. It was a genuine hang glider in which the operator suspended himself from two bars that ran down from the upper wings and passed under his armpits. The tail support rods were also attached to these bars.

The cruciform tail of the new glider was of special interest. Both Cayley and Alphonse Pénaud had observed that a fixed tail, properly positioned on a flying model, would provide a useful degree of stability in the pitch axis. In such a case, the center of lift for the wing and tail combination remains constant even if slight changes occur in the attitude of the machine. When struck by a gust, such a craft will tend to return to level flight.[21]

Herring had made use of this principal in the flying models he had built since 1891. He had also introduced the combination of fixed horizontal and vertical tail surfaces, attached at a slight negative angle of incidence by a willowspring, to the Langley aerodromes.[22]

He chose to retain his now classic cruciform tail in the case of the new glider. This time, however, the tail was placed on an universal joint, guyed in place with wires that ran forward to the main body of the craft, where they were attached to springs. Under normal circumstances the tail would remain stationary and keep the glider flying in a steady attitude. When struck by a gust, the tail would "give" in the opposite direction, applying a force that would tend to return the craft to straight and level flight.

The finished glider was simple and elegant, a distinct contrast to the complexity of the wing-rocking *Katydid* or the birdlike Lilienthal machines. It was small, 31 pounds; but this simple craft, with its clean, lightweight structure, provided "the basis for all externally braced biplanes."[23]

In view of the importance of this glider in the evolution of the flying machine, the credit for its design is a matter of some interest. In 1900 a dispute arose between Chanute and Herring as to who had contributed most to the design. In articles and speeches describing events on the dunes in 1896 and 1897, Chanute gave his associate sole credit for the development of the automatic stabilizing tail, but intimated that he himself had been responsible for the rest of the craft.[24]

Herring disagreed. He argued that what was to become known as the "two-surface machine" had been the direct outgrowth of a small "aspirating kite" that he had built and flown during the first period at Miller. This kite was a monoplane device with an early form of the Herring stabilizing tail. The New Yorker claimed that Chanute's only contribution to this most successful glider was restricted to the decision to build a man-carrying machine with superposed wings to test the stabilizing mechanism. Herring continued,

> I have never seen why you [Chanute] should . . . appear to claim the whole credit for the invention of the two surface gliding machine, since its success depends wholly upon the efficiency of the regulating mechanism which was my work and furthermore I made the designs for the original two surface machine alone and

Katydid in the air.

at my home. I put them on paper as a scale drawing in the course of one afternoon in your study.[25]

Chanute's memory of the circumstances leading up to the construction of the machine was different:

While we were still in camp I made and gave you [Herring], on cross section paper, a sketch of the two surfaced machine with a Pénaud tail to serve in building the 1896 machine. This you assigned as a reason why I should join you in applying for a British patent, at the time that I disclaimed any share in the design of the propelling arrangements.[26]

While it is impossible to exactly apportion credit for the design, it is apparent that Herring had a stronger case than Chanute was willing to concede. As early as 1891–1892 Herring had constructed a monoplane flying model powered by twisted rubber strands that clearly embodied important features that would appear in the 1896 Chanute-Herring two-surface glider, notably the general wing shape and cruciform tail unit.[27]

A biplane version of this original model, probably built in 1893, was intended for use with a small steam engine. This craft bore an even closer resemblance to the 1896 glider. Langley had been particularly impressed when Herring made flights of up to 25 meters with this model, powered by rubber strands, at the Smithsonian in October 1895.[28]

The kite that Herring flew on the beach at Miller, Indiana, in 1896 was a direct descendant of these two models. The resulting glider was basically an enlarged version of the models and the kite. It represented a design that Herring had been evolving over a four- or five-year period. Chanute approved the idea, funded construction of the craft, may even have suggested the original triplane configuration, and certainly recommended the trussing; but the basic design elements were probably contributed by Herring.

By the time the group was ready to return to the Lake Michigan shore, Butusov's *Albatross* was complete. The *Albatross* was a very large machine with a wing span of 40 feet and a chord of 7 feet. A large kite surface, or "aeroplane," was placed horizontally over the wings. The angle of incidence at which this kite struck the air could be varied by the pilot. The vertical, longitudinal "keels" of balloon cloth, each 3 feet high and 8 feet long, extended from the bottom of the wings to the pilot's position.

The operator was housed in a boatlike frame in which an 8-foot running board was provided. He could, therefore, exercise control over the rise and fall of the glider by moving to the front or rear on this narrow platform. In addition, he could bank the craft by leaning about 3 feet over either side of the cockpit. Both a rudder and elevator were provided on the rear of the machine, to be operated by control lines that ran to the pilot's position. The lifting surfaces of the *Albatross* totaled 266 square feet and weighed 160 pounds. A glider this large could not be launched in the normal manner. Butusov decided, therefore, to construct a large trestle with tracks that ran downhill into the face of the prevailing wind.[29]

Chanute, Herring, Avery, Butusov, and Rickets were prepared to return to test flying with the three new gliders by mid-August 1896. In order to avoid alerting reporters, who had plagued the party during June and July, Chanute had chartered a small ship, the *Scorpion,* to carry the men and machines to the test site near Miller. On August 20, the *Katydid* and the triplane glider were loaded at the Pestigo Dock on the Chicago lakefront, after which the *Scorpion* moved to the Seventy-first Street pier, where Paul Butusov and the *Albatross* were taken aboard. The boat remained tied in south Chicago overnight and arrived off the "experiment hill" at 12:30 P.M. the next day. A Mr. Cord met the *Scorpion* with a flatboat. All of the equipment was unloaded by 1:45. Tents were pitched, and general camp chores were completed by the evening of August 21.

Miller had proved "too public" during the previous trials, so the group chose to move 5 miles down the shore to an area

where the hills were higher, the solitude greater, and the path more obscure to the railroad, which it reached at a sandpit station consisting of a single house, and called Dune Park. The distance from our camp was about two miles, through a series of swamps, woods, and hills, so that imposing visitors not infrequently got lost.[30]

The reporters who did discover the site agreed with Chanute's description of the area. A newspaperman with the *Chicago Inter-Ocean* remarked that to locate the camp was "about as hard a task as a man can put his hand to."[31] Moreover, the site was protected by a "phalanx" of mosquitoes and cacti.

Disaster struck the camp as a storm blew in from the lake the morning after their arrival. The tents were blown down, the men soaked, equipment damaged, and provisions ruined. The three wings of the triplane glider, on which work had begun the previous evening, were hopelessly smashed. August 22 was spent drying equipment and awaiting the arrival of a new tent from Chicago.

Another storm raged that night. But the skies had cleared by 9:00 A.M., when Chanute returned to the city to purchase supplies. The rest of the party spent the night at a local fisherman's home. Avery, Rickets, and Butusov began assembling the *Albatross* and its launching trestle on Monday, August 24, while Herring traveled back to Chicago to select wood for the new wings of the triplane.

Work on Butusov's craft continued throughout the week, and by Saturday, August 29, it was complete except for a few finishing touches. Herring had returned to camp on the previous Wednesday and had finished assembling the fixed wing glider by Saturday, but when first tested that afternoon the craft proved disappointing, exhibiting too much lift on the forward surfaces. At Avery's suggestion, Herring removed the bottom wings of his machine and flew it as a biplane. He was elated by the results. The craft was now stable and supported his weight in glides of up to 97 feet. The "two-surface" or "Chanute-Herring machine" now sported 135 square feet of wing area.

Friday, September 4, was ideal for flying. This fact was apparent to potential spectators as well, for Chanute's friend Joseph Cord appeared with a group of reporters who had hired him to drive them to the camp that morning. Herring's glider was tested first, ten to twelve flights being made. The results, when compared to all of the other trials, were most encouraging. Avery was able to keep the machine in the air for a distance of 253 feet. Herring's best effort of the day was 239 feet. Both of these flights were over twice the best distance previously obtained.

Butusov's inclined trestle was also complete by September 4. This structure consisted of

a pair of tallowed guides or ways, 8 feet apart, descending at an angle of 23 degrees down the slope of the sand hill selected, the top being 94 feet above the lake. The last 10 feet of these launching ways was horizontal, and connected with the sloping portion by a curve of 5 feet radius.[32]

Chanute and the 1896 biplane. Note the side curtains to prevent sideslips and the absence of fabric on the upper tail surface.

The launching ramp faced north into prevailing lake winds. The tracks were supported uniformly 11 feet over the sand. There were no crossties, the two "ways" being each independently supported from the ground. Special "boots" on which the *Albatross* would slide down the ramp had been prepared.

Some time was spent in putting some pieces of missing cloth onto the glider, after which it was discovered that the two "boots" were not operating correctly. Once this problem had been overcome, the *Albatross* was tested with 65 pounds of sand. The machine was slightly damaged, and a defect in the wings was discovered. It was decided to forego further testing until some braces were completed.

The wind had freshened on September 9, and the *Katydid* was suspended between two trees so that the wing movement that was intended to provide stability and control could be checked and adjusted. Once Chanute was satisfied that the craft was safe, Herring prepared for a flight. While still making preliminary hops to prepare for full-scale glides, he was lifted by a sudden gust and tossed to the ground. As a result, the rear wing was broken. The repaired multiplane was next taken out for trial on September 11. The wind was blowing from the north at a speed of 22.3 miles per hour. Herring made a number of fine flights during the morning, including one of 148 feet in seven seconds, a second of 166 feet in 7.5 seconds, and a third of 172 feet in 7.8 seconds. Avery had a successful morning as well, with one glide of 174 feet in 7.6 seconds and another of 188 feet in 7.9 seconds.

By noon the wind had freshened and was blowing from the west at 31 miles per hour. Conditions seemed perfect, and the Herring glider, now a biplane, was flown with phenomenal results. For the first time the Chanute group equaled the results obtained by Lilienthal. Avery's efforts of the afternoon included flights of 199 feet in eight seconds and 256 feet in 10.2 seconds. Herring's flights were even more encouraging. He covered distances of 234 feet in 8.7 seconds, 320 feet in 9 seconds, 235 feet in 10.3 seconds, and 359 feet in 14 seconds.

Effort was concentrated on minor changes in Chanute's multiplane glider and Butusov's machine on September 12. The Russian returned to the dunes on Saturday, "worn out with two sleepless nights" in Chicago nursing his sick child. The *Albatross* was assembled by 4:00 P.M., but heavy fog prevented tests and the men were forced to remove portions of the cloth to avoid damage in the event of high winds during the night. Chanute, Avery, Butusov, and Rickets became quite angry with Herring, who refused to work with them on the large machine. The independent New Yorker had flown his biplane once again, covering 359 feet on one glide.

On September 13, a Sunday, the crew once again returned to Chicago. The following day brought rain storms all over the northern Midwest, and Chanute remained in town. Herring called on him at 1:00 P.M. with serious complaints.

Herring said that he "disbelieved Paul's [Butusov's] having flown with his machine; that he considered it [the *Albatross*] highly dangerous, and sooner than be a party to its testing he preferred to withdraw."[33]

Chanute had received complaints from both Avery and Rickets about Herring's high-handed manner, and realized that only by accepting his resignation could he hold the rest of the party

Gliding down a slope in the biplane.

together. He accepted the loss of the man whom he considered
to be his most valuable assistant. But even his seemingly endless
store of patience was exhausted when Herring ran to Manly of
the *Chicago Record* with a full account of the "disagreement."

Chanute realized that Herring's fears for the safety of the
Albatross were only an attempt to mask his real reason for with-
drawing from the experiments. He believed that the success of
the two-surface glider had opened the way to powered flight. In
November 1896, Chanute described the events of mid-Septem-
ber to James Means:

> Mr. Herring did not prove satisfactory. He left me . . . giving as
> his reason that he did not want to countenance by his presence
> the pending test of a third machine, designed by Wm. Paul [Butu-
> sov]. . . . I think the real reason is that he knew I would not
> consent to apply a motor to a full sized machine, believing this
> to be entirely premature, while he was at the time so elated by our
> joint success and the unwelcome (to me) advent of the newspaper

The Albatross *ready for launch.*

reporters, that he thought success within his grasp. He told me that he intended to build at once a full sized machine with a gasoline motor of his invention, with the assistance of a syndicate of newspapers or from the proceeds of public exhibitions. I understood that he had applied to Barnum and Bailey's circus, but had been unable to make an arrangement.[34]

Chanute returned to Dune Park on Tuesday, September 15, to resume testing. Butusov's *Albatross* was placed on top of its launching ramp, and the rails tallowed in preparation for a flight. With Butusov in the cockpit checking the balance of the craft a sudden wind lifted the entire apparatus some 2 1/2 feet into the air, buckling a brace and forcing cancellation of further trials that day. September 16 was spent in repairing the *Albatross,* but Avery was able to make several glides with the multiplane.

In the interest of safety it was agreed to test the Butusov glider as a kite, with sandbags simulating the pilot's weight. Preparations for these trials were complete by Thursday, September 17. A bridle had been placed around the fuselage of the *Albatross,* and a single main line ran from this device down the incline to a post 250 feet from the end of the tracks. The line passed through a swivel at this point. The men were to grab it and run at right angles to the direction of flight in order to keep the machine in the air. In addition, volunteers manned shorter ropes tied to the wing tips and the nose and tail. Chanute cut the release rope at 12:35 and the huge craft sped down the ways and into the air. It flew slightly to the right at an altitude of 15 to 20 feet, touching the earth after it had traveled roughly 100 feet. Some damage was done to the keel and stanchions, but all repairs were complete within two hours. The Chicagoan was relieved, for "the experiment seemed to indicate that the apparatus is stable, and will not come down so as to endanger the operator."

The Butusov glider was once more pulled to the top of the ramp on September 25. Released at 3:00 P.M., it slid down the track and ground to a stop on the level portion. It was positioned once again, this time with 90 pounds of sand but no pilot on board. A rope was attached to the nose to pull it into the air. As the *Albatross* rose from the track it nosed toward the southwest, banking into a group of trees on the left. The left wing was smashed, but Chanute believed "if a man had been in the machine he would not have been hurt." The test was especially disappointing, however, for the Butusov glider had demonstrated that "it will glide, not soar."

The men broke camp for the final time after the destruction of the *Albatross.* They had enjoyed thirty days active flying time. No accurate count of the actual number of flights was kept, but the total probably exceeded a thousand, if the very short jumps were included.

Chanute and his companions had demonstrated that Lilienthal's efforts could not only be repeated but improved upon. During a single summer, these men had built and flown the most advanced glider in the world. To the general public it appeared that mankind now stood on the threshold of flight. The men involved were not so certain.

10

Herring Alone, 1896–1898

The flying-machine movement in America had reached its high-water mark during the summer and fall of 1896. From May through December of that year the nation's newspapers had reported a series of stunning accomplishments in aeronautics. It was a season of triumph for the men who had gambled their lives and reputations on the possibility of heavier-than-air flight.

After more than a decade of effort, S. P. Langley had successfully launched two of his steam-powered aerodromes on flights of up to three-quarters of a mile over the Potomac. Octave Chanute and his associates had repeatedly demonstrated the superior performance of their biplane glider as they skimmed down the slopes of the Lake Michigan dunes. In New England, C. H. Lamson, A. A. Merrill, and Samuel Cabot had made well-publicized glides in machines of their own design, while William Randolph Hearst manufactured his own headlines by sponsoring flight tests of a Lilienthal glider on a Long Island estate. Even the publication of James Means's second *Aeronautical Annual* had excited much favorable comment in the press.

Public enthusiasm for flight approached a peak in the wake of these widely reported successes. Scores of eager young mechanics across the nation, their imaginations fired by accounts of the progress being made in aeronautics, were hard at work on strange-looking contraptions designed to carry them into the sky. Even the most skeptical members of a generation that had witnessed the advent of the telegraph, the telephone, and the horseless carriage were slowly coming to realize that they stood on the threshold of the air age.

The fact that well-known inventors like Thomas Edison, John Holland of submarine fame, and Alexander Graham Bell were taking a serious interest in flight was also a major factor in promoting popular interest in flight.[1] Newspaper editors were quick to comment on the new wave of flying-machine enthusiasm that was sweeping the nation. The *Portland Oregonian* noted that "the serious attention given to the airship by scientific men has done much to inspire a belief that aerial navigation belongs to science, not crazy speculation." A *Boston Herald* reporter remarked that "there never was a time when so much genuine interest was taken in the subject of aerial navigation as at the present day," while the *Toledo Bee* opined that the belief that flight would be accomplished in the near future "is general even in the most perfect minds." Clearly, Simon Newcomb and other scientists who had so long doubted the possibility of flight were fast becoming a minority.[2]

Yet the summer of 1896, which seemed filled with promise, was also a turning point. The leaders of American aeronautics, unable to sustain the momentum of their drive toward powered flight, entered a two-year period of indecision and uncertainty. Having demonstrated the possibility of heavier-than-air flight with their models and gliders, these men realized that an even greater effort would be required to overcome the enormous obstacles blocking further progress toward a successful full-scale airplane. They were tempted to accept the honors for what had already been accomplished and step aside to allow others to face the continued risk of ridicule and disgrace that still lay in wait for the unsuccessful flying-machine experimenter.

S. P. Langley adopted just such a cautious stance, publicly announcing his retirement from aeronautics in the fall of 1896 while initiating a quiet search for potential funding to support the construction of a man-carrying aerodrome. If conditions for success remained ripe and if sufficient money became available, he could re-enter the field, for in spite of his desire for a respite Langley believed that the airplane was within striking distance for a man with enough cash and a will to succeed.

Octave Chanute was less optimistic. His published account of the 1896 glider trials focused not on the success achieved, but on the unexplored territory that lay ahead. The final goal of powered flight was, he concluded, "as yet very distant." Convinced of the need to achieve absolute stability with a glider before undertaking work with a powered machine, Chanute was prepared to abandon the 1896 biplane in favor of a new multiplane craft featuring another automatic control system.[3]

While neither Langley nor Chanute seemed willing to lead an immediate all-out assault on powered flight, younger men, individuals with less to lose and more to gain, were eager to forge ahead. Augustus Moore Herring, the most important of these figures, was to emerge as the most active and successful flying-machine experimenter in the United States during the closing years of the nineteenth century.

Herring was scarcely a newcomer to aeronautics. By the fall of 1896 he was the most experienced glider pilot in the world and a seasoned contributor to flight technology. The first American to build and fly a copy of a standard Lilienthal machine, Herring had also served as chief aeronautical assistant to both Langley and Chanute. The "regulating" cruciform tail that he had developed was widely regarded as a major factor in the successful designs of both men. The 1896 Chanute-Herring glider had been a direct descendant of the small rubber- and steam-powered monoplane and biplane models he had built and flown as early as 1894.

Herring had emerged from this period a bitter and frustrated man. For years he had worked in a subordinate role, overshadowed by employers whom he regarded as less talented than himself. His disappointment had festered as Chanute and Langley failed to allow him complete control over their aeronautical research.

Nor had the frustration been one-sided. Langley had dismissed Herring in December 1895, after only seven months' employment, convinced that the young engineer was incapable of following instructions. Chanute expressed his dissatisfaction in a letter to James Means, written after Herring's precipitate departure from the camp at Dune Park before the end of the 1896 glider trials. Noting that both Langley's "cast iron ways" and his own softer approach had failed to hold Herring in check, Chanute concluded that "he tries very sulkily those experiments that do not originate with himself, and is, as he admits, very obstinate."[4]

Chanute's refusal to begin planning for a powered version of the 1896 biplane forced Herring's decision to strike out on his own. He believed, as had Lilienthal, that the addition of a light-weight power plant to a successful hang glider would enable an experimenter to extend his time in the air, moving slowly toward a genuine airplane capable of sustained flight under the control of the pilot. Herring was sure that, unencumbered by the constraints imposed by an employer, this approach would place him in the lead in the race for powered flight.

After his break with Chanute in September 1896, Herring began a search for a new patron to support the work on a powered hang glider. His first thought had been that a news-paper syndicate might fund the effort. He also considered the possibility of charging admission to a hang-gliding exhibition, suggesting to Barnum and Bailey's officials that glider drops would prove a popular circus attraction. When neither of these prospects materialized, he contacted foreign aeronautical experimenters who might sponsor the venture.[5]

Unwilling to halt his work during the search for long-term financial assistance, Herring invested $150 of his own funds in the construction of a large triplane glider that he hoped would prepare the way for a powered machine. Completed during October 1896, the new machine featured three superposed wings with a span of about 15 feet and a 5-foot chord. The total surface area was about 227 square feet. As usual, the peak of the camber fell at the midpoint of the chord. The craft stood about 8 feet high from the bars supporting the pilot to the top of the third wing. It was some 12 feet long from the leading edge to the tip of the regulating cruciform tail at the rear of the glider.[6]

In addition to its larger size, a number of other features distinguished this craft from the triplane/biplane flown by the Chanute party earlier in 1896. The cruciform tail was still mounted on a universal joint so that it could be moved in any direction by a gust of wind, thus restoring the machine to straight and level flight. This time, however, a compressed air mechanism had been added to speed and strengthen the reaction of the tail to a gust. In addition, the two support bars for the pilot's arms, which had extended straight down at right angles from the wing in the Chanute glider, were now angled in to give the operator better leverage for swinging his weight.

Flight-tested at the old Chanute camp on the dunes, the triplane was a success. After a little practice, Herring was able to make glides of up to 927 feet, more than doubling his best flights with the Chanute craft. In winds of over 30 miles per hour, he reported that the new glider was sometimes lifted 40 to 50 feet above the line of flight. On two occasions he had been carried to an altitude of 40 feet above his starting point. With the new machine, Herring also found that he was able to turn in the air for the first time. This ability to make quartering flights was a major factor in extending the length of his glides, enabling him to follow the curve of the slope to pick up rising currents.

Herring was also pleased with the performance of his compressed-air-powered automatic control system. He found that in moderate winds the triplane would fly a level path for the first 100 feet or so after leaving the hillside. Unless he attempted a turn to follow the slope, the craft would begin a gentle descent toward the sand once it had cleared the air currents over the hill. If the pilot wished to increase his speed, he had only to move forward an inch or two on the support bars to find himself "sailing downward . . . at a tremendous rate." Striking an ascending current, the pilot would feel the weight on his arms increase. To correct for this rise, or for that matter for a descent or the rise of either wing tip, the pilot had only to extend a leg in the appropriate direction to restore his balance. Some 300 flights were made with the triplane without difficulty or danger.

Toward the end of the test period, as Herring's funds were approaching exhaustion, trials were conducted that would lead directly to a powered version of the glider. A bag of sand was fastened between the two lower wings. During a series of flights, the weight of the bag was gradually increased from 12 to 41 pounds without materially decreasing the length of an average glide, although some difficulties were encountered with higher landing speeds as the weight increased. Herring now had some idea of the power that would be required to pull the machine into the air, the additional weight that could be devoted to the engine, transmission, and propellers, and the handling problems that might be encountered with the additional weight.[7]

For Herring, the future seemed clear. Adequate financing was now the only barrier to his rapid progress toward powered flight.

By mid-June 1897, however, the fund-raising effort had not borne fruit. Hard pressed for money to support his family, Herring reluctantly accepted an offer from the ever-patient Chanute to conduct preliminary tests that would lead to the construction of a new, stable multiplane glider. Herring, certain that he was close to success, had kept the news of his experiments with the triplane a secret from Chanute. He now had little choice but to shelve his own plans and return to work for Chanute in order to make ends meet. Moreover, Chanute's plans did hold some promise of financial reward. The older engineer, still in search of perfect automatic stability, suggested constructing a five-wing multiplane glider in which the wings would be free to rock on a central pivot in response to gusts. If the craft was successful, a 40-foot catapult launcher would be built and admission charged to a series of public glider flights.[8]

The new association between the two men was to be short-lived, however. Herring found himself unable to develop any enthusiasm for the Chanute project while his own dreams of powered flight languished. Two weeks after re-employing Herring, Chanute returned from a business trip to find his assistant working not on the experimental program outlined for him, but on plans for a portable gold dredging machine designed to survive the rigors of the Chilkoot Pass. Chanute regarded this as "so palpably absurd" that he dismissed Herring, convinced at last that "his mind naturally revolts at following other men's ideas."[9]

One possibility remained open to Herring. While still in Chanute's employ, he had received an order for a copy of the 1896 biplane from Matthias Charles Arnot, a young Elmira, New York, banker who also agreed to provide money for flight testing the new glider. Herring hoped that, through careful cultivation, Arnot's largess might be extended to include the powered-aircraft scheme.

Only six years out of Yale, Matthias Arnot was fascinated by the way in which technology was reshaping his world. This interest had led him to try his own hand at the mechanic arts, constructing lightweight engines for bicycles, developing a private telegraph system, and designing and installing the first telephone line in Elmira. A typical dilettante, he stood in awe of the professional engineers who were overcoming barriers of time and space. In contacting Herring, Arnot seemed to ask nothing more than an opportunity to play a financial role in solving one of the great mechanical problems of the age.

With Arnot's initial payment in hand, Herring immediately placed an order for a glider with J. S. Avery, the carpenter who had constructed the 1896 biplane. The new machine was also to be a biplane, in spite of the recent success with the triplane in October. It is difficult to fathom Herring's reasoning in returning to the older configuration. Intent as he was on impressing Arnot, Herring may have been afraid to allow his new patron to fly the higher-performance triplane. He may also have been unwilling to reveal the improvements embodied in the triplane until Arnot was firmly hooked as a patron of future attempts at powered flight.

Thus, the 1897 Herring/Arnot glider bore such a close resemblance to the Chanute/Herring biplane of the previous year that Chanute used drawings and photos of the two crafts interchangeably. The new machine was constructed of black spruce. The wings and tail were covered with fabric placed only on the upper side of the surfaces. As in 1896, it was rigged in a Pratt truss with piano wire. The regulating tail was not fitted with the compressed-air mechanism featured on the triplane, but the angled pilot support bars were retained.[10]

While preparing to test the new glider, Herring had accepted an engineering position with the Truscott Boat Yard of St. Joseph, Michigan. Herring, his wife, and two children moved to a large house at 413 Church Street in this small Lake Michigan port lying next to Benton Harbor at the mouth of the St. Joseph

Herring (right) and companions relax during the 1897 glider trials on the Indiana dunes.

River in the late summer or early fall of 1897. Not only would the move ease the family's financial problems, but it would physically remove Herring from Chicago aeronautical circles dominated by Octave Chanute. St. Joseph also boasted machine-shop facilities that would be required for work on the powered machine. Moreover, a narrow beach fronting the lake could serve as a preliminary test site for both the Arnot glider and an eventual engine-driven craft.[11]

Avery delivered the new glider to Herring in late August 1897. After assembling the craft and trying a few short hops from the beach, Herring informed Arnot that he was ready to begin serious test flying. The banker arrived in St. Joseph soon thereafter, and by early September 1897 the two men, joined by Henry Clarke, a Philadelphian whom Herring hired as an assistant, had pitched a camp among the shifting sands of the Indiana dunes, some 2 miles north of the small railway station at Dune Park, Indiana.

With their camp established, Herring and Arnot wasted little time in preparing for the first flights with the new glider. Herring's initial trial, on September 3, was made from a 40-foot slope into a 15-mile-per-hour wind and covered 200 feet. The following day he was turning in distances of up to 300 feet in the teeth of a 40-mile-per-hour gale. By Friday, September 5, 600-foot flights were being reported.[12]

Chanute and Means, who had been invited to visit the camp during this period, were most impressed. In later years Means's son would recall that his father was so enthusiastic about Herring's performance that he could talk of nothing else for days after his return from the dunes. Even Chanute was beginning to question the haste with which he had abandoned a design that Herring was able to use so successfully.

Herring proved as adroit in handling the press as he did in controlling his glider. Whereas reporters had been forced to ferret the story out of Chanute the previous year, Herring made certain that all of the Chicago papers were informed that trials were being held and that every courtesy was shown to visiting newsmen. The result was a series of articles describing the exploits of the group in the most favorable terms and predicting a bright future for a powered version of the glider being demonstrated.

The reporters took special delight in describing the appearance of the craft to their readers. One of the newsmen, apparently at a loss for words, likened it to the double-tiered "whatnot" shelf found in so many homes of the period. They marveled at the craftsmanship that had combined the spruce frame, piano-wire rigging, and silken wing covering, varnished to "drum tight" perfection, into a machine that would carry a man aloft.[13]

On several occasions Herring invited particularly daring reporters to try their hand at gliding. One of these neophytes described his adventure in what is perhaps the finest available account of the emotional experience of a flight in one of these primitive hang gliders.

> The machine weighs only twenty-three pounds, but it is as big as the bay window of a cottage. . . . Once underneath the machine one finds himself standing on a wide plank which rests on the sloping side of a sand hill. The hill is about 100 feet high and steep enough. . . . You face the wind as squarely as possible and shift

The most strenuous part of gliding—the trudge up a dune.

the machine to and fro until you feel that it is balanced fairly on your arms. You are suddenly aware that the broad expanse of varnished silk above your arms is trying to get away from you with each gust of the freshening wind. At the same time you remember the caution to keep the front edge of the machine depressed until the instant of your departure from earth. . . . Just at this time, when one finds himself steering down the side of a steep hill and sees a stump sticking out of the sand at the bottom, he wonders whether he will hit it or miss it in his downward flight. He sees a small tree, and shudders at the thought of landing in its top. One of his friends about half way down the hill comes suddenly into his range of vision, and is cautioned to move a half mile to the side. In the meantime a sickening fear comes over one that he may lose his balance and plow a long and deep furrow in the sand with his nose . . . one takes four or five running steps down the plank and jumps off expecting to drop like a stone to the sand. To his surprise and pleasure he experiences about the same sensation felt by a man when taking his first ascension in an escalator. There is the queer feeling of being lifted from beneath. . . . The wind rushes in the face of the opertor like a hurricane and hums through the network of fine wire that forms part of the framework with a high shrill note. . . . All these things are noted in a moment of dread, for the earth is rising all the time, as though to strike one.[14]

On September 11, another reporter filed a story extolling the virtues of the glider. He claimed to have covered 225 feet on his first attempt. He also witnessed Herring make successful flights of 250, 275, 290, and 310 feet in a matter of a few minutes. The experimenter was extravagant in describing the capabilities of a powered version of the frail glider. He envisioned regular flights from Chicago to New York on which the craft would make only four stops to refuel and would travel at 40 miles per hour.[15]

Herring saw the successes of 1896 and 1897 as proof that his basic glider was sufficiently stable to be flown as a powered machine. The problem of financing the next step remained, however, since Arnot now seemed uncertain as to whether he could provide further assistance. In desperation, Herring turned to Chanute, who, though unwilling to provide personal support for a venture that he considered premature and dangerous, would at least explore the possibility of raising capital from other sources. With Means's assistance, he approached Colonel Albert Pope, a bicycle manufacturer who would later turn to the production of automobiles. The two men felt that Pope, who was interested in mechanical innovation, might be willing to channel funds to the experimenter who seemed most likely to develop a successful flying machine. This would, they presumed, be Herring. Pope was interested in the proposition but refused to supply all of the money required. He suggested that a consortium of industrialists might be formed, but Chanute's experience with finance and aeronautics had taught him that the chances of creating such a group were minimal.[16]

When Chanute reported his failure, Herring contacted the newspaper entrepreneurs James Gordon Bennett and William Randolph Hearst, either of whom might be willing to underwrite his expenses in exchange for an exclusive story. Even Herring must have been a bit surprised when both of these men answered his initial letter. Bennett was sufficiently interested to hire a Chicago engineer to investigate and report on the project. Herring followed up the favorable report with a request for $7,000 in return for sole rights to an account of the world's first airplane flight. The price proved too steep for the publisher, however.[17]

Finally, as all other prospects were disappearing, Arnot decided to continue his support of the Herring effort, offering a total of $3,000 to be paid in ten monthly installments. There would be an even split of any exhibition profits, and Arnot would have the honor of being the second man to fly the finished machine. In addition, at Chanute's urging, Herring insisted that his benefactor provide him with an insurance policy to be paid to his family in the event of his death. Arnot also took out a $35,000 policy on his own life, naming Herring the beneficiary. This money was to be used to carry on the work in Arnot's name. After years of waiting, Herring was at last free to concentrate all of his energies on a powered flying machine.[18]

Herring's plans for a powered hang glider had changed little since the triplane experiments of the previous year. Immediately after the final flights with the 1896 triplane he had prepared and submitted a set of patent drawings and specifications for a compressed-air-powered flying machine. The craft closely resembled the triplane, but was to be larger. A small seat was provided for the pilot, and a set of wheels were included for landing. Two propellers, a tractor, and a pusher were carried at the leading and trailing edges of the two lower wings. They were to be driven on a single shaft by two bottles of compressed gas.[19]

Herring realized that such a "minimum flying machine" would not represent a final solution to the problems of powered flight. He was convinced, however, that even short powered hops would attract attention and generate the funding to support a long-term effort.

The prospect of success had never been brighter. The triplane glider that would serve as a basis for the powered craft was the most sophisticated heavier-than-air flying machine developed to date, and money was now available to complete the work.

Herring received a serious blow in January 1898 when his patent application was rejected by an examiner who regarded the apparatus "as incapable of practical use." The inventor had presumed that he would have official protection for his ideas before publicly demonstrating an operating machine. Overcoming his disappointment, he realized that there was little choice but to proceed with the work while attempting to reverse the patent-office decision.

The airframe, a straightforward construction job presenting few problems for an experienced carpenter, was to be farmed out to the local Truscott Boat Yard. Herring would devote his full attention to the one element that would set this machine apart from all of its predecessors—the power plant.

The engine problem had consumed most of Herring's attention since the conclusion of the triplane flights in October 1896. On the basis of the glider tests, he calculated that a 3-horsepower power plant generating a little over 32 pounds of thrust would be required for sustained flight.

With this goal in mind, Herring went to work on a pair of

Otto cycle gasoline engines. Each was a two-cylinder water-cooled power plant with a 3-inch bore, a 3-inch stroke, and a single valve for each cylinder. Ignition was automatic, although a spark from a Rhumkoff coil was required for starting. Constructed of tempered tool steel, each engine produced about 2 1/2 horsepower, roughly two-thirds of that required to power the machine. In addition to the basic 12-pound weight of the engine, a 14-pound fly wheel, a 2-pound gasoline tank and carburetor, and a 10-pound ignition and storage-battery unit would raise the total flight weight of the power plant to 38 pounds.

Thus, one engine would produce insufficient horsepower to keep Herring's craft in the air, while two engines would be too heavy. In addition, the engines proved tempermental and untrustworthy. With money in hand, Herring was looking for short-term success, and the development of a suitable internal combustion engine looked like a long-term venture.

An interim power plant would be required. The steam engine seemed too "flimsy," uncertain, and dangerous. The easiest solution was to revert to the very simple compressed-air motor included in the patent application. When complete, the two-cylinder power plant weighed only 12 pounds and developed between 3 and 5 horsepower. A single compressed-air cylinder measuring 7 inches in diameter by 2 feet in length would provide power for thirty seconds of operation.[20]

Herring was forced to make serious modifications in the design of his machine because of the deficiencies of the new power plant. The horsepower was marginal, at best. In order to insure that he would be drawn into the air at all, the weight and drag of the machine would have to be reduced. This was accomplished by abandoning the triplane configuration in favor of a double-deck wing.

It was to be a chancy proposition at best. Conditions for success were far from optimal, but Herring was so anxious to make the attempt that he accepted the limitations. He was gambling that even a short powered hop would be seen as a minimum demonstration of powered flight in a manned machine and would attract sufficient cash to permit continued work on the remaining difficulties.

The airframe and engine were ready for trial by July 1898. The Truscott carpenters had done a masterful job. With the exception of the missing upper wing, the machine was based on the 1896 patent drawings. The biplane wings had a span of 18 feet and resembled "broad, shallow gutters turned upsidedown and set one above the other about a yard apart." One of Herring's standard cruciform tails, fitted with the automatic stabilizing mechanism used on the 1896–1897 gliders, completed the airframe. It is not clear whether the compressed-air actuating mechanism employed on the 1897 triplane was retained on the powered craft.[21]

The engine and compressed-air cylinder, carried between the wings, drove two 5-foot propellers. One of these, a tractor, was placed on a shaft in front of the wings, while a pusher was positioned on the same shaft at the rear. The finished aircraft weighed only 88 pounds.

The operator would begin a flight by lifting the machine on his shoulders like a normal hang glider, facing into the wind, starting the engine and taking a few steps forward. Once in the air he could draw his feet up and sit on a small platform set beneath the lower wing. Skids were provided for landing, although some thought had also been given to placing wheels on the craft.

With a potentially successful flying machine on hand, Herring now encountered a series of minor problems that forced repeated postponements of the flight tests. The balky gasoline engine he had borrowed to power his homemade air compressor required constant attention. As the weather deteriorated with the approach of winter, he continued to battle a plague of leaking valves, faulty compressor packing, and an engine that seemed determined to stall at the very moment full pressure was attained in the tank.

The frustrating months of ground testing, repair, and gradual improvement were relieved during A. F. Zahm's visit to St. Joseph in late September. Zahm, who had built an enviable reputation in aeronautics during the years since he had helped Chanute organize the International Conference on Aerial Navigation, bolstered Herring's sagging confidence with praise and a judgment that the compressed air flying machine appeared airworthy.[22]

As October began, Arnot was on hand in St. Joseph. Chanute had been informed that flights could be expected at the next break in the weather. It came on the morning of October 10.

Sam Lessing, the operator of a hot dog stand on the north side of Broad Street near Silver Beach, noted that Herring arrived early that morning at the South Bathing Pavillion, which served as a makeshift hangar. Lessing didn't know Herring well—few St. Joseph residents did. Several of his neighbors later recalled feeling sorry for the "Professor." He seemed a nice enough young fellow, but had always been too aloof and stand-offish for local taste. As Lessing watched with interest, Herring, who was dressed in dark overalls and a knitted cap, raised the large door of the hangar and walked inside. With Arnot's help he lowered the wings from their resting place in the rafters. After puttering with the compressor motor for a few minutes, the two men carried the wings and tail section separately to the south end of the building, where a brass tube leading to the air compressor was attached to the compressed-air reservoir nestled between

Herring's powered hang glider of 1898. The wheels were later replaced by skids.

the wings. The first quick pops of the gasoline engine that drove the compressor rose to a deafening roar that continued for a full fifteen minutes, as 600 pounds of air were forced into the cylinder.

This time there had been no mishap. Herring's compressed-air tank was full. With the tail bolted in place, the small craft was moved to an open area of the narrow beach.

Herring, who had worked for years to arrive at this moment, must have felt a bit uneasy as he crawled beneath the wings, fitted his arms through the support bars and stood upright, testing the balance of the machine. With the propellers rapidly turning in the 20-mile-per-hour wind, he took a few brief steps forward, engaged the engine, and was pulled into the air. Skimming along a yard above the sand, his knees tucked up beneath the shrieking engine, Herring sailed into the wind for some 50 feet before settling gently back to the sand. He was elated. While he hadn't achieved a sustained flight, the frail machine had moved into the wind under its own power. The disappointments of the past months were forgotten during these heady moments when success seemed within his grasp.[23]

Rather than risking a second attempt with so few witnesses, Herring ordered the machine taken back into the shed. The next time it lifted from the beach, he intended to have Octave Chanute witness the event.

Summoned by telegram, Chanute arrived in St. Joseph by the night boat from Chicago, only to return home disappointed the following evening. The favorable wind of the previous day had died, and no flights could be made. The calm of October 11 was to cost Herring dearly. For the rest of his life Chanute, the one respected figure who might have publicized the effort and encouraged and financed further progress, would remain convinced that Herring's compressed-air flying machine was incapable of even short hops. Chanute's faith in Herring had completely soured. His conviction that powered flight remained a very distant goal had solidified.

As the winds blowing off Lake Michigan freshened in late October, Herring prepared to try his machine a second time. On the morning of October 22 it was removed from the hanger and brought to rest near the air compressor once again. A small crowd gathered to watch as Herring faced into a 26-mile-per-hour wind. As before, he was swept into the air after a few brief steps. A reporter for the *Niles Mirror* described the events of the next few seconds.

> "During the flight, which lasted eight to ten seconds, Herring's feet seemed to . . . almost graze the ground, while the machine skimmed along on a level path above the beach. The landing was characterized by a slight turning to the left and slowing of the engine when the machine came gently to rest on the sand."[24]

The craft had flown 73 feet at an altitude of not much over a yard and a speed characterized as "remarkably slow." Indeed, the ground speed had probably not been more than 5 or 6 miles per hour, but the airspeed may have been five times as high. Herring was "pleased with the result."

Winter weather closed in on St. Joseph, and Herring informed reporters that he would return to the shop to prepare an improved aircraft and engine to be tested in the spring. The short duration of the 1898 hops had apparently convinced him of the need for increased horsepower, for in February 1899 he was describing to Carl Dientsbach, a New York journalist and aeronautical enthusiast, some experimental steam engines that he had constructed. The best of these engines developed 8 horsepower for a weight of only 17 3/4 pounds, including boiler, cylinders, burners, pipes, and boiler covering. Herring explained that while the gasoline engine was best "for a perfected machine . . . steam or compressed air is undoubtedly best in a first experimental apparatus." He also admitted that his powered machine had introduced many new difficulties, "particularly in the area of steering and control."[25]

By the spring of 1899 Herring's confidence was waning. As he had intimated to Dientsbach, the heavier steam engine would require a larger machine, and "wholly unexpected" control problems loomed on the horizon. But by taking slow, careful steps, these difficulties might be overcome.

Any hopes for such a long-range effort were dashed by destruction of the experimental engines, tools, and equipment in a fire that spring. Arnot, who had decided to support the 1898 tests at the last moment, now found that his interest and enthusiasm were rapidly draining away. During the next two years the banker would continue to provide some funds, and would launch a crusade in Herring's behalf when it appeared that Octave Chanute might be attempting to take sole credit for the basic biplane glider design. Never again, however, would he finance the construction of a full-scale machine. Herring's bid to achieve powered flight had come to an end.[26]

Arnot's premature death from peritonitis on July 31, 1901, brought Herring's years of estrangement from Chanute to a close. The two men were able to settle their differences and resume a vestige of their old relationship, but Herring's attention was now redirected toward money-making projects. The publication of a magazine, *Gas Power,* aimed at an audience of budding motorists, and the manufacture of motorcycles became his primary concerns. Discouraged and disheartened, he would not return to aeronautics in any serious fashion until after the Wrights had flown.

In later years Herring and his supporters, notably the aeronautical writer and sometime airplane builder James V. Martin, were to publish accounts in which the two short hops at St. Joseph were seen as a major step toward powered flight. They denounced those who had "robbed" Herring of the credit he deserved for having pointed the way to the airplane. In fact, Herring's 1898 motorized machine represented nothing more than the culmination of the hang-gliding tradition. Having made his brief powered hops, he found himself at a technological dead end. The primitive and ineffective body-shifting control system so limited the available wing area that the craft could barely carry the weight of a pilot let alone an engine. Woefully underpowered, the little biplane was incapable of sustained flight. The belief that an inventor could move toward a genuine airplane in slow, easy stages had been proven false. But the notion that a revolutionary approach would be required if progress were to continue was very slow in coming.

In fact, the revolution had already begun. As Herring sur-

veyed the ashes of his workshop in the spring of 1899, two brothers, several hundred miles south of St. Joseph, were preparing
to fly a small kite. As it rose and fell, dipped and recovered at
the command of its operator, this kite gave notice that Wilbur
and Orville Wright had leapfrogged the short-term hurdles that
had stymied everyone else. The brothers from Dayton had no
interest in powered hang gliders. They were out to invent the
airplane.

11

Two Gentlemen from Dayton

By the end of the nineteenth century there was little doubt as to Octave Chanute's status as "the grand old man" of international aeronautics. As his reputation for generosity, patience, and fair play in dealing with younger experimenters spread, he began to receive a flood of letters from would-be flying-machine inventors around the globe. Many came from untutored mechanics who asked for everything from money to a sympathetic ear and a pat on the back.

In spite of the amount of time consumed by the task, Chanute was always careful to answer each letter, for he could never be certain that one of these unsolicited correspondents might not become a major contributor to flight technology. His patience was amply rewarded on May 13, 1900, when his mail included a pale-blue envelope postmarked Dayton, Ohio.

The letterhead informed him that the correspondent, Wilbur Wright, was, with his brother Orville, the proprietor of the Wright Cycle Co., 1127 West Third Street, Dayton, Ohio. A direct fellow, Wright came straight to the point, admitting that "for some years I have been afflicted with the belief that flight is possible to man." This "disease," he continued, "has increased in severity and I feel that it will soon cost me an increased amount of money, if not my life."[1]

It was the opening line of a correspondence that would span the remaining decade of Chanute's life and chronicle the final steps toward the invention of the airplane.

Wilbur and Orville Wright hold an almost unique position in the history of technology. It is impossible to overemphasize the magnitude of their achievement. Their own brilliant insight and inspired research strategy, perseverance and determination enabled them to move beyond their contemporaries with amazing rapidity. They were engineers of genius, the inventors of the airplane in a much truer sense than Morse can be said to have invented the telegraph, Fulton the steamboat, or Edison the incandescent lamp. Yet at the time of their initial contact with Chanute there was little to indicate that the Wrights were extraordinary. Wilbur, age thirty-three, with only 140 pounds distributed over a spare 5 foot 10 inch frame, had a thin, emaciated look. His face was narrow and angular, with thin lips, a long nose, and a high, domed forehead. His eyes, "a superb blue-grey, with tints of gold that bespeak on ardent flame," still retain their flash and sparkle in stilted studio photographs taken over three-quarters of a century ago.[2]

Wilbur was aloof, quiet, occasionally uncommunicative, and withdrawn. His favorite niece recalled that "when he had something on his mind, he would cut himself off from everyone. At times he was unaware of what was going on around him."[3]

He was a voracious reader and a superb speaker and writer. While he always sought to be presentable, his sister Katharine often found it necessary to remind him that his clothes needed pressing or that certain items of apparel were inappropriate or didn't match.

Orville, four years younger, was quite different. He was short and dapper, with a sporty mustache. Friends regarded him as the sort of polite fellow who was always the last through the door. Relatives recall the pride he took in his appearance. "I don't believe there ever was a man who could do the work he did in all kinds of dirt, oil and grime and come out of it looking immaculate. At the rear of the bicycle shop . . . Orville, in collar

The brothers Wright, 1910.

and bow tie, donned his work apron of blue and white ticking, and sleeve cuffs reaching to his elbows to work on parts of the plane, and always when the job was finished he'd come out looking like he was right out of a band box."[4]

Orville was the dreamer and idealist. He was both a born tinkerer and an inspired engineer, forever seeking to improve the operation of a mechanism, whether it be a child's toy, a typewriter, a bathroom shower, or an airplane.

The key to the success of the Wright brothers was the way in which they were able to mesh their personalities into a functioning unit.

Their father commented that "they are about equal in their inventions, neither claiming any superiority above the other, nor accepting any honor to the neglect of the other."[5] But perhaps Wilbur provided the clearest statement of their relation-ship.

> From the time we were little children my brother Orville and myself lived together, worked together and, in fact, thought to-gether. We usually owned all of our toys in common, talked over our thoughts and aspirations so that nearly everything that was done in our lives has been the result of conversations, suggestions and discussions between us.[6]

The Wrights were born to a family with deep roots in Middle America. Their father, Milton Wright, had met and married Susan Koerner while he was a teacher and she a student at Hartesville College, a United Brethren school in Indiana. Their seven children, including twins who died in infancy, were born over the next two decades as the couple moved through a series of church posts in Indiana, Ohio, and Iowa.

Wilbur, the third son, was born in 1867 in Millville, Indiana. Orville was born in 1871 in the house at Number 7 Hawthorne Street, in Dayton. Katharine, the youngest child, followed in 1874.

With Milton Wright, a rising churchman, frequently absent on business, Susan Wright became the central figure in the lives of the three youngest children. Her death of tuberculosis in 1889 was an enormous blow to the family, particularly to Wilbur, who had devoted himself to her care during her months of decline.[7]

Neighbors watching Wilbur and Orville grow into young men might easily have concluded that the Wright boys were having a difficult time finding their place in life. Wilbur seemed particularly aimless. An athlete and active participant in school activities as a teenager, he was struck in the mouth while play-ing a game of hockey on a frozen Dayton pond in 1885. Serious complications suffered in the wake of the accident forced Wil-bur to live as an invalid for over five years. He lost most of his outside interests and withdrew into himself—reading, thinking, and dreaming. His older brother Reuchlin voiced the concern of family and friends when he inquired of Katharine, "What does Will do? He ought to do something. Is he still cook and chambermaid?"[8]

Orville was involved in a variety of activities during his late teens and early twenties, most of which involved printing, a technology that had fascinated him since childhood. These ventures were never very profitable, however, and Orville, like his brother, continued to search for an agreeable way of making a living.

They found it in the bicycle. By 1892, the safety-bicycle craze was sweeping the nation. Nor was the enthusiasm difficult to understand. The bicycle offered inexpensive transportation for every person. A young workman provided with his own set of wheels could not only travel back and forth to work on his own schedule, but could range far and wide on Sunday outings with his best girl. This new freedom of movement was exhilarating, creating a mindset and a demand for improved vehicles and good roads that paved the way for the automobile.

The Wrights were quick to put their natural mechanical abilities at the service of Dayton cyclists. They opened their first shop for the rental and repair of bicycles in 1892. Within four years they had moved to the location on West Third and had begun assembling and selling cycles under their own brand names, Wright Flyer, St. Clair, and Van Cleve.

Frugal, industrious, and friendly, the brothers prospered. They seemed to be settling into the pattern typical of the small businessman of the period. Yet they remained dissatisfied. They felt unchallenged, their potential untapped by the routine of the bike shop. One has the feeling that both men, but particularly Wilbur, were casting about for a challenge against which to measure themselves. The airplane was to furnish that challenge.

Like other Americans, the Wrights could hardly ignore the subject of flight during the summer of 1896. Langley, Chanute, Lilienthal, Lamson, and others were fast becoming standard fixtures on newspaper front pages. It was the death of Lilienthal in August that first sent the brothers on a search for books on flight, but they found little beyond a few volumes on ornithology and the never too trustworthy or detailed news accounts.

By the spring of 1899 they had completely exhausted the limited aeronautical resources of their own home and the Dayton Public Library. Their reading had taught them very little about the current state of flight technology, but it had, as Wilbur remarked, "convinced me more firmly that human flight is possible and practical." More important, they had decided that this was to be their problem.

Their first step was to expand their reading program. On May 30, 1899, Wilbur wrote to the Smithsonian. Describing himself as "an enthusiast, not a crank," he requested assistance in obtaining books on prior aeronautical experiments. Richard Rathbun, Langley's administrative assistant, replied promptly, sending reprints of articles by Mouillard, Lilienthal, and Langley and information as to how the Wrights could obtain Langley's *Experiments in Aerodynamics,* Chanute's *Progress in Flying Machines,* and Means's *Aeronautical Annual*s.[9]

This was scarcely the first time that the Langley organization had responded to such a request. Like Chanute, the Smithsonian staff took pride in providing information and assistance to young experimenters. But this time the effort had a special meaning. It is ironic, but important to note, that the gift of a handful of pamphlets to these two Dayton brothers was one of the most significant Smithsonian contributions to the invention of the airplane, almost as important as the decade of aerodromic research leading up to the flights of Nos. 5 and 6.

The receipt of the Smithsonian material marked the beginning of the Wright aeronautical effort. For the first time the brothers were able to study the work of their predecessors in detail.

What they found was at once disappointing and encouraging. They were impressed by the fact that so many great minds had taken a serious interest in flight, but they were appalled to discover that aeronautical theory remained a confusing mass of speculation and guesswork that offered little guidance to newcomers. One of the early marks of the Wright genius, however, was their ability to winnow a few useful ideas from this morass.

The Wrights were entering the field at an ideal moment. The first period of serious active aeronautical endeavor was at an end. The work of Lilienthal, Langley, Chanute, Maxim, Herring, and Pilcher had reached a logical conclusion. For the first time muddled theory could be supplemented by hard experience. It was this experience that would provide the Wrights with a starting point.

It was clear to them, for example, that flight tests of manned gliders, as advocated by Lilienthal, Chanute, and others, offered a more rational path toward success than did the use of scale models. Moreover, they believed that the success of Lilienthal guaranteed the accuracy of the air-pressure tables that he had developed for use in planning the wing surface area of a flying machine. The structural problems that had plagued Lilienthal seemed to have been solved by the classic two-surface machines Chanute and Herring had built and flown in 1896 and 1897.

Thus, the Wrights believed that, at the very least, they had found a small bit of firm ground from which to begin their own work. More important, their review of previous work enabled them to identify the most important problem blocking the route to success—control.

They were opposed to the system of automatic control and stability envisioned by Chanute, Langley, and others that supposedly would free the pilot from dealing with the balance of his machine. They resolved that the operator of their craft would have a control system that would give him absolute command over every motion of the glider.

The Wrights' background in the bicycle business had been a key in turning their attention to the control problem. The tie between these two modes of conveyance was closer than many had supposed. As early as 1896 a Binghamton, New York, editor had noted that "the flying machine problem is liable to be solved by bicycle inventors." James Means had also commented on the importance of the bicycle. "To learn to wheel one must learn to balance," he remarked, adding that balance was, after all, the key to success in flight. Lilienthal agreed, noting in a letter to Means that "I think that your consideration of the development of the flying machine and the bicycle and the analogy between their development is quite excellent. I am sure the flying machine will have a similar development."[10]

For the Wrights, the first problem was to devise that control system. The weight-shifting acrobatics of the hang-glider school would not do. Not only had this technique led to the death of Lilienthal, but the resulting limitation of surface area had prevented the development of a craft capable of making long glides. Instead, the Wrights searched for a mechanical system that would enable the pilot to alter the aerodynamics of his machine at will to maintain perfect balance in every axis with little physical effort.

Wing warping was the answer to control in the roll axis. As Wilbur remarked to Chanute: "My observation of the flight of buzzards leads me to believe that they regain their lateral balance, when partly overturned by a gust of wind, by a torsion of the tips of the wings. If the rear edge of the right wing tip is twisted upward and the left downward the bird becomes an animated windmill and instantly begins to turn, a line from its head to its tail being the axis."[11]

Whether in fact the idea of imparting a helical twist across the wings was derived from bird observation, or from idly toying with a long cardboard inner-tube box, the resulting wing-warping technique was the first and most important of several keys to the Wright success. The idea was not new. Two Englishmen had patented related systems during the nineteenth century, both of which were quickly buried and forgotten in government files. At least one American experimenter had even made use of wing warping in a large kite built and flown at New Haven, Connecticut, in 1898.

The inventor of the kite, Edson Fessenden Gallaudet, a Johns Hopkins Ph.D., was an instructor of physics at Yale. A childhood interest in bird flight had led to a careful reading of the aeronautical literature when he was an undergraduate. In 1897 he began a period of intensive research that he hoped would lead to the construction of a full-scale flying machine.

Gallaudet realized that the development of an effective means of balancing an airplane was the most important problem faced by flying-machine experimenters. He chanced upon wing warping, as would the Wrights the following year, entirely on his own. Gallaudet's first aircraft, a large kite, was specifically intended to prove the effectiveness of the technique.

Work on the wing-warping kite began in spring 1898. Complete and ready for trial in early November, it featured biplane wings with an 11-foot span. The four wings composing the upper and lower surfaces were built with four ribs each, a wooden leading and trailing edge, two internal stringers, and a central spar tied to the warping mechanism. The wings were covered with fine-grade linen doped to a yellowish finish. The wings and tail were guyed to a central pylon structure constructed of four square wooden rods. A horizontal tail was carried on a wooden boom at the rear of the craft. The whole apparatus was mounted on two metal floats. The finished kite measured 7 feet from nose to tail, and stood 5 feet 6 inches high. It weighed 25 pounds.

Gallaudet planned to incorporate two electric motors to operate the control mechanism. Both motors were to be powered by stranded electrical cable running to the ground. One of the motors would move the elevator up or down to force the kite to climb or dive. The other was to manipulate the wing-warping mechanism. But the motors were not employed during the tests. The elevator remained fixed on test flights, while the wing-warping mechanism was operated by cords from the ground.

Gallaudet's wing-warping mechanism differed significantly from that employed by the Wright brothers. The three ribs of each wing of the kite were fixed to a spar running through each about two-fifths of the way back from the leading edge. The two spars running through the bottom wings were attached to 4-inch-diameter gears that meshed with a central pinion. When the pinion was turned in either direction, the gears and shafts would impart a helical twist to the lower wings. The warping effect was communicated to the upper surfaces by the outboard wing supports.

When complete, the kite was moved to Branford, Connecticut, where Gallaudet's father maintained a second house on Long Island Sound. The flight tests were conducted in secrecy. No newspaper reports of the activity appeared, and Gallaudet remained quiet about the outcome. Fortunately, his father, a lifelong diarist, did leave an account of the trials.

The first test took place on the afternoon of November 6, 1898, when the kite was taken out in a small boat for tests of the floats. One week later, on Saturday, November 12, the two men were ready for a flight. Edward Gallaudet rowed while Edson pushed the kite on its floats in front of them. As the wind began to stiffen they anchored the boat. The kite rose into the air, bobbed about for a short period, then fell off into the water on one wing. Edson immediately removed the floats and hauled the craft aboard. The damage was so slight that it was repaired within an hour after reaching shore. The kite was then placed in storage for the winter.

Gallaudet hoped to resume work in the spring of 1899, but his colleagues were to intervene. News of his aeronautical experiments had leaked to other members of the department, and he was instructed to halt his work on "flying gimcracks" or look elsewhere for employment. Discouraged and anxious to protect his reputation as a solid engineer, Gallaudet agreed to halt his work.

The kite remained in storage at various Gallaudet homes, and was eventually moved to the Gallaudet factory before being donated to the Smithsonian Institution in June 1921.

In later years Gallaudet was to recognize the error of his easy capitulation to the criticism of his colleagues. He had "faltered." In a 1934 article he remarked:

> I have always greatly regretted that I did not file a patent on this machine. While it was not a practical flying machine, it showed a structure which was later found to be of great importance. I did not realize this at all.[12]

The 1898 kite had been an extraordinarily advanced device, the first in the world to embody the wing-warping principle that would lead others to success.

A year later Wilbur and Orville Wright independently fixed on wing-warping control. With no knowledge of Gallaudet's earlier work, they constructed their own simpler kite to explore the operation of the principle for themselves. Wilbur flew the kite in late July 1899, while Orville was on a camping trip. The only witnesses to this first series of Wright test flights were a group of small boys who fell to the ground to avoid being hit by the kite as it dipped and rose at Wilbur's command.

Convinced they were on the right track with a control system that gave them a great advantage over others, the Wrights immediately began to plan for a man-carrying version of the kite.

On the basis of the Lilienthal lift tables and data provided by the eighteenth-century English experimenter John Smeaton on the resistance, or drag, of a flat plate held vertically in the wind, the Wrights calculated that a machine with slightly more than 150 square feet of wing area should support its own weight and that of a pilot in a 16-mile-per-hour head wind.

Like the 1899 kite, this first full-scale Wright machine would bear a rough resemblance to a box kite. Structurally, it was a derivation of the 1896 Chanute-Herring glider. With a wing span of about 17 1/2 feet and a 5-foot chord, the finished craft would weigh 50 pounds.

Its most interesting feature was the large canard, or forward elevator, set directly in front of the lower wing. The Wrights correctly reasoned that this forward surface would provide a more instantaneous control response. The great advantage of the forward elevator, however, was in preventing a nose dive in the event of a stall. On a number of occasions this feature saved the brothers from serious injury. In addition, it would provide the pilot with a means of gauging the angle of the machine to the horizon and cushion the shock of a nose-down crash.

Much has been made of the importance of wing warping in the Wright story. In fact, until 1902, the brothers had little opportunity to explore seriously the operation of the wing-warping mechanism and thus remained ignorant of the need for a rudder. During their first two seasons, the use of the elevator to practice fore and aft balance was more important than roll control in practical terms.

In the design of their airfoil the Wrights also departed from tradition. They chose a camber of 1 in 22, in which the chord, or width of the wing, was twenty-two times the distance from the chord to the peak of the arch. This peak was placed much closer to the leading than the trailing edge in the manner of the airfoils developed by the English experimenter Horatio Phillips than in the manner of those developed by Lilienthal, Chanute, and Langley, which were perfect arcs. This was an intuitive decision, made in the hope that they could reduce the travel of the center of lifting pressure on the wing. Eventually the Wrights would discover that the increased resistance that resulted with arc airfoils as the angle of incidence (the angle at which the wing met the air stream) approached the horizontal resulted in the center of pressure moving rapidly to the rear of the wing. Other experimenters had assumed that the center of pressure would move straight forward to reach the leading edge when the wing was parallel to the air stream. The Wright design reduced this motion and made control in pitch, the up and down axis, simpler.

The 1900 Wright machine was designed to be flown as a kite from a tower with the lines running from the ground over pulleys at the top to the airplane. In this way the brothers hoped to gain hours of experience in the air, learning to balance their aerial steed.

The 1900 Wright glider being flown as a kite.

The 1900 glider, their first attempt to construct a machine that would carry a man into the air, was important. One of the central keys to the Wright success was their instistence on sticking to this basic design. Unlike Chanute, who moved rapidly through a series of varied designs, the Wrights were to develop an initial configuration that they could fully explore and alter as they met and mastered one difficulty after another. Thus, they were able to progress step by step, fine-tuning their machine by building each new discovery into the basic glider design. Unlike Chanute and others, they did not begin anew each season, but went to the field with a craft that had been improved upon the basis of experience and with an opportunity to face new problems. Whereas Langley simply altered the weight, balance, and power elements of his basic design, the Wrights treated their machine as an organic whole, each element of which was interrelated. Each new bit of knowledge was incorporated as their flight experience grew. Their rapid progress was due to their ability to exploit fully the potential of a basic structural configuration.

It was at this point, as their plans for the first glider were taking shape, that Wilbur made contact with Chanute. From the beginning Chanute seems to have sensed that the Wrights were different from other young experimenters he had befriended and supported. They consistently refused his offers of financial assistance, insisting on their own independence, yet welcoming the opportunity to discuss complex issues with the older, more experienced engineer. While Chanute was to make no technical contribution to the Wright gliders, his interest, friendship, and moral support was to prove of extraordinary value, encouraging the brothers to remain at work when they threatened to withdraw from the field in defeat.

By spring 1900, anxious to build and fly the glider they had planned on paper, the Wrights began their search for a test site. Chanute suggested San Diego, California, St. James City, Florida, or the sand hills scattered along the Atlantic coast of Georgia and South Carolina. Letters to the U.S. Weather Bureau, however, revealed an apparently ideal site—Kitty Hawk, North Carolina, a small fishing village located on the northern leg of the Outer Banks, a narrow ribbon of sand that parallels the North Carolina coast, separating the Currituck and Albemarle Sounds from the turbulent waters of the Atlantic. Kitty Hawk offered steady winds, gently rolling sand slopes, and isolation—the conditions required for what the Wrights described as their "scientific kite flying."

On September 3, 1900, Wilbur informed his father of his intention to build and fly a glider. Three days later he boarded a Big Four passenger train for the first leg of the journey to Kitty Hawk. He carried a bundle of fabric that had been carefully sewn to cover the surfaces of the glider and most of the wooden parts and metal fittings for the machine, except for the long spruce wing spars. Too unwieldy to be carried aboard the train, Wilbur planned to have these cut to order in Norfolk. Orville was to follow later if he could hire temporary help to watch the bike shop.

Wilbur finally docked at the small wharf in Kitty Hawk Bay at 9:00 P.M. September 12, after a harrowing journey that included a near drowning during a sudden storm on the sound. Early the next morning he had his first view of the place.

Kitty Hawk was one of the most isolated spots on the East Coast. It included a church, a store, and a handful of unpainted frame houses. A U.S. Weather Bureau facility and life-saving station rounded out the place.

Initially, Wilbur lodged in the home of William Tate, a Currituck County commissioner and leading citizen of the area. After Orville's arrival on September 20, the two moved into a tent camp near the Tate home. In 1901, 1902, and 1903 they transferred operations 4 miles down the beach to the Kill Devil Hills, a range of sand dunes that got their name, according to a nineteenth-century Norfolk editor, "because sailors say it is enough to kill the devil to navigate this part of the sound." At the new site the Wrights' only immediate neighbors were the crew of the U.S. Lifesaving Service's Kill Devil Hills station, located on the Atlantic beach roughly a mile from the brothers' camp.[13]

Between 1900 and 1903, the Wrights would develop a real affection for the Kitty Hawk area and its residents. For the brothers, their annual trek to Kitty Hawk was always an adventure.

Living conditions on the Outer Banks came as something of a shock to the Wrights. The ever-present sand sifted through the smallest cracks. Insects, particularly mosquitoes, infested the area. As Orville reported in 1901, "They chewed us clear through our underwear and 'socks.' Lumps began swelling up all over my body. . . . Misery! Misery!"[14]

Nor were weather conditions the best. Arriving at Kill Devil Hills in 1903, the brothers discovered that a February storm had lifted their original hangar from its foundations. Having repaired the original structure and completed work on a new building, they were assaulted by a gale of such ferocity that the immortal words of an Oberlin College football coach were called to mind: "Cheer up, boys, there is no hope."[15] Each fall, cold weather set in. In a letter to his father in 1903, Wilbur commented that "in addition to . . . 1, 2, 3, and 4 blanket nights, we now have 5 blanket nights, & 5 blankets & 2 quilts. Next comes 5 blankets, 2 quilts & fire; then 5, 2, fire & hot water jug. . . . Next comes the addition of sleeping without undressing, then shoes & hat and finally overcoats."[16] A makeshift stove constructed of a carbide can provided some heat, but filled their living quarters with smoke so thick that the brothers were forced sit on the floor to eat. When the soot on the ceiling began dropping onto their plates, they added legs, a chimney and dampers to the stove, which eased the situation considerably.

While in camp each season the Wrights were faced with the perennial problem of the Kitty Hawkers—food. There were few food stores in the village. A few residents attempted, with little success, to maintain small vegetable patches, but wild game and fish were the dietary staples. Even here the locals had some difficulties. Fish were abundant, but the need for cash guaranteed that most of the tons of fish caught off the banks each year would be shipped north to Baltimore.

Game laws were ignored. Anything that ventured forth on four legs or two wings offered an acceptable target. Ingenious blinds were devised from which thousands of wild fowl and migratory birds, including the vanishing egret and tern, were slaughtered. Like the fish, most of the birds were shipped north for sale.

The "Kitty Hawkers" were never quite sure what to make of the Wrights. They were likable, friendly enough young men, invariably well dressed and polite to a fault. Yet the natives remained dubious of these fellows who spent their vacation skimming down the dunes on enormous white-winged contraptions. After all, as one of their number recalled in later years, the "bankers" were a practical, hard-headed lot who believed "in a good God, a hot Hell, and more than anything else . . . that the same good God did not intend that man should ever fly."[17]

The 1900 flying season was something of a disappointment. The Wrights' plans to spend extended time gaining experience aboard the machine did not materialize. The craft was flown almost exclusively as a kite. While occasional manned tethered flights and a few short free glides were made, the machine was sent aloft unmanned far more often, usually loaded with chains. Scales on the kite lines provided a means of measuring the lift and drag of the glider, while the anemometer of the neighboring weather station gave an accurate reading of wind speed. This data would eventually prove more useful than any flight experience the Wrights might have gained during their first short stay in Kitty Hawk. It enabled them to make precise—and disturbing—comparisons between the actual performance of their machine in the air and its ideal performance on paper. The glider provided less lift and less drag than had been expected. Nevertheless, the brothers believed that their basic wing-warping technique had been demonstrated once again.

They left Kitty Hawk on October 23 confused and befuddled. Orville remarked that they had tried the machine "with tail in front, behind, and every other way. When we got through, Will was so mixed up he couldn't even theorize. It has been with considerable effort that I have succeeded in keeping him in the flying business at all."[18]

Disappointment notwithstanding, the brothers had enjoyed both their stay on the banks and the intellectual challenge of the flying puzzle. The total cost of their first machine had been only $15, and the trip itself could be written off as a vacation. The experiments had proven fairly safe and there seemed no reason not to plan for a return trip with a new and larger glider the following year.[19]

By May 1901 the Wrights were once again full of enthusiasm, describing their plans to Chanute in detail. The 1901 glider would be "built on exactly the same plans as our last year's machine, but will be larger and of improved construction in its details."[20]

The Wrights had chosen the simple expedient of increasing the surface area to provide more lift. The span of each surface would be 22 feet, with a 7-foot chord. The elevator was 4 feet by 5 feet, raising the total surface area, once a cutout had been provided for the pilot on the lower wing, to 315 square feet. Its total empty weight was about 98 pounds.

In an effort to further increase the amount of lift, the Wrights increased the camber of the wings from the 1 in 22 of 1900 to 1 in 17. It was the largest glider anyone had attempted to fly.[21]

Chanute immediately began planning a visit to Dayton. Since the summer of 1896 he had been searching for a means of establishing a second glider camp. He saw in the Wright brothers an opportunity to recapture the excitement of his earlier experimental group. The Wrights would serve as the core of the new unit, with several other young experimenters augmenting the group.

Edward Huffaker, who had resigned his position at the Smithsonian in December 1898, was once more working for Chanute, constructing a model of a new biplane soaring machine designed to explore further the wing rocking automatic stability system favored by Chanute. The finished model would be flown either as a kite or powered by rubber strands. It was tested in the hills of Huffaker's native east Tennessee, where cross currents and gusts provided a perfect test of stability. Chanute had been encouraged by the performance of the model, but Huffaker was less certain, remarking that "much ought to be left to the skill of the operator."

Nevertheless, the model had enabled Huffaker to investigate a variety of aerodynamic phenomena, including ground effect, the cushion of air that provides extra lift as a machine approaches the ground. More important, Huffaker discovered that the center of lifting pressure on a cambered surface did not continue moving toward the leading edge with a decrease in the angle of incidence, the angle at which the airfoil met the air stream. Rather, the center would move forward, then move rapidly toward the rear. The Wrights, who made the same discovery independently, considered it a major step toward understanding equilibrium.[22]

During the summer and fall of 1900, Chanute, still preferring multiplanes to biplanes, ordered Huffaker to begin work on a full-scale five wing glider. As it approached completion the following spring, Chanute invited Huffaker to Chicago, where Avery could teach the Tennessean the fine points of hang-glider operation.

Chanute also hoped to involve George A. Spratt in testing the new craft. Spratt, the newest of Chanute's disciples, was a young farmer living in Coatesville, Pennsylvania. He had first contacted Chanute in early January 1900. Chanute was impressed by a series of experiments conducted by the young Pennsylvanian, but noted that he was untrained and would require guidance. When an attempt to persuade Langley to provide support Spratt's experiments from the Hodgkins Fund proved unsuccessful, Chanute offered Spratt money to study the movement of the center of pressure on a curved surface. In addition, he promised to finance the construction of a suitable glider to be designed and constructed by Spratt. Chanute was soon urging the Pennsylvanian to devise methods of testing the lift and movement of the center of pressure on a cambered wing in both artificially induced currents, as in a wind tunnel, and by means of a whirling arm operating in the open air.

In addition, Chanute had taken a serious interest in Lamson's manned kite and was considering the possiblity of commissioning the Maine experimenter to build yet another craft. The Chicagoan planned to hold a series of competitive trials to determine which of the gliders was most successful, but his visit with the Wrights in Dayton on June 26, 1901, convinced him that the preliminary plans for his own tests should be scrapped and all effort directed toward assisting the brothers.

Chanute continued to Chucky City, Tennessee, after his stop in Dayton to inspect the large five-wing machine and to persuade Huffaker to travel to Kitty Hawk to assist the Wrights. Chanute was not satisfied with the new craft. Huffaker had introduced a number of unnecessary complications that weakened the structure, leading Chanute to believe that it "will not stand long enough to test the efficiency of the ideas in its construction." Chanute, who had always preferred the known strength of traditional construction materials to experimentation with new building techniques, had chosen to use thick paper tubes for the framing of the new glider. In addition, the wings could be folded for ease in transportation. He now feared that the convenience obtained through this innovation was hardly worth the concomitant loss in wing strength.[23]

In spite of its deficiencies, Chanute decided to test the new craft at Kitty Hawk. He wrote Wilbur on June 29, commenting that he would abandon the five-wing craft without a trial under normal circumstances, but offered to send the machine and its builder to Kitty Hawk "if you think you can extract instruction from its failure." He would, in addition, send Spratt as an observer and assistant.[24]

Wilbur responded on July 1, 1901, informing his Chicago friend that while they would be glad to have the company of Spratt and Huffaker at Kitty Hawk,

> we could not permit you to bear the expense of . . . [the] trip merely to assist us; if, however you wish to get a line on his [Spratt's] capacity and aptitude and give him a little experience with a view to utilizing him in your own work later, we will be very glad to have him with us, as we would feel that you were receiving at least some return for the money expended.[25]

Chanute replied, "I will be compensated by the pleasure given him, even if I do not utilize him hereafter." The Wrights, it appeared, would have company at Kitty Hawk.

The brothers left Dayton to begin their second flying season on July 7, 1901. The enlarged machine made it necessary to construct more permanent facilities at the camp site. In 1900 they had lived in a tent large enough to house the glider as well as themselves during inclement weather. A rough hangar would be required for the new craft. Work on this structure began soon after their arrival. When complete, it measured 16 feet by 25 feet and stood 6 1/2 feet high at the peak of its low pitched roof. The building was roofed with tar paper and featured large doors at either end, hinged at the top so that they could be swung out and supported by props.

The Kill Devil Hills had altered since the previous year. The summit of the big dune was almost 25 feet lower than it had been, and the slope was now roughly 45 degrees to the south and 11 or 12 degrees to the north. The permanent camp was established some 1,500 feet from the hill. Huffaker, who had arrived on the scene by July 19, commented to Chanute, "No better spot for experiment could be imagined." Spratt was detained by a harvest on his farm, and did not arrive until July 25.[26]

With camp building complete, work began on both the Wright and Chanute aircraft. The weather was so warm that the three men commonly worked all morning and rested in the shade during the afternoon.

The Wrights noted disadvantages of the Kill Devil Hill site as compared to the old location closer to Kitty Hawk. Fresh water was simply not available, and a well had to be drilled. The insects that infested the dune country proved to be a more serious problem.

Storms were also a major problem in 1901. The day before the Wrights landed in Kitty Hawk a 93-mile-per-hour gale had swept across the Outer Banks.

Huffaker was most impressed by the ingenuity and competence of his companions. Their opinion of his ability was decidedly lower. Wilbur described the engineer in a letter to Bishop Wright on July 28.

> He is intelligent and has good ideas but little execution. His machine, which he built for Mr. Chanute, is a total failure mechanically. . . . He is astonished at our mechanical facility and, as he has attributed his own failures to the lack of this, he thinks the problem solved when these difficulties are overcome, while we expect to find further difficulties of a theoretical nature which must be met by new mechanical designs.[27]

Launching the 1901 glider.

The Wrights began gliding on July 27. They had hoped that their enlarged craft would surpass the performance of its predecessor, but problems became immediately apparent. Control was still far from certain. On one occasion the machine climbed to the point of stalling, with Wilbur making a recovery and safe landing at the last minute. Seventeen flights were made the following day. During the best of these, the machine covered 315 feet in 19 seconds at 13 miles per hour. Huffaker found such a performance almost unbelievable, but the Wrights were disappointed. The glider was simply not performing as well as they had expected. In addition, the control problem, which they had considered solved after 1900, was still with them. For the first time they began to consider the possibility that the published data on lift and drag on which they had based their craft might be inaccurate.

Wilbur wrote a discouraging assessment of the new craft in his diary on July 30, noting that the lift was only one-third that predicted by the tables. This was especially disappointing, since it meant they could not fly the machine in low winds.[28]

In an effort to cut the resistance, the Wrights removed the wings and began streamlining the leading edge. This work was in progress when Chanute arrived to inspect the camp on August 1. In addition, king posts that could be used to alter the camber of the wing were added.

By August 8 the trials had resumed, and for the first time Chanute witnessed flights with the Wright glider. The best flight of the day covered a distance of 335 feet and was made into a 25-mile-per-hour wind. This trial concluded with a nose dive into the ground. The operator was thrown forward breaking a number of rudder ribs on the aircraft and bruising his eye and nose. Chanute departed on August 11, and the discouraged brothers broke camp eleven days later. The 335-foot glide that had almost ended in disaster had been the most successful of the season.[29]

After their return to Dayton, Katharine noted "they haven't had much to say about flying. They can only talk about how disagreeable Huffaker was." The brothers had found Spratt to be a pleasant companion, but Huffaker had proved very difficult. While in camp, Spratt's funny stories and pleasant company had served to ameliorate Huffaker's abrasiveness. Once the Pennsylvanian had departed in mid-August, the situation had become intolerable.[30]

Wilbur identified Huffaker's major flaw as a tendency to make "character building" rather than hard labor the great aim in life. The Daytonians had also been discomfited by the Tennessean's disregard for his personal appearance. Wilbur indicated this fact in a letter to Spratt.

> Mr. Huffaker left Sunday. He looked rather sheepish on departure, which I attributed to the fact that he was still wearing the same shirt he put on the week after his arrival in camp. Well, some things are rather more amusing to think over than to endure at the time.[31]

Langley would have sympathized. It should, perhaps, be noted that the Wrights, like the secretary, were fastidious dressers.

They faced each day of their isolation in the gritty, mosquito-ridden environment of the remote beach with fresh linen, a tie, and clean celluloid collar.

The brothers had, at least, found Huffaker's flying machine to be a source of amusement. Wilbur later sent a series of photos of this bedraggled craft to Spratt.

> I enclosed a few photos. That of Huffaker's machine you will please not show too promiscuously. I took it as a joke on Huffaker but afterward it struck me that the joke was rather on Mr. Chanute as the whole was his. If you ever feel that you have not got much to show for your work and money expended, get out this picture and you will feel encouraged.[32]

The Wrights were confused and discouraged. The performance of their machine remained far below expected levels. The control system with which they had been so pleased after 1900 had demonstrated that a number of anomalies remained to be solved. The realization that the scientific tables in which they had placed total confidence were incorrect was their most serious problem, however. This meant that in addition to solving the mechanical difficulties, they would be forced to undertake basic research as well. The additional task seemed so hopeless that the Wrights came very close to abandoning their aeronautical work during late summer 1901.

Chanute, recognizing that the Wright brothers were the most promising enthusiasts with whom he had worked to date, was determined to prevent their withdrawal from the field. He wrote on August 29, 1901, inviting Wilbur to address the Western Society of Engineers, a prestigious professional organization in Chicago. Wilbur was Chanute's guest while in Chicago and offered a graphic description of the older man's study. Katharine relayed the account to her father.

> Will declares [that the room] was ten times dirtier and more "cluttered up" than yours ever was. . . . It seems that he has models of flying machines suspended from the ceiling so thick that you can't see any ceiling at all.[33]

The two men had a long discussion on the merits of Lilienthal's work with airfoils. After Wilbur's return to Dayton, the brothers began to question the validity of their own results. Lilienthal and Smeaton were, after all, experts in the field. The brothers continued to be puzzled by poor performance of their machines that had been based on the published data. Wilbur muted his original firm position on the accuracy of the tables when he edited his Chicago speech for publication and began to consider the possibility of conducting his own laboratory experiments. The time had come to determine just how much lift and drag could realistically be expected from various airfoils.

The Wrights were about to begin the most important two months of their aeronautical career. The research that they undertook during November and December 1901 would provide the necessary engineering data on which the first successful airplane would be based.

The first step was to develop the apparatus with which to conduct the experiments. Initial tests were conducted with the model airfoils attached to the rim of a bicycle wheel mounted horizontally in the wind. When this proved inadequate, the device was bolted to the front of a bicycle that could be ridden at high speeds while the rider observed the reaction of the test surfaces. The brothers very quickly realized that neither of these two methods were trustworthy.[34]

Orville then constructed a makeshift wind tunnel, using an old starch box some 18 inches long. A plate of glass was placed over a cut-out section of the top of the box so that detailed observations of the interior could be made. A metal rod was placed on a pivot inside the small structure. A cambered surface was placed vertically on one end of the rod, while a plate was attached to the other. Each of the surfaces employed measured 1 inch by 3 1/4 inches. "When exposed to the wind the vane took up a position to one side of the line of the wind direction thus showing that the curve required a less angle of incidence than the plane." This primitive tunnel was in use for only one day, but it demonstrated in rough that their misgivings with regard to the established tables were well founded.[35]

Work began soon after on a more sophisticated device that

would enable the brothers to conduct more reliable tests on which tables could be based. The second tunnel was a wooden box some 6 feet long, 16 inches square on the inside. A fan powered by a home-built one-cylinder gas engine was placed at one end. The air from the fan passed through an open wooden grid designed to provide a uniform current in the tunnel.

The experiments were complete by early December. In addition to their studies of lift and drag, the Wright's had obtained data on aspect ratio (the ratio of width to span in wings) and the proper gap between the wings of a biplane. The brothers, having acquired a tremendous advantage over other experimenters,

A replica of the Wright wind tunnel.

decided to return to Kitty Hawk with a new machine that would embody their discoveries.

The wind-tunnel experiments of 1901 epitomize the methodical, meticulous attention to the collection of relevant scientific and engineering data that characterized the Wrights' approach to aeronautics. They had a firm notion of what the problems were and how they could best be attacked; and, having gathered the required information, they were quick to incorporate it into their craft.

Chanute was particularly anxious to provide financial assistance during the winter of 1901–1902. On December 19, for example, the Chicagoan offered to contact his friend Andrew Carnegie in an effort to raise $10,000 to support the work of the Wright brothers. Wilbur replied that while Chanute's concern was appreciated, the brothers preferred to continue the experiments solely with their own resources. Only in this way, they argued, could they ensure that their business would always remain their central concern. Wilbur did offer a number of suggestions as to how men of great wealth might contribute to aeronautics, however. He argued that the establishment of a "Croesus Fund for the Promotion of Aeronautical Science" that could offer grants and publish results would be especially useful. A second possibility would be the establishment of a permanent prize "of a considerable amount" to be awarded to a successful airplane meeting "rigid tests." The interest on the principal could be awarded annually "to the most valuable improvement or contribution to aeronautical science made during the year."[36]

Chanute understood the Wrights' caution. "You are eminently right in saying that there is a limit to the amount of neglect which a business will endure," he commented. I discovered that in 1897 when after spending some $10,000 in experimenting and assisting others to experiment, I found some danger of losing the business which gave me bread and butter. Since then I have been more cautious."[37]

Wilbur Wright was following Chanute's lead in encouraging the efforts of other experimenters during spring 1902. He was particularly anxious to assist Spratt in his attempts to build a large glider. When Chanute approached Langley for a Hodgkins Fund grant for the Pennsylvanian, Wilbur added his recommendation. In addition, the Daytonian assisted Spratt in setting up his own wind tunnel and sent examples of the airfoils tested during the fall of 1901. When Langley refused to make a grant to Spratt, Wilbur sent a letter commiserating with his friend. He made little secret of his opinion of the secretary's efforts.

> I am sorry that Mr. Langley has not adopted Mr. Chanute's suggestion to help you in your experiments with an appropriation. I sometimes think that Mr. L. is a little bit jealous of M. Chanute and takes pleasure in slighting him in such a way as this. However, it may be that he is honest in his refusal. If he had many like Mr. Huffaker in his employ I would not blame him for not having much confidence in outside work.[38]

In addition to his grants to Huffaker and Spratt, and the attention that he was devoting to the Wright brothers, Chanute was drawn back into direct contact with Herring early in 1902. The long period of strained relations between the two men had at least been glossed over. Chanute, who continued to view Herring as a man of some mechanical ability and much experience, was willing to overlook his personal shortcomings in order to give him yet another opportunity to fly.

Chanute contacted Herring in May 1902 with a request for an estimate on rebuilding the 1896 multiplane glider. Herring replied that $44.45 would cover the cost of the materials while 410 man-hours at 34 cents an hour, brought the total cost of the project up to $183.85. Chanute would provide the frame of the original machine and $150 with which to rebuild the rest of the craft. It was clear from the outset that Chanute planned to fly the new glider with the Wrights at Kitty Hawk during the coming season.[39]

By July 7, Herring had completed the wing framing and most of the wooden parts. He estimated that the original 37 pounds could be reduced by 9 or 10 pounds. He told his employer, "I am rather proud of [the] work so far as it is probably lighter and neater than any of the machines so far built." Chanute had also planned to have Herring build yet another two-surface glider, but realized by July 20 that he could not afford the additional expense.[40]

Chanute also contracted with Lamson for the construction of a glider to be test-flown at Kitty Hawk. Chanute had met the experimenter during a vacation in Pasadena, where Lamson had established a jewelry store after his Maine flights. Lamson had patented an oscillating wing "kite" in 1901. Chanute was sufficiently impressed to finance the construction of a man-carrying version. When delivered at Kitty Hawk on October 8, the craft had a 20-foot wing span and a 4-foot chord.[41]

Once again Chanute hoped to use the camp at Kitty Hawk as a means of training other enthusiasts in gliding. Plans were made for Spratt's return, but Huffaker had proved so distasteful to the Wrights that his continued presence for another season was out of the question. Chanute considered both Avery and Herring as prime candidates to test his two new gliders and sought the opinion of the Wright brothers on the matter. Wilbur replied that he would prefer Avery "because several things I have heard about Mr. Herring's relations with Mr. Langley and yourself seemed to me to indicate that he might be of somewhat jealous disposition and possibly inclined to claim for himself rather more credit than those with whom he might be working would be willing to allow." Nevertheless, he remarked that the final choice of assistant was up to Chanute and agreed to accept whomever he sent. Chanute chose Herring.[42]

By mid-August the Wright brothers were hard at work on their full-scale glider. Katharine described the scene in the house at 7 Hawthorn Street in a letter to her father.

Will spins the sewing machine around by the hour while Orv squats around marking the places to sew. There is no place around the house to live but I'll be lonesome enough by this time next week and wish that I could have some of their racket around.[43]

The pair left Dayton at 9:00 A.M. on August 25 and arrived at Kitty Hawk on the afternoon of Thursday the twenty-eighth. They immediately set to work refurbishing the building constructed the year before at Kill Devil Hill. Having chased a number of "hungry razor backs" from camp, they enlarged the kitchen and added a sleeping loft with wooden beds to replace the cots used during earlier seasons. Battens were placed over cracks in the structure to keep the wind, sand, and mosquitoes out. Construction of the glider began on September 8 and required only eleven days. The 1902 machine featured biplane wings with a 32-foot span and a 5-foot chord. The camber was initially fixed at 1 to 25. It also featured a single fixed vertical surface at the rear measuring 5 feet by 14 inches and the usual forward elevator.

By September 21, the brothers were able to complete some fifty glides. Most of these were limited to distances less than 200 feet to give the pilots an opportunity to acquaint themselves with the behavior of the new craft. Orville commented that they were becoming reasonably adept, and could make such flights with the wing tips "practically level."

Their first potentially serious accident occurred on September 23, when Orville crashed from an altitude of 25 to 50 feet. While gliding normally, one wing tip had begun to rise. When the operator attempted to correct the situation the craft fell off on the low wing. "The result was a heap of flying machine . . . with me in the center without a bruise or scratch." Nevertheless, seventy-five glides had been successfully made at the time of Orville's "slight catastrophe," and the Wrights were sure that their control system was approaching perfection.[44]

Repairs were completed by September 25. Four days later twenty-five flights were made in one day. On the longest of these Wilbur covered 230 feet and remained in the air for thirteen seconds. By October 3 the record distance had stretched to 320 feet and the time aloft to twenty-five seconds. The Wrights were building a record of experience in the air that surpassed that of any previous experimenters.

The problem that had resulted in Orville's crash on the twenty-third continued to plague them. Occasionally when one wing tip would rise and normal warping control was effected to return to level flight, the opposite would occur. The low wing tip would dip even lower, corkscrewing the glider to earth. Orville finally concluded that the new fixed tail was responsible. He reasoned that when one wing fell too low, the rudder, rather than assisting in the correction, presented so much of its surface

Wilbur aboard the 1902 glider.

to the air that it made the situation worse, slowing the speed of the affected side to the point of stalling. He suggested making the tail movable so that the operator could adjust its angle to meet any situation. Wilbur argued that this would only add to the confusion of flying the craft, and countered by recommending a mechanical link between the wing-warping mechanism and a movable rudder, so that the two would automatically operate in concert.

The final problem had been solved. The 1902 glider, after the alterations of October 1902, was essentially the world's first successful airplane. These improvements, when coupled with the growing skill and experience of the two pilots, opened the way to flights of what seemed fantastic length. On October 20 Wilbur was able to cover 552 feet in just over twenty-five seconds. By the twenty-third, glides of 540 feet had become common, and distances of up to 622 feet were occasionally attained.

Four other men were in camp with the Wrights during the fall of 1902. Lorin Wright and George Spratt had come to assist and observe. Chanute and Herring arrived on October 5. The two men immediately set to work assembling the multiplane glider that Herring had shipped earlier from St. Joseph. The craft was complete the following day. Herring made two flights with the craft on October 6. On the second glide he traveled some 200 feet at a ground speed of 16 to 18 miles per hour. The right wing was damaged in landing, necessitating repairs that were finished late that evening. Herring discovered that he was unable to coax his glider into the air on days when the Wrights were making flights in excess of 250 feet. All tests of the multiple-wing craft were discontinued after October 11, by which time the overwhelming superiority of the Wright glider was apparent. Orville ascribed the failure of the multiplane to structural weakness and poor construction. He noted that the distortion of the wings under the stress of normal flight was a particular problem.

The inadequacy of Herring's workmanship led Chanute to bring their eight-year association to an end. The two men continued to correspond after fall 1902, but Chanute was never again

Wilbur (left) and Dan Tate, a local helper, launch Orville in the 1902 glider.

to employ Herring. The Chicagoan described his reassessment of Herring's capability in a letter to Langley.

> I have lately gotten out of conceit with Mr. Herring, and I fear that he is a bungler. He came to me in July, said that he was out of employment and urged that I let him rebuild gliding machines "to beat Mr. Wright." I consented to building new wings for the multiplane machine, but could give it no attention, as the work was done at St. Joseph, Mich. Herring adapted new forms of wings and reduced the total weight from 33 1/2 lbs. to 27 lbs., but when the machine was tried by him in N. Carolina it proved a failure, and he said he did not know what was the matter.[45]

The Lamson oscillating wing glider arrived at Kitty Hawk on October 8. Herring test-flew this craft on a number of occasions, but he enjoyed as little success with it as he had with his own. The experience of 1902 had demonstrated to Chanute just how far the Wright brothers had advanced beyond Herring, Huffaker, Lamson, and others whom he had always viewed as the most talented of experimenters. After this date, all of Chanute's efforts would be directed toward assisting the Wrights and publicizing their achievements.

The doubts that had plagued the Wrights after 1900 and 1901 were erased by the experience of 1902. They realized for the first time that they were within striking distance of final success. Wilbur outlined their plans for Chanute on December 11, 1902.

> It is our intention next year to build a machine much larger and about twice as heavy as our present machine. With it we will work out problems relating to starting and handling heavy weight machines, and if we find it under satisfactory control in flight, we will proceed to mount a motor.[46]

12

The Great Aerodrome

Publicly, Samuel Langley brought his aeronautical work to a close following the spectacular flights of Nos. 5 and 6 in May and November 1896 but his withdrawal from the field was little more than a façade. Privately, Langley scarcely paused to catch his breath and bask in the glory of his success before launching a drive to raise funds with which to begin work on a full-scale, man-carrying aerodrome.

In a letter to Chanute in June 1897, the secretary expressed his desire to continue the work and raised the question of financial assistance: "If anyone were to put at my disposal the considerable amount—fifty thousand dollars or more—for . . . an aerodrome carrying a man or men, with a capacity for some hours of flight, I feel that I could build it and should enjoy the task." Langley was so confident of success that he believed he would be in the air "within two or three years from the time such means are put at my disposal."[1]

In a second letter to Chanute that December, Langley put the matter more bluntly: "If you hear of anyone who is disposed to give the means to such an unselfish end, I should be glad to meet him."[2]

Langley realized, however, that his only real hope of continuing his work toward a manned aerodrome was federal support. As early as October 1897 he had prepared a confidential memo for the Smithsonian files outlining his plans for a full-scale machine to be used in the event "that I may called upon officially to pursue these investigations in the interest of the Government." The secretary opened with the comment that "the results already accomplished on May 6, 1896, and November 28, 1896, make it as nearly certain as any untried thing can be, that . . . a larger machine of the same model . . . [can] carry a man or men."

This being the case, his basic plan was simply to "scale up" the 1896 models to man-carrying dimensions, modifying the proven design "only as the changed scale and the presence of a man may demand."[3]

It all seemed so simple—deceptively simple. The general configuration of the successful flying models could remain unchanged. Even the system of catapult-launching the machine over the Potomac could be retained to take full advantage of the lessons of 1896.

But some major changes would be required. Steam-engine technology would probably prove inadequate for a craft sporting as much as 1,200 square feet of wing area. Initially, Langley envisioned powering what was already becoming known at the Smithsonian as the "Great Aerodrome," with a pair of internal combustion engines, each developing 12 horsepower.

In order to hold together the experienced team of engineers and craftsmen that had produced the model aerodromes, Langley drew on miscellaneous Smithsonian funds to underwrite preliminary studies, such as B. L. Rinehart's design work on an experimental gasoline engine. Meanwhile, the secretary continued to explore every avenue of financial support within the federal government. The breakthrough came as a result of the efforts of Langley's old friend Charles D. Walcott of the U.S. Coast and Geological Survey.

The two men met on March 21, 1899, to discuss common problems. The conversation turned to the possible use of the aerodrome in the impending war with Spain. When Langley informed Walcott of the need for $50,000 to $100,000 to perfect a large machine, the geologist suggested that the president should be made aware of the military potential of the airplane and offered to approach McKinley on Langley's behalf. He suggested that a presidential board composed of authorities like Chanute, Thurston, and General Nelson Miles of the Signal Corps might be appointed to consider the secretary's plan and to report on the military utility of the craft. Langley sent a memo to Walcott two days later, restating his belief that an enlarged version of No. 5 or 6 could carry a man in flight "for a time and distance which would render them important factors in land and naval warfare," and approving the idea of a board of inquiry.[4]

But the secretary stated a number of conditions. He would insist on complete control of any funds allocated and would not undertake the task unless he were placed in complete control of the project. Adequate safeguards, such as standard bookkeeping practice, would, of course, be observed. It would, he remarked, "be nearly useless to attempt this construction under the restrictions ordinarily imposed by an act of Congress." Langley also demanded that absolute secrecy be maintained. If the government chose to accept these stipulations, he would agree to donate his own services.

Walcott approached John Addison Porter, President McKinley's secretary, with the request that he bring the matter before the chief executive. McKinley was interested and requested photos of the models in flight. These were immediately produced, and McKinley suggested that Walcott carry his case to Secretary of War George Mickeljohn. Walcott met with Micklejohn on March 25 and persuaded him to create the board. He also contacted Assistant Secretary of the Navy Theodore Roosevelt, who also agreed to participate.[5]

The panel included Walcott and Alexander Graham Bell, who were to serve ex officio. Major G. W. Davis of the Ninth Infantry and a Major Craig of the Signal Service would represent the Army; Charles W. Davis and Stimson J. Brown of the Naval Observatory were appointed by Roosevelt. The men were "to meet and examine into the Langley flying-machine, and to report whether or not you think it can be duplicated on a larger scale, and to make recommendations as to its practicality, and to prepare estimates as to the cost."

The board met at the Smithsonian on April 6. Langley exhibited his successful models and discussed alterations that might be necessary in a larger machine. He remarked, a bit ingenuously, that

> while he was by no means eager to assume so much care and responsibility, he would, if the Government desired, undertake the construction of an aerodrome which he believed would not only fly, but would transport a man, with some reserve lifting power, for a considerable course.[6]

The secretary warned that while the aerodrome would not "be at once an engine of war . . . it would certainly develop into a very important one." He requested $50,000 and restated his insistence that he not be hampered by unnecessary restrictions or a government comptroller.

The board required only one week to deliberate and offer a favorable report. Their decision was hastened by the fact that the Spanish-American War had begun April 24, 1899, only five days earlier. The members agreed that Langley's proposed craft could provide "a practical success in the sense that it was able to make an aerial voyage of considerable length in any required direction . . . within the period the hostilities might be supposed to last."[7]

But Langley's search for funding was still not complete, since this group had no power to appropriate funds. He now had to carry his plans before the Board of Ordnance and Fortification.

Created by a congressional appropriation act of September 23, 1888, the Board of Ordnance and Fortification considered problems common to the Army Ordnance Department, Artillery, and Corps of Engineers. Moreover, the board was designated as the proper body to "make all needful and proper purchases, investigations, experiments and tests to ascertain with a view of their utilization by the Government, the most effective guns, small arms, cartridges, projectiles, fuses, explosives, torpedoes, armorplate, and other implements and engines of war."[8]

In the absence of any other agency specifically assigned the task of military research and development, this responsibility was gradually assumed by the Board of Ordnance and Fortification. In 1898, Nelson Miles, commanding general of the Army, was serving as chairman of the board. Other members included General P. C. Haines, General Royal T. Frank, Major F. H. Phipps, and Congressman Joseph N. Outhwaite of Ohio. Lieutenant Isaac Newton Lewis served as secretary and performed general staff duties for the group.

Langley was informed that the next meeting of the board would be on June 14 and was prepared to present his plans at that time, but the members did not receive their copies of the joint Army-Navy Committee recommendations until June 20. The secretary was then preparing to leave for his annual summer visit to relatives and friends in Europe, so action on the matter was temporarily deferred.

Serious work on the great aerodrome began after Langley's return early in October 1898. The secretary remarked in his private waste book that while the negotiations with the Army might "come to nothing," he was now determined to proceed "as far as the limited means allow."[9]

It soon became apparent that the power plant would again be Langley's primary concern. In June 1898, letters were dispatched to several automobile companies, requesting estimates for a six-cylinder internal combustion engine capable of producing 12 horsepower at 600 to 800 revolutions per minute. The total weight was to be under 60 pounds, and the engine would be required to operate for up to three hours without overheating. The price was to be under $2,100.

When these initial inquiries failed to produce an interested builder, a search was instituted for a smaller firm with experience in the design and construction of lightweight internal combustion engines capable of meeting the requirements. On November 3, 1898, Richard Rathbun, Langley's secretary, sent a letter to Stephen M. Balzer, a New York inventor, inviting him to accept an order for a 12-horsepower motor weighing not more than 120 pounds complete with flywheel, water jacket, water, and all accessories. Balzer, a native of Hungary, had built the first automobile in New York City in 1894. The three-cylinder, rotary, air-cooled, internal combustion engine that powered this car first attracted Langley to Balzer.[10]

The prospect of a brand-new undertaking forced the secretary to return to the task of selecting an assistant. Since Herring's departure in late 1895, Langley had placed a number of men, including Huffaker and Reed, in charge of the aerodromic work. But no one had been able to satisfy his demand for perfection.

Familiar with all of the major American experimenters, Langley chose to hire an engineer who had not yet become actively involved in flying-machine work. On May 9, 1898, he wrote to Robert Thurston at Cornell for advice on the matter. Could Thurston recommend a "young man who is morally trustworthy ('a good fellow') with some gumption and a professional training" who might be interested in a Smithsonian position?[11]

Thurston recommended a Sibley College senior, Charles Matthews Manly, a native of Staunton, Virginia. Manly enrolled at the University of Virginia but transferred to Cornell in his sophomore year, majoring in electrical and mechanical engineering. He became one of Thurston's favorite pupils and was allowed to accept the position with Langley a month before he was to have graduated, receiving his degree *in absentia*. In Manly the secretary had finally found his ideal assistant. Their relationship was to be one of the most successful and fruitful that Langley would ever enjoy.

The secretary intended his large aerodrome to be a scaled-up version of No. 5. But there were several alternatives that should be explored. He was still intrigued, for example, by the possibility of using biplane rather than monoplane wings. In addition, he realized that modifications in the launching system might be necessary. Reed was therefore instructed to rebuild the engines of Nos. 5 and 6 so that these models could serve as test vehicles.

New methods of controlling the flight of the manned machine were also developed during summer and early fall 1898. Like Chanute and Herring, Langley was convinced that the wind gusts aloft were so treacherous that human reflexes would be unable to cope with them. He intended to provide the pilot of the aerodrome with a movable rudder for turning and an elevator to control climb and descent. All other controls were to be fully automatic. The wings were to be set at a high angle to the fuselage to provide some measure of automatic stability. Moreover, the secretary suggested three more complicated systems employing feedback mechanisms.

Langley's interest in the possibility of applying a gyro-stabilized platform as a reference for an automatic control device dated to his earlier work with the small aerodromes. The discussion of the virtues of the gyroscope continued throughout the months when the great aerodrome was being planned, but no serious attempt was made to translate the secretary's thoughts into a practical means of guaranteeing equilibrium.

While in France during summer 1899, Langley conceived a second self-correcting system for maintaining a constant attitude. He suggested that the tail of the aerodrome be attached to the main fuselage by means of a rolling carriage, free to move to the front or rear. Thus, when the aircraft nosed up or down, the sliding section would move to change the center of gravity. But Manly successfully persuaded his employer that this method was questionable at best and would prove very difficult to perfect on a practical basis.[12]

The assistant countered with a suggestion that was almost adopted. He recommended the use of a heavy pendulum controlling a servomechanism that would operate the Pénaud tail. The idea generated a great deal of enthusiasm, and drawings were prepared to illustrate how the device could be applied to the great aerodrome. As more essential problems arose with the engine and airframe, however, the secretary decided that the first test flights of the manned craft should be made with a much simpler elastic tail similar to those used on Nos. 5 and 6. Once basic success was demonstrated by a straight-line flight, the Smithsonian staff could return to the development of a more complex and effective system of automatic attitude control.

Lieutenant Lewis of the Board of Ordnance and Fortification contacted Langley for the first time on November 2. Lewis called on the secretary at the Smithsonian the following Saturday and was given a complete tour of the shop facilities. Langley also provided him with information on recent developments in military aeronautics. Lewis remarked that the board had discussed the potential of the aerodrome at some length on two occasions during the summer and seemed willing to appropriate the required sum. Langley was pleased but pointed out that no preliminary flight tests with the large models on hand could be expected before spring. The two men agreed that Langley would appear before the board at its next meeting to present his drawings and to answer questions.[13]

The secretary met with the group in Room 363 of the War Department on November 9, 1898. He spoke for forty-five minutes, emphasizing that he alone was responsible for the aerodromic work and that the Smithsonian Institution could not be obligated in any way. He insisted on being given complete control of any funds appropriated and restated his desire for complete secrecy. The members of the board viewed photos of the flights of 1896 and promised Langley a prompt decision.[14]

It proved impossible to keep word of the meeting from leaking to the press. The secretary was horrified to find a story concerning the government's interest in the aerodrome splashed across the front page of the *Washington Post* on November 11. The paper reported that "the Board of Ordnance and Fortification has decided to institute an investigation of the possibilities of flying machines for reconnoitering purposes and as engines of destruction in time of war." Readers were further informed that a grant of $25,000 had been awarded.[15]

Even more alarming was the fact that the *Post* article had named General Adolphus Greely, head of the Signal Service, as the man selected to lead the enterprise. Langley was simply to place his knowledge and experience at the Army's disposal. Langley informed Lewis that such a relationship was out of the question. Lewis immediately responded with an apology and the assurance that if the money was appropriated, the secretary would be in complete control of the project.

On December 10, Langley sent a final memorandum to Lewis in which he outlined the conditions that must be met before he would accept funding from the board. The secretary would retain all rights to the final machine. General Greely, the chief signal officer, through whose office the money would flow, would be required to pay any and all bills that were approved and forwarded to him. Furthermore, there was to be no publicity, and Langley would be free to publish his results where and when he chose. On December 11, Lewis informed Langley that both Greely and the board had agreed to the conditions and had approved a grant.[16]

There was a minor misunderstanding with regard to the amount of the appropriation, however. The secretary assumed that the board had voted the full $50,000, while the official report makes clear that only half this sum was initially awarded. It was the understanding of the members that an additional $25,000 would be withheld until the original sum had been expended and some judgment as to the progress of the work could be made. Langley, however, was to remain unaware of this problem for some time.

The secretary's immediate problem was to finalize plans for the engine. Balzer had expressed an interest in building a power plant to meet the specifications outlined by Rathbun, and had sent one of his three-cylinder rotaries mounted on a tricycle to the Smithsonian. In addition, he had traveled to Washington early in November to discuss terms with John Watkins, curator of the Smithsonian's mechanical collections, and Manly. Both men were favorably impressed and recommended "that unless some better offer should be received for the gas engine from other manufacturers, the contract should be closed with Mr. Balzer." During the course of the meeting, Manly informed the New Yorker that the secretary had reduced the acceptable weight for a 12-horsepower engine from 120 to 100 pounds.[17]

Balzer planned to build a five-cylinder version of his automobile rotary. The engine was to have a 4 1/4-inch bore and a 6-inch stroke. The exterior of the cylinders was to feature spiral cooling fins to conduct heat away from the hot lower sections more efficiently than the traditional parallel vanes. The engine would run as an air-cooled rotary to avoid the use of the heavy radiator or water jacket. The flywheel required for smooth operation with a stationary engine could also be eliminated.

Manly was also intrigued by the possibilities of the rotary engine. The torque created by the whirling power plant could be put to use by placing two engines so that they would spin in a direction parallel to the motion of the aircraft, thus giving it the benefit of the additional momentum.

Balzer was in touch with Langley once again on December 5, having cut the required 20 pounds from his initial proposal. He promised to deliver the finished engine within ten weeks for a price of $1,500.

Langley contracted for the engine, assuring Balzer that he would also be asked to provide a second if the original proved satisfactory. In addition, Balzer also received a contract for the central section of the aerodrome, including the airframe, propeller support arms, transmission gears, and shafting, in order to guarantee a successful interface of these elements with the engine.[18]

By February 7, the secretary was anxiously inquiring as to when the first horsepower tests might be run. Langley paid a personal visit to New York in late March and reported that he was "much pleased" by Balzer's progress. The first extensions of the delivery date were approved in early May, but the Smithsonian staff had not yet realized the severity of the problems their contractor was encountering.

Preliminary drawings of the aerodrome itself were complete by May as well. Since the size of the central fuselage had been dictated by the size and placement of the two engines, work had actually begun on this portion of the craft late in December 1898.

As originally designed by Reed, each of the four wings of the craft included a leading edge, central spar, and twenty-eight ribs. A large cruciform tail was to be placed on the rear of the machine. A bowsprit and guy posts were to be employed in anchoring the many wires that would brace the wings. Three sets of wings were to be constructed. Two of these would fly on the craft while the extra set would be available in case of an emergency.

A working model of the new launch mechanism was also under construction during the spring of 1899. This device would support the models from beneath as they were propelled down

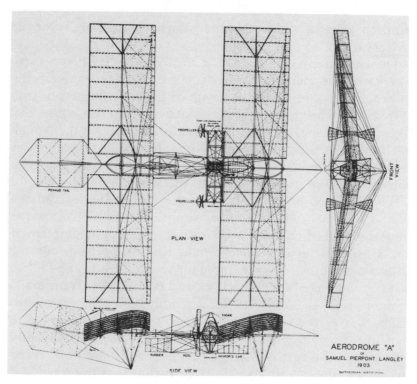

The great aerodrome.

a 24-foot track. At the moment of launch it would fold down to avoid striking any portion of the departing aerodrome. If the new design proved satsifactory, work would immediately begin on a full-scale mechanism for the great aerodrome.

Nos. 5 and 6 were fully reconditioned and ready for flight by February 6, but ice on the river prevented immediate testing. Langley ordered that a third model, a 1:8 scale replica of the new aerodrome design, also be built as an unpowered vehicle to be used in launch tests.

Reed had begun drawings for an enlarged houseboat in December. A suitable barge measuring 40 feet by 60 feet had been obtained, and on April 1 a contract had been let for the construction of the required superstructure and work areas for $3,075. This work had been completed by May 1899. The houseboat required only the addition of the launcher to prepare it for the task ahead.[19]

The barge remained docked at the Washington Navy Yard, where work began on the superstructure that was to support the launcher. A 15-ton turntable revolved on a circular track supported from the side walls of the structure on the houseboat. This platform measured 48 feet square, and carried the launch rail itself and a 5-foot gauge track 80 feet long. The turntable was provided to avoid the necessity of constantly shifting the position of the large scow to face into the wind.

When the old boat had been in use during the tests of the models, the small aerodromes had simply been carried out of the doors and placed on the launcher on the roof. Langley realized that a different arrangement would have to be made for the full-scale machine. A large trap door was built into the roof so that the complete fuselage, wings, and tail could be transferred straight up to the launch rail for assembly. Once the great aerodrome was placed on board, however, it proved impossible to maneuver through the trap door. Two large doors were finally cut through the rear of the house. The aerodrome was backed out of these doors onto a small barge anchored at the rear. This was then pulled alongside, and the pieces of the aerodrome were lifted to the roof of the main scow with a block and tackle.

Additional tests were necessary before work could begin on the launcher itself. The secretary left Reed in charge of the work when he departed for Europe in spring 1899. Although he realized that problems were developing with the engine, all other matters seemed to be well in hand. He expected the power plant to be shipped by Balzer any day. In addition, all preparations seemed to have been made for tests of the new launch mechanism with the refurbished Nos. 5 and 6. The old houseboat used during the first series of trials that had ended in November 1896 was no longer usable, and a new small scow was constructed for the flights with the models.

Manly now began preparations to return downriver with Nos. 5 and 6 and the 1:8 scale model to test the biplane wings and the new launcher. Widewater, Virginia, was chosen for the new series of flights. The crew arrived at the site for the first time on June 7, 1899. No. 6 was carried to the roof and placed on the new catapult. The device consisted of a car with three major struts that gripped special points on the frame of the aerodrome when the clutch was engaged. As in 1896, the craft was driven down the track both by the action of its own propellers and a spring mechanism operating through pulleys. As the aerodrome reached the end of the track, traveling at something close to flying speed, it passed over a cam that disengaged the craft from the car.

Flight tests were conducted between June and August 1899 with the refurbished Nos. 5 and 6 using both monoplane and biplane wings. Flights of up to 2,500 feet were achieved, demonstrating the practicability of the launcher to Manly's and Langley's satisfaction. The tests also demonstrated the superiority of the monoplane wings, which, although less rigid and more difficult to brace than the biplanes, proved far more successful in flight.[20]

Reed's 1:8 scale model of the great aerodrome remained to be tested, however. This craft was intended to explore the proper placement of the launch rods on the full-scale model and to check the balance and control system to be applied to the manned aircraft. The model had been hurriedly constructed and was very crude. The fuselage tubing was simply wired together, with solder applied at crucial points, but the machine seemed very sturdy and airworthy. Serious thought was given to constructing a liquid-air engine for the model. These plans were eventually abandoned, and the 1:8 scale craft was launched from the houseboat in August 1899, as a simple glider. It was also flown as a kite with the string attached at the point where the propellers would revolve in the great aerodrome. The model was lost when it fell into the water and was sunk by a passing boat.[21]

Both Langley and Manly were pleased with the summer's work. Nos. 5 and 6 had proved themselves once again, and were oiled and packed away for the last time. The superstructure of the large houseboat was complete by November, and construction of the full-scale launcher based on the successful design used during the latter portions of the 1899 flights could begin.

It seemed to the Smithsonian crew that they were at last within striking distance of success. In reality, their problems had only begun. Over three years were to elapse and more than $50,000 spent before the great aerodrome was complete.

Work on an experimental set of wings for the great aerodrome had proceeded in the Smithsonian shop while most of the staff were absent at Quantico during the summer of 1899. These wings were spread with sand to simulate the loading to be encountered in flight and proved inadequate for the task.

Langley had visited Clément Ader in Paris during the summer. He had been unimpressed by Ader's flying machine, but was intrigued by the manner in which the Frenchman had developed a light, strong framework for the fuselage and wings. Ader's practice of routing out or hollowing the wooden wing ribs in order to lighten them while preserving their strength was particularly interesting. This technique was applied in the redesign of the wings for the great aerodrome that followed the failure of Reed's original wings. A series of tests were conducted on the strength of various ribs and other wooden component forms for the wings, and alternative techniques for guying the wings were also tested.[22]

All of these tests were complete by October 23, 1899, and a new full-scale wing was constructed soon thereafter. When guyed in a manner similar to that which would be employed on the great aerodrome, it was able to support up to 231 pounds of sand without appreciable deformation. Since this weight was thought to be 1.5 times as great as the pressure to be encountered during normal flight, the wing was judged satisfactory, and five mates were ordered built at once, two of which would serve as spares.

Each of the wings for the great aerodrome was 24 feet long and had an 11-foot chord. The leading and central spars were hollow, as noted, and had an outside diameter of 1.5 inches at the junction with the fuselage. Both spars had a uniform diameter to the midpoint of the wing, after which they tapered to an outside diameter of 1 inch at the tip. Each wing had ten ribs, spaced 30 inches apart. A wooden strip was tacked across the trailing edge, both to keep the rib tips in position and to hold the cloth in place. The wings were designed to be easily disassembled and stored.[23]

While problems with the houseboat, launcher, control system, and wings were being resolved, the situation with the Balzer engine was rapidly moving from bad to worse. Manly paid a surprise visit to the Balzer shop on July 14, 1899. He found that the Langley engine was in precisely the same condition as it had been in at the end of April. The principal difficulties were with the ignition system. Balzer was using one of his own three-cylinder automobile engines to perfect a system of "jumping" the spark to each cylinder rather than making a direct contact in the proper sequence.

Manly believed that the experiments were necessary and that Balzer would eventually perfect the engine, but he did inform the secretary that the New Yorker faced serious financial difficulties that would slow progress.

Balzer had spent all of Langley's initial payments and all of the capital acquired through the sale of his automobiles and engines but was, according to Manly, in touch with several promoters interested in financing the production of autos, and hoped that sufficient funds to renew the Langley project would be forthcoming. Manly summarized his opinion of Balzer in a letter written to the secretary in July 1899: "That the man is a master mechanic there is no doubt, and that he has a very wonderful engine there is also no doubt, but he seems utterly lacking in business ability."[24]

Manly was continually exasperated by Balzer's vacillation. One day he would seem certain that he was on the verge of success, the next day he was just as sure that all work to date would have to be scrapped.

At Manly's insistence Balzer finally ran one cylinder of the engine and found that it developed 4 horsepower. This seemed promising for it indicated that the complete engine would develop something over 20 horsepower. If this could be accomplished, a single engine could power the aerodrome. Manly was again hopeful, and redoubled his efforts to force Balzer to complete the power plant.

By late August Balzer was again complaining of financial

difficulties that were retarding work on the rotary. Manly responded with an advance of $500 on the final purchase price of $1,500.

Progress on the engine continued as slowly as before the allocation of new funds. The lubricating system and ignition mechanism were new sources of difficulty. Nor was Balzer able to report the completion of the other elements of the aerodrome for which he had contracted.

With time on their hands, Langley and Manly decided to investigate the unknown problems that might result from the difference in scale between the models and the manned craft. Since the preparation of the airframe seemed to be proceeding satisfactorily, the two men set the staff to work on a powered quarter-scale replica of the large machine. A 1 1/2-horsepower engine to power the model was ordered from Balzer late in October 1899. Manly and Langley undoubtedly believed that this expression of confidence in Balzer's work would spur the contractor to greater effort and would provide him with much needed operating capital. In fact, the additional tasks simply made it that much more difficult to concentrate on the central problem of the large rotary engine.[25]

Langley's account books show that by September 7, 1899, he had spent $24,765.63 on the aerodrome project. On September 12 he requested that Lewis provide the remaining $25,000 so that work could continue. Lewis replied on October 8, informing Langley for the first time that an official appropriation would be required to free the second allocation and requested an official visit of inspection to the Smithsonian before making a final decision on the continuation of the project. The secretary was anxious to impress the group and arranged a formal presentation for November 12.

Members of the board arrived at the institution at 2:30. Langley opened the session with a discussion of the work completed to date and his hopes for the future. The group was then taken to the South Shed, where Balzer, who had arrived from New York the previous evening, had set up the incomplete five-cylinder engine. The carburetor had not arrived, however, so that Balzer was reduced to turning the engine over by hand to demonstrate its operation to the guests. In addition, the inspectors were allowed to view the models and those portions of the wings and frame that had been completed.

Finally, the men were taken to the Eighth Street Wharf, where the secretary's "floating machine shop" was docked. Langley believed that the inspection had been a great success. "They appeared to be very much pleased with the condition of things, especially the engine. Balzer received the congratulations of the party for turning out such a magnificent piece of work." As a result of the visit the allocation of the second $25,000 installment was approved on December 18, 1899.[26]

Balzer returned to New York with his engine immediately after the inspection, promising a test of the horsepower within a week. Langley continued to wait for the results of the test until January 3, when Manly was once more dispatched to New York to study Balzer's problem. He reported to the secretary that the ignition system was still not functioning properly, although trial runs of up to 800 revolutions had been conducted without overheating. The New Yorker still faced financial difficulties, and Manly convinced Langley that one more advance of $400 would be sufficient to complete the job. The young assistant took pains to make clear to Balzer just how far he had gone to retain the secretary's support for the engine. "I have had to practically guarantee this amount myself and further assure the Secretary that the engine will be ready for its official test by the third of February. Now pray don't disappoint me."[27]

The situation had not improved by March 20, when Manly attempted to explain Langley's misgivings to Balzer.

> You must realize that there is a limit to the number of times that a man of the Secretary's experience will allow himself to be given assurance that everything is progressing as well as possible, and then after waiting several months, things are in practically no better shape than they were before, without losing confidence in the person giving him such assurance, and I fear that unless this large engine is completed very soon that it may be the means of the Secretary losing all confidence in my judgement and advice.[28]

As Manly feared, Langley was at last losing confidence in Balzer. In a memo to his assistant dated April 6, 1900, he pointed out that after months of effort they were still not sure whether the engine would develop sufficient horsepower to propel the aerodrome or whether two engines would be required. He intimated that he was considering the possibility of beginning a search for a new engine. Before taking such drastic steps he sent an additional $500 in advance money through Manly and offered to return to the board with a request for an appropriation beyond the $50,000 if necessary.[29]

Horsepower tests were finally run in May 1900. At 700 revolutions per minute the Balzer engine produced only 8 horsepower. Work continued, but it seemed impossible to gain the extra 4 horsepower required by the contract, and there seemed no hope to run the power plant as long as promised. To make matters worse, Balzer's workmen, who had not been paid for some time, walked out on May 11, and Langley was forced to dispatch Smithsonian machinists to New York.

Langley had finally given up. When he left for Europe in June 1900, he took Manly and George B. Wells, a Smithsonian machinist, with him. The men were ordered to visit facilities in England and on the Continent and to bring themselves up to date on light-engine technology. The secretary believed that such a detailed examination of European developments might uncover an existing power plant that could be adopted for use with the aerodrome.

The men met with Maxim, probably the most experienced aeronautical engine builder in England, who strongly advised against continuing work on the rotary engine. Contact was made with a number of other engineers, notably the Comte De Dion, whose single-cylinder rotary had been successfully used in a number of self-propelled vehicles, primarily the De Dion–Bouton tricycle.

But Manly continued to believe that the first $1,500 already invested in the Balzer power plant had not been in vain. He returned to New York in mid-August and immediately visited Balzer's shop, only to discover that the result of a month's work had been a drop from 8 to 6 horsepower.

While Manly still believed in the potential of the engine, it was now obvious that he must terminate the relationship with Balzer. He ordered the engine shipped to Washington, where he would personally supervise the transformation of the Balzer rotary into a fixed radial. That is, rather than having the engine and propeller revolve around a stationary crankshaft as in the Balzer original, the five cylinders would now remain stationary while the pistons turned the crankshaft. This would necessitate major changes, such as the provision of a cooling system, but it was apparent that such a radical breakthrough was required to produce the necessary horsepower. Manly prepared a temporary water jacket, and by September 11 he had obtained "750 revolutions per minute with the horsepower varying between twelve and sixteen."[30]

It was necessary to expand the shop facilities at the Smithsonian once work on the full-scale engine had been transferred to Washington. In addition to the responsibility for both the power plant and airframe of the great aerodrome, Manly had also brought the quarter-scale engine back from New York. By February 1, 1901, the staff had grown to seven machinists and three carpenters. The monthly salary for these men amounted to $835.60. This quickly became the major drain on the Board of Ordnance and Fortification account, that had already been sadly depleted by the houseboat contract and the money that had been spent on the two Balzer engines. Langley, Manly, Watkins, and Rathbun also devoted the major portion of their time to aerodromic work, but these men were carried on the normal Smithsonian rolls.[31]

Manly's insistence that the Balzer engine be run as a radial and his improvements in the sparking mechanism, valves, and cooling system raised the power plant output to 18 horsepower by March 2, 1901. Even this vast improvement, which was more than double Balzer's most successful result, was still insufficient to propel the full-scale machine.

In a report to Lewis dated September 6, 1900, Rathbun reported: "Generally speaking, it may be said that the aerodrome is now about ready for its first trial, with the exception of the engine."[32] The four large wings and the spares were finished.

The frame had been ready to receive the engine for some weeks, and the steering mechanism and tail could be attached at any time. The houseboat had been delivered in May 1900, and the superstructure and launch mechanism were complete. The Navy had supplied the anchor and auxiliary equipment, while the Army had detailed a soldier to guard the craft. The lighthouse tender *Maple* was prepared to tow the boat down the Potomac to Widewater on short notice.

Throughout this period the secretary remained in touch with Chanute, discussing theoretical issues in general and keeping up to date on other developments in American aeronautics. Langley seemed particularly interested in the work of Herring and the Wright brothers. He also met with Means, Rotch, and other members of the Boston circle with some frequencey. These men introduced the secretary to C. H. Lamson and other kite experimenters in whom he took a real interest. Like Chanute, Langley offered some financial support to less affluent investigators by farming out portions of his own experimental program. Lamson, for example, provided kites to be tested by the secretary. At one point Langley was seriously considering hiring the Maine enthusaist to construct a set of experimental wings. Albert A. Merrill was employed in 1901 to construct a test apparatus and to conduct a study of the lift obtained from various airfoils. The secretary was sufficiently intrigued by the Wright investigations to offer a grant, but his overtures were rebuffed by the Daytonians, who steadfastly refused to accept any outside financial assistance. Langley's generosity did have limits, however. When Chanute requested that the secretary consider underwriting the aerodynamic studies being conducted by George A. Spratt, Langley refused, arguing that his earlier experience with amateurs like Spratt had not proved fruitful.[33]

Manly was also drawn into the wider circle of the American aeronautical community after 1898. He became a frequent correspondent of Chanute's. As noted in the case of the Whitehead machine, he also took a specific interest in the work of other experimenters. Neither the secretary nor his assistant was willing to provide any information on the progress of the aerodrome, however. While they were anxious to remain abreast of current work in the field, the most knowledgeable aeronautical experimenters remained ignorant of developments at the Smithsonian.

Emphasis shifted to the completion of the quarter-scale model as work on the large engine seemed to continue interminably. The model had originally been something of a make-work project intended to keep the shop workers busy until the large engine was perfected and the construction of the full-scale frame could be continued. The small craft was designed to solve some of the remaining technical problems as well. It would provide a final test of the launch system and would indicate the aerodynamic changes resulting from the enlarged scale. The problem of correct balance could also be studied. This was of crucial importance, for the safety of the pilot would depend on the inherent lateral stability of the great aerodrome. Thus the performance of the quarter-scale model assumed greater significance as the date of a manned flight drew nearer.

The wings and frame of the model were complete by June 1900. As in the case of the great aerodrome, however, work came to a standstill as a result of Balzer's inability to perfect the engine. The changes that Manly proposed for the model engine closely paralleled those that he had outlined for the large power plant, but some short cuts were taken to save time. Whereas water jackets were constructed to cool the large engine, the small version was operated without a cooling system. Consequently, it proved impossible to run the quarter scale for more than thirty seconds at a time. After this point the cylinders became so hot that spontaneous ignition occurred. Manly believed that once the aerodrome was moving through the air, the effect of the slip stream would act as an effective coolant, making longer periods of operation possible.[34]

The first flight tests of the quarter-scale mode were held on June 19, 1901. The small houseboat had been towed downstream to Widewater, where preparations for the launch were complete by 5:15 P.M. The aerodrome made four flights of 100, 150, 300, and 350 feet on this occasion. Manly realized that he had been incorrect in assuming that the 1 1/2-horsepower engine was capable of keeping the model aloft and returned to Washington deter-

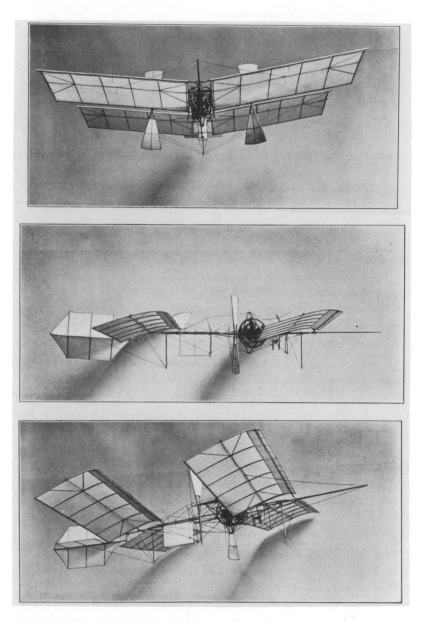

Three views of the quarter-scale aerodrome.

mined to alter the gear ratio in an effort to produce at least 2 horsepower. The time required to make these alterations and difficulties with the naphtha engine that powered the test launch prevented further attempts at flight with the machine until the great aerodrome was finished. Manly and Langley agreed that even the short hops of June 1901 had been sufficient to demonstrate the basic stability of the craft.[35]

The secretary faced yet another major crisis during fall 1901. On October 15, Manly reported that the $50,000 appropriation from the Board of Ordnance and Fortification had been exhausted. Langley was, of course, completely unwilling to abandon the work when success seemed so close. Once again, Alexander Graham Bell came to his rescue.

In June 1890 Bell had presented the secretary with $5,000 to be spent on any sort of physical research undertaken at the Smithsonian. Dr. Jerome Henry Kidder, a Washington physician, had willed a similar amount to the institution at the time of his death in 1889. Like the Bell gift, the Kidder bequest was to be used for any research deemed appropriate by the secretary. Langley had held these funds in reserve for over ten years to meet an emergency such as he now faced. With Bell's enthusiastic approval, the aerodromic work continued with money drawn from the two accounts. Even this sum proved insufficient,[36] however, and Langley was eventually forced to withdraw an additional $13,000 from the Hodgkins Fund.[37]

Manly offered a full report of the status of the project as the Board of Ordnance and Fortification account was closed.

> The general condition of the work may be summed up by saying that everything now awaits the completion of the engine, so that extended trials may be made with it working in the frame in order that the strength of the frame may be determined—besides the test of several other minor parts which will depend on the working of the engine, and judging from past experience with the models, it will be reasonable to expect that many defects will come out when these trials are made with the engine working in its place, and that some reconstruction along several different lines will probably be necessary though just how much, of course, it is impossible now to say.[38]

Steady work on the large engine resumed once the quarter-scale model was packed away. Manly had raised the output of Balzer's basic power plant to 22 horsepower by June 28, 1901. In order to achieve this level of performance he had installed new lightweight pistons, a new ignition system that permitted smoother running, and the permanent cooling jackets on the cylinders.

The secretary and his assistant realized that even with the increased power, the engine was still, at best, a marginal product. Having determined that it would be too difficult and expensive a task to build a mate, the only alternative was to search for ways to increase the horsepower of the Balzer engine.

As early as November 1900, Manly had received Langley's approval to increase the displacement from 380 cubic inches to approximately 540 cubic inches. This required casting five new, enlarged stainless-steel cylinders and cast-iron cylinder liners. Naturally, new water jackets were also required.

When tested once again on October 2, 1901, Manly discovered that several of the jackets leaked badly and would have to be removed and replaced. The discovery that three of the cylinder heads also leaked water was even more serious, and necessitated an order for completely new castings.

At the time the engine was removed from Balzer's control in August 1900, a total of $1,850 had been spent. By November 8, 1901, Manly's reconstruction had raised the total cost of the power plant to $5,130.[39]

Manly was still not satisfied with the performance of the power plant and continued work with the ignition, carburetion, and other elements until, on April 28, 1902, he finally achieved an output of 41 horsepower. The engine represented a new device. Manly had so altered the original power plant that there was very little of Balzer's work left with the exception of the basic engine block. The Manly-Balzer engine had finally reached its finished state, although more than a year of additional tinkering and minor alteration remained before it would be used in an actual attempt at manned flight. Manly described the power plant as it appeared at this point in the fall of 1902.

The flying weight of the engine, including all accessories, I think will come very close to 200 pounds, of which 130 pounds is for the actual engine itself, 20 pounds for the two flywheels, 25 pounds for the cooling water, 17 pounds for the condenser, 1 pound for the pump, 3 pounds for the sparking coil, 9 pounds for the sparking dynamo or battery, besides a few minor water connections, electrical wires, etc.[40]

The flywheels were used to insure smoothness of operation. The "condenser" to which Manly refers was, of course, the radiator. The total engine was 37 inches in diameter and 19 inches wide. It featured a 5-inch bore and a 5.5-inch stroke. A surface carburetor was employed, and a battery, induction coil, and spark plugs composed the ignition system. There can be little doubt that the Manly-Balzer engine was the most advanced lightweight internal combustion engine in the world, but its utility as a power plant for the great aerodrome remained to be demonstrated.

The great aerodrome and its power plant were basically complete by mid-November 1902. Langley described the state of affairs to Lewis:

Everything is ready, and were there still time this season, a flight would be made, but I do not expect one until after the ice has gone; then I, who have never known any great initiatory trial without some mischance, look for what I call our "first smash." When every human care has been taken, there remains the element of the unknown. There may well be something that forethought has not provided for, and I expect it, but excepting for the fact that a human life is now in question, I could make it without fear at all.[41]

By March 1903 Manly was performing regular tests of the engine mounted in the airframe. The power plant was consistently operating at 45 horsepower, turning the twin propellers at a speed of 575 revolutions per minute.

The aerodrome was now complete. The airframe had been constructed in two sections. The central portion was usually referred to as the main frame. It measured 58 feet, 5 inches from the tip of the bowsprit to the point where it connected to the Pénaud tail. The major strain was to be borne by two 50-millimeter tubes that ran the length of the frame. The midrod that had formed the backbone of the smaller models now served only as a point of attachment for the wings.

Four "pyramid" guy posts, two on top of the machine and two on the bottom provided a means of guying the frame and wings into a fairly rigid structure. The lower "pyramid" served a second function as the primary point for attaching the aerodrome to the launch car.

The cruciform tail attached at the rear was free to move only in a vertical plane. A smaller rudder was placed on the underside of the craft, immediately forward of the leading edge of the rear wings.

The aviator would sit in a cloth-covered "car" set between the two forward wings. A great deal of thought had been given to the possibility of strapping him into a specially constructed seat, but these plans were abandoned in the interest of allowing the pilot to make a safe and speedy exit should the need arise. This was to prove a wise decision.

The operator was provided with two control wheels in his cockpit. One controlled the rise and fall of the tail and, it was hoped, the aerodrome. Springs were placed between this wheel and the tail in order to compensate for the shock of sudden wind gusts. Once in the air, this control was to be used in the manner of a trim tab. The tail would automatically adjust to maintain level flight under normal conditions, but the wheel could be employed under extraordinary circumstances or in the event that the aerodrome had been improperly balanced fore and aft before take-off.

The second control wheel was also placed on the right side wall and operated the rudder. Shock springs were also employed in this system. Finally, the pilot had sufficient freedom of movement so that shifts in his weight could be used to control and balance the machine. In addition to these flight controls, the operator was provided with a throttle to be used in adjusting the engine speed.[42]

Both Manly and Langley realized that the problem of stability

(Left to right) Langley, Manly, Reed, and Cyrus Adler stand beneath the aerodrome on the roof of the houseboat.

and attitude control was far from solved. They believed, however, that these arrangements would suffice to keep the aerodrome in the air for a reasonably short flight. Once basic success had been demonstrated to everyone's satisfaction, a more thorough investigation of control methods could be undertaken.

The selection of a pilot for the aerodrome had been resolved in June 1901. Langley had a clear idea of the qualities that would best suit a man to operate the machine.

I have repeated to Mr. Manly what I have frequently said, and what I understand to be of importance in the man who takes this first flight, that provided he understands the working of the levers which are to make the machine go faster or slower, point higher or lower, any engineering knowledge . . . is of less consequence than a general clear head and ability for quick decision and action united with a most important quality implying the absence of

nervousness which for want of a better word I will call unper-
turbability, a quality which prevents a man from losing his head
at the critical moment.[43]

The secretary was anxious to give Manly an opportunity to
be the first to fly the aerodrome, but the engineer seemed reti-
cent. Langley noted that Manly offered his services, but was
"not anxious to press them." Other applications had been received from potential pilots. R. H. Chapman, a young man employed by the Geological Survey, was a particularly promising
candidate. Chapman was not familiar with the aerodrome or the
dangers involved in flying the craft. The secretary decided to
invite the young man to attend the flight trials of the quarter-
scale model and then begin a period of intensive flight training.
Manly finally settled the question with a memo of June 1, 1901,
to Langley, in which he remarked that "I am now . . . ready to
occupy this position." Given this firm expression of interest on
his assistant's part, the problem of selecting a pilot for the aerodrome was resolved.[44]

A final test of the balance of the quarter-scale model was to
precede the manned attempt. The houseboat used during the
1899 trials was no longer fit for service, so the shorter launch rail
for the model was placed on the roof of the large boat with the
track for the large aerodrome. The model was in the same condition as during its first trial, but on this occasion it was flown
only as a monoplane. The houseboat was towed downriver to
Widewater on June 14. Langley's long-standing policy of withholding information from the press did not prevent local news-
papermen from covering what promised to be one of the most
important stories of the century.

The quarter-scale aerodrome was ready for flight testing by
August 8. The wind was blowing from the east southeast at 12
miles per hour when the craft was launched at 9:30 A.M. The
machine flew roughly 350 feet, then began a shallow bank
through a quarter circle. It remained in the air for 27 seconds
and covered 1,000 feet before it entered the water. Manly was
disappointed with so short a flight, particularly since the engine
had not operated smoothly. One of the mechanics admitted to

The quarter-scale aerodrome in flight.

having overfilled the gasoline tank, which explained the uneven output of the power plant, and the aerodrome had seemed well balanced. Manly decided, therefore, to forego further tests with the model and proceed with launching the great aerodrome.[45]

Seventeen years of effort stood behind the Langley machine, which was judged complete and ready to carry a man into the air by early September. While both Langley and Manly realized that the craft was deficient in many respects, they were certain that it was capable of straight flights for short distances.

But Langley and his staff would not have the field to themselves as the fall of 1903 approached. Five hundred miles to the west Wilbur and Orville Wright were hard at work putting the finishing touches on their own powered flying machine. Like the Smithsonian crew, the Wrights were certain that they were close to the final success. They had more reason for confidence.

13

December 1903: The Month of the Flying Machines

Shortly after 2:30 P.M., December 8, 1903, the tugs *Bartholdi* and *Joe Blackburn* pulled away from a wharf at the foot of Eighth Street in southeast Washington with a large, flat-bottomed houseboat in tow. The vessels moved downriver through sheets of floating ice to an anchorage off Arsenal Point, near the confluence of the Potomac and Anacostia rivers. A midday calm had given way to winds gusting up to 20 miles per hour—hardly ideal conditions for men struggling to bolt a cruciform tail and four large wings to a steel-tube fuselage mounted on a catapult on the roof of the houseboat.

Charles Matthews Manly was in charge of this operation. He took particular care with these final preparations for he was about to trust his life to the ungainly machine resting on the launcher. If the events of the next few hours unfolded as planned, Charles Manly would become a very famous man. He would be remembered as the pilot of the world's first successful powered airplane.

Samuel Pierpont Langley watched the activity from the deck with some apprehension. This was to be the second trial of his great aerodrome.

The great aerodrome, ready for flight, rests on the catapult.

The first attempt had been made two months earlier, near Widewater, Virginia, close to the site where the model aerodromes had been test-flown.

On September 8, one of the propellers had broken at the hub during an engine test run, smashing into the frame. By October 7, with repairs complete, the crew was again ready for a trial. This time preparations proceeded smoothly. After the preliminary engine run-up, the great aerodrome was ready for flight. Manly, huddled in the small cockpit, was ready as well.[1]

Again starting up the engine, and bringing it up to full speed and finding that it was developing over 50 horsepower, I gave the order to release the car on which the machine rested. This was done and the car started down the track under the combined impetus of the launching springs and the propellers of the aerodrome.

Manly (in the control car) and Reed (in the straw hat) prepared the great aerodrome.

The aerodrome, its forward wings already collapsing, sweeps over the cameraman on October 7, 1903.

Just as the end of the track was reached and at the moment when the machine should have become entirely free from the launching car, I experienced a slight jerk and discovered immediately that the machine was plunging forward and downward at an angle of 45 degrees. Finding that there was not time to shut down the engine before striking the water, I prepared for the plunge, since it seemed that nothing could be done to obviate it.[2]

A Washington reporter provided a much more graphic description of the scene, remarking that the aerodrome entered the water "like a handful of mortar."[3]

The front wings were crushed as the machine entered the water. The rear wings and rudder were broken while the craft was being towed back to the houseboat. Manly, however, was uninjured.

Langley was bitterly disappointed. Nevertheless, he retained his belief in the ability of the machine to fly, rationalizing its initial failure as the fault of the launch mechanism, not the aircraft. In fact, the crash may well have been the result of some defect in the catapult, in which case the secretary had only

October 7, 1903. The aerodrome entered the water "like a handful of mortar."

himself to blame. For it was his own insistence on recreating the precise conditions of 1896 that led to the great aerodrome's being subjected to the enormous strains inherent in a catapult launch. While a precise structural analysis of the craft is probably impossible to obtain at this point, the weakness of the smaller models suggests that the scaled-up version was incapable of even marginal flight. The decision to compound the basic difficulty of getting this overly complex, structurally weak and underpowered craft into the air by boosting it from a complete standstill to flying speed in only 70 feet was, to judge the matter kindly, unwise.[4]

The repairs required were far beyond the capacity of the light machine shop housed on the boat, so the crew returned to Washington, where two months of feverish effort were directed toward preparing the great aerodrome for another trial.

Once again on December 8, a small group of invited witnesses from the Smithsonian, the Coast Survey, and the Army Board

Raising the remains of the aerodrome following the October launch.

of Ordnance and Fortification were on board the houseboat with Langley. In addition, Dr. F. S. Nash, an Army contract surgeon, was present to provide emergency medical services.

By 4:30 the weather was deteriorating. The overcast winter sky was darkening rapidly, and the gusts had begun to shift direction so that it became impossible to keep the boat pointed into the wind. In a hurried conference, Langley and Manly agreed that the test could not be postponed. It might be weeks before significant improvement in the weather could be expected, and funds were not available to allow for such a delay.

Manly quickly stripped his outer clothes. He would make the flight dressed in a union suit, stockings, light shoes, and a cork-lined jacket. Whether he succeeded or failed, he faced the prospect of a second landing in the frigid Potomac and he had no intention of being weighed down by heavy garments. The young engineer stepped through the tangle of brace wires and struts into the small fabric-sided cockpit. He seated himself on a board facing the right side of the machine, his hands resting on two small wheels mounted on the right wall of the cockpit. These controlled the up and down motion of the tail and operated the rudder on the underside of the fuselage. As Manly ran the engine up, the invited guests joined members of the Washington press corps in a number of small boats from which they had a good view of the proceedings and were in a better position to offer assistance if rescue attempts were required.

Satisfied with the sound of the engine and the operation of the controls, Manly gave the signal to Reed, who released the catapult at 4:45. He sped down the rail, felt a sharp jerk and immediately found himself staring straight up at the sky as his aerial steed flipped into the water on its back. Manly hung from the cockpit sides with his hands, so that he entered the water feet first. In spite of his precautions, he found himself trapped beneath the surface with the cork-lined jacket caught on a metal fitting. Ripping the garment off he struggled through the maze of broken wood and wire only to reach the surface beneath the ice sheet. He dove again, finally emerging in free water some distance from the floating wreckage, just in time to see a work-

man plunge under the remains of the machine in a rescue attempt.[5]

Both men were quickly fished out of the water and carried to
safety aboard the houseboat. Manly was uninjured but so frozen
that Dr. Nash was forced to cut the clothing from his body.
Moments later, wrapped in warm blankets and fortified with
whiskey, this genteel son of a university president startled the
group by delivering a "most voluble series of blasphemies."[6]

Langley and Manly puzzled over the accident for days, but
were unable to satisfy themselves as to the cause. The two men
were simply unwilling to accept structural weakness as the
probable explanation.

The failure of the aerodrome was a direct result of Langley's
approach to engineering. From the earliest period of his work
with models, the secretary had struggled to hold weight to such
an absolute minimum that the strength of his craft was marginal. His insistence on attempting a "minimum" straight-line
flight in which the pilot was scarcely more than a helpless passenger illustrated his readiness to cut corners and take enormous leaps into the unknown. This becomes even clearer when
it is noted that Langley had given no serious thought to the most
basic problem of all—landing. Every landing would be a crash
landing and the pilot, seated in his flimsy, cloth-sided cockpit,
would be the first thing to touch down. At best, Manly could
look forward to repeated drenchings, but if the machine strayed
over land the pilot faced unavoidable disaster.

Finally, in addition to structural shortcomings and leapfrogged problems, the Langley aerodrome seems to have har-
bored unrecognized aerodynamic defects. Raymond Bispling-
hoff, a leading aeronautical engineer, has singled out the craft
as a classic case of aeroelastic or wing-torsional divergence.
That is, the flexible wings of the aerodrome were given a
corkscrew twist as the center of lifting pressure moved rapidly
toward the trailing edge at the moment of launch. The flexibil-
ity and enormous wing area of the machine magnified this
twisting action until the inadequate wing supports failed.[7]
Those who have argued that the great aerodrome could have
flown if only Langley had abandoned the catapult are wrong.

The machine was structurally and aerodynamically unsound.

Langley had been right on one point, however. The reaction to the disaster of December 8 was as immediate and harsh as he had feared.

When the secretary returned to the Board of Ordnance and Fortification, his request for additional funds was refused. The board could hardly have reacted in any other fashion, for it was coming under heavy fire from congressional leaders.

On January 23, 1904, Representative Robinson of Indiana had opened a direct attack on the power of the board: "The War Department—the Board of Ordnance and Fortification in that Department—has permitted an expenditure for scientific purposes of thousands in a vain attempt to breathe life into an air-ship project which never had a substantial basis."[8]

Robinson characterized Langley as "a professor . . . wandering in his dreams of flight . . . who was given to building . . . castles in the air."[9] Representative Gilbert Hitchcock of Nebraska joined the battle in support of Robinson on January 27 when he inquired of James A. Hemenway, chairman of the House Appropriations Committee, "if it is to cost us $73,000 to construct a mud duck that will not fly 50 feet, how much is it going to cost to construct a real flying machine?"[10]

The Langley aerodrome had become a symbol around which a general discussion of the government's role in funding science and technology was developing. Following Hitchcock's remarks, Robinson expanded his earlier discussion of this issue and again pointed to the aerodrome as a case in point.

> I realize . . . that Professor Langley is a learned man. He is erudite in scientific matters. He knows a vast amount about extinct animals and stuffed birds. He is at home with the *Pterodactyl Ornithostoma*. . . . But I see no reason, and the taxpayers of the country can see no reason . . . why at national expense he should be constituted and established a modern Darius Green.[11]

Representative Hemenway disagreed, pointing out that members of the House "got up and laughed" when the original appropriation for the telegraph was requested.[12]

The central theme of the discussion revolved around the wisdom of general appropriations that gave civil servants or military officers the right to make specific allocations. In essence, Robinson and Hitchcock were protesting the system that had been developed by the Board of Ordnance and Fortification for promoting research in those areas of military technology that the members felt held the most promise. Robinson took special issue with the board's description of the aerodrome as an instrument of war, remarking that "a regiment of them would not conquer the Fiji Islands, except, perhaps, by scaring their people to death."[13]

Once again chairman Hemenway came to the secretary's defense.

> If [the aerodromes] could sail over the enemy's camp and see what he had there in the way of men and fortifications, and ascertain all about him, and still be out of danger themselves, that would be an instrument of war more formidable than any that the world has ever yet seen.[14]

Robinson retorted that if steps were not taken to curb research spending,

> some one will influence some Department to test the principle of erecting buildings beginning with the roof . . . [or] will be promoting with Government aid a plan to feed spiders on glue and bluebottle flies to make it weave a fabric of strength and color.[15]

The nation's newspapers also became a forum for the debate. The *Brooklyn Eagle* on March 13, 1904, featured an article in which Representative Hitchcock was quoted as saying, "You tell Langley for me . . . that the only thing he ever made fly was Government money."[16]

Samuel Langley's eighteen-year search for a successful airplane ended in the Potomac on December 8, 1903. He had spent thousands of dollars and man hours in a vain attempt to purchase immortality. Major N. W. Macomb of the Board of Ordnance and Fortification spoke for many Americans when he remarked in his final report on the Langley project that "we are still far from the ultimate goal, and it would seem as if years of constant work and study by experts, together with the expenditure of thousands of dollars, would still be necessary before we can hope to produce an apparatus of practical utility on these lines."[17]

One of the men who would prove Major Macomb and Langley's newspaper and congressional critics wrong boarded a train in Dayton, Ohio, on December 9, the morning after the Langley crash. Orville Wright carried with him a new propeller shaft that would be fitted to another flying machine that had been conceived, designed, and constructed far from the glare of publicity that surrounded the Smithsonian effort.

While waiting to board the train that morning, he had purchased copies of newspapers carrying the details of the Langley disaster. These accounts came as no surprise to him, for the Wrights had long believed that there was little hope for success with the Langley machine.

Still, both brothers must have felt a great deal of sympathy. As Wilbur Wright recalled several years later, "I cannot help feeling sorry for him. The fact that the great scientist, Prof. Langley, believed in flying machines was one thing that encouraged us to begin our studies. It was he that recommended to us [the readings that] started us in the right direction in the beginning."[18]

The Wrights had returned to Kitty Hawk in 1903 confident that their three years of experience had carried them to the brink of success. During the previous winter and spring they had overcome two final obstacles, producing an engine and propellers to power the 1903 airplane.

These were more difficult tasks than the brothers had at first supposed. In the case of the propeller, they had always presumed that a trip to the library for a review of marine-screw theory in engineering texts could serve as a basis for their own design. They discovered, in fact, that virtually the only useful bit of data available on ship propellers was the fact that their efficiency was dependent on the total volume of fluid that passed through the blades each revolution.

The 1903 Wright flyer rests on the sand in front of the hangar. The smaller building to the right served as living quarters.

Once again the Wrights were forced to resort to their own engineering genius to solve a problem that other experimenters had almost completely ignored.

They immediately abandoned the traditional view of the propeller as an "air screw," whirling through the air as a wood screw moves through a board. Rather, the Wrights reasoned that a propeller was actually a rotary wing in which the lift was vectored into thrust to move the aircraft forward. Using the information employed in wing design, they carefully analyzed each propeller section to determine the optimum camber for the particular speed at which that section would be sweeping through the air. The result was the world's first true aircraft propeller, a device whose performance could be precisely calculated.[19]

In the case of the engine, the Wrights had correctly decided that the state of the art of power-plant design was sufficiently advanced so as to guarantee the ready availability of a suitable motor. Since Langley's difficulties with the Manly-Balzer engine were discussed previously, this point may not be obvious. The secretary sought to move into the air by brute force, attaining the highest possible power rating for the lowest weight. For Langley the development of this ideal power plant had, in practice, almost replaced the flying machine as the basic goal.

The Wrights, however, had shown their usual good judgment in expending almost all of their effort on the air frame and control systems and reducing the engine problem to realistic proportions. They differed from all of the other enthusiasts in their realization that power plants were already available to power an airplane, if effort were concentrated on the efficiency of the lifting surfaces, the propellers, and the reduction of air resistance.

The time and energy that Langley spent on his very successful engine was wasted because of the inefficiency of the aerodrome and propellers. The Wrights, with their enlightened view of the airplane as a complex technical system, realized that each element of the total machine had to be separately evaluated in order to judge where the real problems lay. This attitude prevented them from too heavy a concentration on the particular problems and permitted a continued drive to develop subsystems that would mesh to form a complete and efficiently operating machine.

The Wrights had originally intended to purchase an engine. They contacted a number of manufacturers but were unable to find a company that would meet their specifications at a price that they considered reasonable. The brothers decided that they could produce the engine themselves and avoid straining their limited budget. Charles Taylor, a machinist in the bike shop, was to be responsible for much of the work. The finished power plant was a four-cylinder gasoline engine with a 4-inch bore and stroke. Fully equipped for flight, it weighed 140 pounds. Under optimum conditions it developed 16 horsepower during the first fifteen seconds of operation, after which it dropped to 12 horsepower.

The engine was first tested on February 12, 1903. During a run on the thirteenth the bearings froze. New aluminum cylinders were added in late April, and by early May they believed their engine to be complete. The brothers were pleased with its performance. In fact, the 1903 Wright engine was crude and inefficient. Langley's power plant was far superior. But the poor showing of the engine was a matter of little consequence, for it was sufficiently powerful to propel their machine into the air, all that would be required of it.[20]

The necessary elements were now in place, and the Wrights finally applied for a patent on March 23, 1903. The application embodied the control features present in the 1902 glider. The engines and propellers were not patented.[21]

The brothers had been among the most open members of the community prior to this time. The essentials of their system had been freely shared with Chanute and others. Their camp at Kitty Hawk had been thrown open to those men whom they had every reason to believe were their closest rivals in the search for a flying machine. This pattern changed after fall 1902.

The major factor leading to this change was the realization that they had invented the airplane. Before 1902 the Wrights had viewed themselves as contributors to a body of knowledge upon which eventual success would be based. The breakthroughs accomplished during the winter of 1901 and the demonstration of success on the dunes in 1902 had changed their attitude. Once they recognized how many obstacles they had overcome and how close they were to powered flight, they immediately took steps to protect their interests.

The necessity for withholding key information became even more apparent as other aeronautical leaders began to take a serious interest in their work. Langley, for example, considered visiting Kitty Hawk in 1902. When this proved impossible, he sent what Chanute described as a "cheeky" letter inviting the Wrights to visit Washington to discuss control systems. Chanute could also point to European figures like Captain Ferdinand Ferber, a French enthusiast who had begun to experiment with gliders based on published photos of the Wrights' 1901 craft.[22]

The Wrights' desire to suppress the details of their gliders led to their first conflicts with Chanute. Chanute agreed to refrain from describing the operation of the combined wing warping and rudder mechanism, but remarked that he believed their attempt to maintain secrecy was pointless "as the construction is ancient and well known."[23]

Chanute had spent twenty-seven years studying the various approaches to the flying machine. He may in fact, actually have believed that the theoretical possiblity of such a control system was well known. It seems more likely, however, that he simply failed to understand what the Wrights had accomplished. It is true that his own descriptions of the wing-warping technique were often erroneous. In any case, the Chicagoan had always believed that automatic stability was an absolute necessity. Since wing warping required the intervention of an operator, he had not bothered to conduct active experiments with this or any other active control system.

Having filed for a patent that would finally be granted in 1906, Wilbur and Orville left for their third season at Kitty Hawk early on the morning of September 23, 1903. Arriving in camp on the twenty-fifth, they discovered that the old building had been badly damaged in a recent storm. Dan Tate, a Kitty Hawk friend, remarked that the weather on the Banks had been the worst in memory.

The Daytonians had brought the 1902 machine back with them. They intended to continue practicing with the old craft while rebuilding the hangar and constructing the 1903 machine. By October 1 they were back in the air with the old glider. Wilbur reported to Chanute that they had developed the ability to soar over one spot for as long as twenty-six and two-fifths seconds. George Spratt had returned to Kitty Hawk for yet another season by the end of October. At this point the three men had finished the 1903 airplane with the exception of the new double-surface vertical rudder. Chanute had also arrived in early November.[24]

The usual collection of minor problems appeared as the Wright flyer neared completion. The brothers discovered that the sprockets, over which the propeller drive chains would pass, refused to remain screwed tight on the shafts. In addition, engine misfires destroyed the synchronization of the propellers. Spratt, who was forced to return to Pennsylvania on November 5, took two damaged shafts with him for repair.[25]

The 1902 glider in the air. Note the wing warping in operation.

During the long evening discussions in camp, Chanute admitted that in spite of his belief in the eventual success of the Wright brothers, he hoped to continue his own research and planned to purchase one of Ader's flying machines. The Wrights, however, were so certain that they were about to get a powered craft into the air that they sent their older brother Lorin precise instructions as to how word of their success was to be presented to the newspapers and wire services.

The propeller shafts arrived back in Kitty Hawk on November 20, but the difficulties with the sprocket remained unresolved, and Orville reported that the day closed "in deep gloom." As a last resort they applied a liberal dollup of a favorite bicycle-tire cement and once more screwed the sprocket onto the shaft. The problem was solved. Now a faulty valve resulted in excess vibration that had also to be overcome.[26]

The airplane was so much larger and heavier than its predecessors that the old method of launching, in which an assistant on each wing tip had pulled the craft into the air, would no longer suffice. In addition, the Wrights wanted to ensure that there could be no question as to whether or not man's first powered flight had been made under perfect conditions. They feared that human assistance in launching would detract from the impact of the flight. For this reason they had designed and built a starting rail. The device was a single track, sheathed with metal and laid on a series of short ties. The airplane would ride down the rail on a small wheeled car placed on the bottom of a crossbar at the front of the craft. Assistants were still positioned at each wing tip to hold the machine in a level position as it ran down the rail. Chanute was delighted with the Wright launch system, noticing that the whole apparatus had cost only $4 while "Langley is said to have spent nearly $50,000 on his starting device which failed."[27]

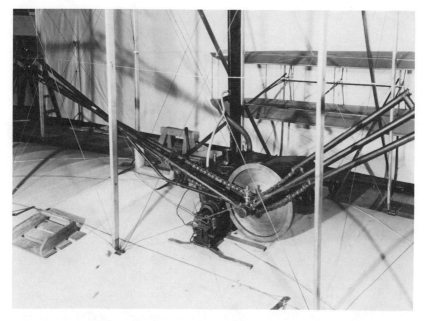

The pilot's position in the Wright Flyer, seen from the rear. The wooden foot rest is to the left, with the hip cradle toward the front, partially hidden by the chain guide.

On November 28, 1903, while running a series of engine tests with the air screws turning at 359 revolutions per minute, the propeller shaft cracked again. After another day spent in unsuccessful attempts to repair the damage, Orville returned to Dayton to obtain brand-new shafts of spring steel. The new shaft was in place by December 11. The winds were too light to attempt to fly the machine, but manned test runs were made late that afternoon. A minor accident required repairs to both the track and tail, so that the first real flight trials were postponed until December 14.

The Wrights had been in camp longer than ever before, and the weather was rapidly deteriorating. If they were to make a flight, they would have to do so soon. For this reason, they prepared to make a powered trial as soon as the damage was repaired on the afternoon of the fourteenth.

By 1:30 P.M. preparations were complete. A prearranged signal was sent to the men at the nearby lifesaving station, and the

The 1903 Wright flyer prior to the unsuccessful trial of December 14.

brothers spent forty minutes on final adjustments. A handful of lifesavers, including Robert Westcott, John T. Daniels, Thomas Beacham, W.S. Dough, and "Uncle Benny" O'Neil, were soon on hand to assist. Chanute was no longer on hand, having returned to Chicago by this time. Wilbur and Orville tossed a coin to see who would have the honor of making man's first powered flight. Wilbur won. After some slight difficulty in preparing for the launch, Will climbed on.

At Wilbur's signal the craft began to move down the track with Orville balancing the right wing and another man on the left. By the time it had traveled 40 feet the two men found that they could no longer keep up with the machine. The airplane rose from its car as it neared the end of the rail. Wilbur nosed up far too rapidly, stalled, and spun into the ground with the left wing from an altitude of 15 feet. One of the skids, the lower rear wing spar, and a main rudder were all shattered. The propeller had made 602 revolutions to carry the machine 105 feet beyond the end of the track. While they had exceeded Herring's 1899 performance, the Wrights had fallen far short of their own goal.[28]

December 15 was spent repairing the craft. A second day was lost when the wind refused to rise to required levels on December 16. When the brothers rose the following morning, conditions were still far from perfect.

The morning of December 17 had dawned cold. The puddles of standing water had frozen over night, and a 27-mile-per-hour wind was blowing from the north. Hoping that the wind might abate, the brothers enjoyed a leisurely breakfast and remained indoors until 10:00 A.M., when they decided to make the trial.

A signal flag was hung out to summon the volunteer ground crew from the Kill Devil station. The Wrights lugged four 15-foot sections of two-by-four, the top of which had been sheathed in metal, to a level area 100 feet west of their buildings. The aircraft, which would ride along this take-off rail on a cart constructed of two bicycle hubs, was taken out of the hanger and prepared for flight. Work in the biting cold was difficult, requiring frequent retreats to the comfort of the carbide can stove, but by the time Daniels, Dough, and A. D. Etheridge arrived from the Kill Devil station, preparations were nearing completion.

Two visitors, W. C. Brinkley, from Manteo and eighteen-year-old Johnny Moore from Nags Head accompanied the lifesavers. Wescott, who had remained on duty at Kill Devil, watched the proceedings through a spy glass, while four miles away Captain S. J. Payne, chief of the Kitty Hawk station, was also training his telescope on the men clustered around the biplane. At about 10:30 A.M. a few drops of gasoline were pumped into each cylinder. The battery required for starting was attached. The engine was allowed to run for several minutes while Wilbur and Orville discussed the situation. One of the witnesses later remarked that "we couldn't help notice how they held on to each other's hand, sort o'like they hated to let go; like two folks parting who weren't sure they'd ever see each other again."[29]

Finally, the two shook hands, and Orville climbed into place beside the engine prone on the lower wing with his feet braced against a board tacked to the trailing edge. His hips lay in a cradle free to move from side to side. To bank to the right, or to raise the left wing tip, he would shift the cradle to the right. This action would impart the correct warp to the wings and turn the rudder to the proper angle. With his left hand, Orville grasped the elevator level that would, hopefully, control the rise or fall of his machine.

His right hand operated a second lever that had only three positions. In the "off" position, it was pointed slightly to the right over the leading edge. When pushed straight forward, it opened the cock connecting the half-gallon gasoline tank to the engine and permitted starting. When Orville was prepared to begin the flight, he would pull the lever to the left, breaking a line that bound the aircraft and wheeled cart to the rail and permitting them to move forward. At the same time the anemometer that served as an airspeed indicator, a stop watch, and a propeller revolution counter were set in motion. The lever was not a throttle, for the engine had only two settings, on and off. Upon landing, however, the pilot would shove the control to the right to shut off the gas, kill the engine, and stop the instruments.

With Orville in place, Wilbur walked to the cluster of witnesses. Daniels was dispatched to man the camera pointed at the end of the rail. The elder brother now suggested that the men "not look too sad, but laugh and holler and clap . . . hands and try to cheer Orville up when he started."[30] Wilbur took his place on the right wing tip, replacing a low wooden bench that had supported the wing up to this point.

At 10:35 Orville moved his left hand back, and the craft began to move slowly into the 27-mile-per-hour wind. The men at the tips had little trouble keeping up with the slow forward speed of the machine. As it rose into the air after a 40-foot run, Daniels clicked his shutter and his companions broke into cheers as instructed. The airplane rose and fell erratically as it sailed forward. After twelve seconds of flight the craft struck the sand at a point about 120 feet from that at which it had left the rail. It hadn't taken very long. The machine hadn't traveled very far, but it had undeniably risen from the ground and flown forward under its own power, landing at a point as high as that from

The triumph of December 17, 1903.

which it had taken off. On this isolated North Carolina beach, a man had flown.

The small crew carried the aircraft back to the rail for a second trial, then retired to the shed for a bit of warmth. Johnny Moore, apparently more impressed by a full box of eggs on the Wright table than by what he had just witnessed, asked one of the station men where the brothers had acquired these treasures. The man jokingly remarked that the Wrights were the proud possessors of a famed chicken that produced eight to ten eggs a day. The men roared when Johnny, who had just witnessed one of the great events of the new century, opined that it was "only a common looking chicken."[31]

At 11:20 the group emerged from the building and Wilbur took his place on the machine for a flight 75 feet farther than the first. Twenty minutes later Orville made his second trial, which lasted fifteen seconds and covered a little over 200 feet. At about noon Wilbur tried again, turning in the best performance yet, a spectacular 852 feet in 59 seconds.

End of the third flight, December 17, 1903.

As the group clustered around the craft, which had been slightly damaged in the last flight, a gust of wind caught the machine and sent it tumbling. Daniels dropped head over heels through the wood and wires, suffering minor bruises. When the craft came to rest it was extensively damaged. Once the witnesses had helped drag the wreckage into the hangar, most returned to the station. One of the witnesses, perhaps young Johnny Moore, raced down the beach toward Kitty Hawk. The additional flights had apparently impressed him, for when he encountered Captain Bill Tate, an old friend of the Wrights and a commissioner of Currituck County, he was yelling, "They did it! They did it! Damned if they didn't fly!"[32]

The Wrights ate a leisurely lunch, then strolled down the beach to Kitty Hawk themselves. They called on old friends in the village to confirm the reports of their success, then proceeded to the lifesaving station where the station telegrapher added a wire to Bishop Milton Wright to a stack of outgoing messages from vacationing duck hunters. The telegram was received in Dayton at 5:27 P.M. that evening, nine days after Langley's disaster on the Potomac. In four short lines it announced the achievement of the age-old dream.

"Success four flights Thursday morning all against twenty-one mile wind started from level with engine power plane average speed through air thirty-one miles longest 57 seconds inform press home Christmas."[33]

Epilogue:

The Old Order Passes, 1905–1948

The Men

William Avery built and flew the last copy of the classic 1896 biplane for his old friend Chanute at the St. Louis Exposition of 1904. Avery, towed into the air by a winch, broke his ankle in a crash and withdrew from aeronautics. Many years later when applying for membership in the Early Birds, an organization for pioneer pilots, he was asked to give the date and place of his first flight. He proudly wrote, "Miller, Indiana—1896."

Alexander Graham Bell became even more closely involved in aeronautics following Langley's failure. In 1907 he organized the Aerial Experiment Association, with Glenn Hammond Curtiss as director of experiments. While his young associates were making aeronautical history with machines like *Red Wing, June Bug* and *Silver Dart*, the inventor of the telephone gradually slipped into the position of a figurehead.

William Paul Butusov struck out on his own after 1896. Seriously injured while flying an "improved" version of the *Albatross* the following year, he remained paralyzed for a number of months. When he encountered Chanute's son Charles on a Chicago street early in the twentieth century, he was greeted with the remark, "We thought you were dead."

Octave Chanute, his role as catalyst and patron complete with the Wright success, remained one of the most revered figures in aeronautics. After 1903 he was to become estranged from the Wrights, convinced that their penchant for secrecy and their insistence on bringing suit for patent infringement were damaging aeronautics. A reconciliation was under way at the time of Chanute's death in 1910.

Edson Fessenden Gallaudet, who had developed the wing-warping technique a year before the Wrights, became a major aircraft manufacturer. His firm, the Gallaudet Aircraft Co., formed the core of what was to become the General Dynamics Corp., one of the giants of the modern aerospace industry.

Augustus Moore Herring, badly shaken by news of the Wright success, was unable to believe that these two newcomers to the field had so quickly solved those problems he had been unable to overcome. In 1908 he was a competitor with the Wrights for the first U.S. Army airplane contract, but withdrew his bid without producing a finished machine. The following year he entered a short-lived partnership with Glenn H. Curtiss that ended in a long-running lawsuit with Curtiss and an out-of-court settlement of $500,000 to Herring's heirs. He died in 1926.

Edward Chalmers Huffaker, whose dirty shirts and makeshift spittoons had so exasperated Langley and the Wrights, continued to search for a perfectly stable airplane at Chanute's expense during the first decade of the new century. He eventually moved to Oxford, Mississippi, where he earned minor fame as a writer and died in 1936.

Samuel Pierpont Langley entered a period of decline after the failure of December 8, 1903. He died following a series of massive strokes in Aiken, South Carolina, in 1906.

Charles Matthews Manly left the Smithsonian in 1905 to enter business. By 1918 he had risen to the position of assistant general manager of the Curtiss Aeroplane and Motor Co. He died in 1927, still planning a final series of flight tests of the Langley aerodrome in which he hoped his son Charles would carry on the family tradition by serving as test pilot.

James Means lost his position as a leading aeronautical publicist with the issue of the *Epitome of the Aeronautical Annual* in 1911. He remained an aeronautical gadgeteer, devising everything from a device for sending smoke signals from an airplane in flight to a flying-machine control system based on the bicycle. He died on December 3, 1920.

John Montgomery returned to California after the Chicago conference. A decade later, in the wake of Langley's failure, he returned to aeronautics with a large tandem wing glider designed to be carried

into the air and dropped from a hot-air balloon. Montgomery abandoned this design when the ex-circus acrobat he had hired to pilot the
machine was killed in a crash and a second novice aviator seriously
injured a short time later. Montgomery himself died in the crash of his
final glider, *Evergreen*, in 1911.

Robert Henry Thurston, who had befriended both Chanute and
Langley and had served as a major professor for Zahm and Manly, died
on October 13, 1903, scarcely two months before the climatic events of
December.

Gustave Whitehead was never to leave the ground, but he did construct several engines that powered other men's flying machines after
1908. He died in 1927, a lonely religious fanatic whose fluid assets totaled
$8.

Orville Wright carried the patent fights against Glenn H. Curtiss
and others to a successful conclusion following his brother's death. As
a result of injuries sustained in a crash during the Army aircraft
acceptance trials at Fort Myer, Virginia, in 1908, he suffered recurring
attacks of sciatica in later years. Orville continued to devote his energies to the defense of the Wright priority as the first to fly. He retained
his boyish enthusiasm for all things mechanical up to the time of his
death in 1948 although he had no further serious impact on the technical development of the airplane after the second decade of the twentieth century.

Wilbur Wright became a figure of almost legendary proportions as
a result of his stunning aerial performances in Europe and America
after 1908. His energies drained by a series of bitterly contested suits,
he succumbed to typhoid fever on May 30, 1912. Biship Wright provided
the finest possible summation of his son's life in a diary entry that
evening:

> This morning at 3:15, Wilbur passed away, aged 45 years, 1 month and 14
> days. A short life, full of consequences. An unfailing intellect, imperturb-
> able temper, great self-reliance and as great modesty, seeing the right
> clearly, pursuing it steadily, he lived and died.

Albert Francis Zahm became a bitter opponent of the Wright brothers. A defense witness for Curtiss during the patent suits, he was also
a major figure in the 1914 trials of the Langley aerodrome. In speeches,
articles, and books written during the half century before his death in
1954 he would seek, unsuccessfully, to prove that others had been
capable of flight before 1903.

The Machines

A handful of the aircraft built in America before 1903 survive in the collection of the Smithsonian Institution's National Air and Space Museum. The Lilienthal glider purchased by William Randolph Hearst is displayed there, while John Montgomery's *Evergreen* awaits restoration at the museum's Silver Hill, Maryland, storage facility with the models Herring constructed for Chanute in 1895. All of Langley's models, with the exception of the successful No. 5, are housed there as well. Chanute's final biplane glider is now displayed at the Musée de l'Air near Paris.

The subsequent history of the great aerodrome and the 1903 Wright flyer are tortuous indeed. Rebuilt by Glenn Curtiss, with the assistance of Zahm, Manly, Walcott and Langley's old Smithsonian associates, the great aerodrome became the center of a controversy that lasted for over thirty years.

Curtiss saw the aerodrome project as a means of escaping the patent suits brought against him by the Wrights for infringement on their flight-control system. If the aerodrome could be made to fly, he could claim that the 1903 Wright airplane had not been the first capable of carrying a man in flight, thus gaining an enormous advantage in court.

In rebuilding the aerodrome, Curtiss incorporated many significant alterations reflecting the advance of aeronautics since 1903. The Langley, now essentially a 1914 airplane, did make a number of short hops, on the basis of which the Smithsonian began to advertise the aerodrome as "the first aircraft in history capable of flight with a pilot and several hundred pounds of useful load."

Orville Wright, carrying on the patent fight alone following Wilbur's death, was incensed by the Smithsonian's refusal to accept the brother's valid claim as the first to fly. As a result of the ongoing controversy, Orville refused to offer the 1903 flyer to the Smithsonian, sending it instead to the Science Museum in London, where it went on display in 1928. Not until 1942 was then secretary of the Smithsonian C. G. Abbot able to convince Orville of a change of heart at the institution. The priceless 1903 flyer, now universally recognized as the world's first airplane, was returned to the United States and given a place of honor in the Smithsonian's Arts and Industries Building, where it was dedicated on December 17, 1948, eleven months after Orville's death.

Visitors enter the new National Air and Space Museum through a gallery entitled "Milestones of Flight." The 1903 Wright flyer holds the central position, hanging suspended in the center of the room, surrounded by other air and space vehicles that have carried mankind on a journey begun at Kill Devil Hills.

Nestled in the upper corner of the gallery, above and to the right of the flyer, is the fifth of Langley's steam-powered flying models. Both aircraft serve as reminders of the tragedy and triumph experienced by the first generation of airmen who took to the skies on fragile wings fashioned by the human mind and hand.

Notes

Chapter 1. Huffman Prairie, 1904

1. Amos I. Root, "Our Homes," *Gleanings in Bee Culture* (Jan. 1, 1905), pp. 36–39.
2. *Liberty Hall and Cincinnati Gazette,* June 26, 1834; *Cincinnati Chronicle and Literary Gazette,* Oct. 25, 1834; *Daily Cincinnati Republican and Commercial Register,* Aug. 23, 1834, and Oct. 22, 1834.
3. John Trowbridge, "Darius Green and His Flying Machine," in Hazel Felaman, ed., *Poems That Live Forever* (New York, 1965), pp. 204–207.
4. Simon Newcomb, "Is the Airship Coming?" *McClure's* (Sept. 1901), pp. 562–565.
5. George Melville, "The Engineer and the Problem of Aerial Navigation," *North American Review* (Dec. 1901), pp. 820–821.
6. John Le Conte, "The Problem of the Flying Machine," *Popular Science Monthly* (Nov. 1888), p. 69.
7. The best treatments of early nineteenth-century aeronautics in the United States are to be found in Jeremiah Millbank, *The First Century of Flight in America* (Princeton, 1941); Tom D. Crouch, "The History of American Aviation, 1822–1905, Part 1," *Aviation Quarterly* (Spring 1976), pp. 8–22.
8. C. F. Duryea, "Learning How to Fly," *Proceedings of the Third International Conference on Aeronautics* (New York, 1894).

Chapter 2. An Engineer Discovers the Airplane

1. Ernest Archdeacon, "Mr. Chanute in Paris," *La Locomotion* (April 11, 1903), p. 225. See also *L'Aérophile* (May 1903), pp. 102–104.
2. L. Mouillard to O. Chanute, Feb. 23, 1892, Box 3, Octave Chanute Papers, Manuscript Division, Library of Congress. Hereafter cited as Chanute Collection.
3. C. H. Gibbs-Smith, *The Rebirth of Aviation in Europe* (London, 1974), covers the period of Wright influence in detail.
4. O. Chanute to L. Mouillard, Feb. 19, 1891, Box 22, Chanute Collection.
5. Details of Chanute's engineering career have been drawn from Box 18, Chanute Collection, and from Alicia Chanute Boyd, "Some Memories of My Father," unpublished ms., Library, National Air and Space Museum.
6. *Leavenworth* (Kansas) *Daily Tribune*, March 6, 1873; *Parsons* (Kansas) *Sun*, March 15, 1873; *Quincy* (Illinois) *Daily Evening Call*, March 10, 1873.
7. "Octave Chanute, A Biographical Sketch," *Cassier's Magazine* (March 1898), p. 448.
8. O. Chanute, "Resistance of the Air to Inclined Planes in Motion," Box 9, Chanute Collection.
9. For detailed treatments of early European aeronautics, see C. H. Gibbs-Smith, *Aviation: An Historical Survey* (London, 1960); C. Dollfus and H. Bouché, *Histoire de l'aéronautique* (Paris, 1932).
10. *Annual Report of the Aeronautical Society of Great Britain* (1867–1877 *passim*); J. L. Pritchard, "The Royal Aeronautical Society: The First Fifty Years," *Journal of the Royal Aeronautical Society* (March–July 1961).
11. Robert Thurston, "The Status of Aeronautics," *Science* (April 10, 1885), p. 295.
12. Israel Lancaster, "A Communication . . . ," *Annual Report of the Aeronautical Society of Great Britain* (London, 1883), p. 59.
13. *Ibid.*, p. 63.
14. *Buffalo* (New York) *Courier*, Aug. 26, 1886. See also *Programme of the Thirty Fifth Annual Meeting of the American Association for the Advancement of Science* (Buffalo, 1886), pp. 48, 109.
15. *Ibid.; New York Times*, Aug. 24, 1886.

Chapter 3. Experiments in Aerodynamics

1. *Detroit Evening News*, Aug. 11, 1875.
2. Biographical Notes, S. P. Langley Papers, Smithsonian Institution Archive; see also, Langley biographical notes in bibliography.
3. S. P. Langley to Simon Newcomb, Oct. 5, 1877, letter series, Simon Newcomb Papers, Library of Congress.

4. S. P. Langley, "The Story of Experiments in Mechanical Flight," *Aeronautical Annual* (Boston, 1897), pp. 11–25.
5. S. P. Langley, *Memoir on Mechanical Flight* (Washington, 1911), p. 7.
6. S. P. Langley, "The Flying Machine," *McClure's* (June 1897), p. 648.
7. Langley, "Story of Experiments," p. 13.
8. *Ibid.*
9. S. P. Langley, *Experiments in Aerodynamics* (Washington, 1891), p. 108.
10. Langley, *Experiments*, p. 7.
11. S. P. Langley, "Aerodromics 1," p. 108, S. P. Langley Collection, Smithsonian Institution. For purposes of footnoting, the author has lumped the consecutively numbered notebooks—or "waste books," as Langley called them—into one collection. The early volumes are held with Langley's Secretarial Papers in Smithsonian Archive, while the later numbers are housed in the Ramsey Room of the National Air and Space Museum Library. Hereafter all these numbered volumes will be referred to as "Aerodromics."
12. Information on the whirling table and all instruments have been drawn from Langley, "Aerodromics 1–2"; Langley, *Experiments*, p. 40; "Dr. Samuel P. Langley's Experiments in Aerodynamics," *Scientific American* (Feb. 18, 1892), pp. 1–2.
13. Langley, "Aerodromics 1"; Langley, *Experiments*, p. 44.
14. F. W. Very to S. P. Langley, Nov. 10, 1888, Box 2, Allegheny Observatory Papers, Smithsonian Archive.
15. Langley, *Experiments*, p. 107.
16. "Langley's Flying Machine," *Aeronautical Journal* (June 1897), p. 8.
17. W. Wright to C. D. Walcott, Dec. 22, 1910, in Marvin W. McFarland, ed., *The Papers of Wilbur and Orville Wright* (New York, 1953), p. 1004.
18. Lord Rayleigh, "Experiments in Aerodynamics," *Nature* (Dec. 3, 1892), p. 322.
19. Cyrus Adler, *I Have Considered the Days* (Philadelphia, 1941), p. 200.
20. Langley, "Aerodromics 10," pp. 48–68 (see especially the entry for Oct. 12, 1896); Langley, *Memoir*, pp. 9–17.
21. Langley, *Memoir*, p. 13; "Aerodromics 10," *passim.*
22. "Aerodromics 10," p. 66.
23. *Ibid.*

Chapter 4. *Chanute and* Progress in Flying Machines

1. "Early Presidents of the Society," *Civil Engineering* (Dec. 1937), p. 871.
2. O. Chanute to M. N. Forney, Nov. 10, 1886, Box 21, Chanute Collection.
3. For all late nineteenth-century European flying-machine experiments, see Gibbs-Smith, *Aviation*, and Dollfus and Bouché, *Histoire*. For individual figures mentioned, see entries by name in Paul Brockett, *Bibliography of Aeronautics* (Washington, D.C., 1910).

4. James Means, "An Editorial," *Aeronautical Annual* (Boston, 1895), p. 69.
5. L. Mouillard to O. Chanute, April 16, 1890, Box 3, Chanute Collection.
6. O. Chanute, *Progress in Flying Machines* (New York, 1894), p. 150.
7. *Ibid.*, p. 151.
8. L. Mouillard to O. Chanute, Nov. 2, 1884, Box 3, Chanute Collection.
9. O. Chanute to L. Mouillard, Nov. 12, 1894, Box 41, Chanute Collection.
10. O. Chanute to L. Mouillard, Dec. 12, 1892, Box 22, Book 30, 205, quoting a letter from the U.S. Patent Office.
11. O. Chanute to L. Mouillard, May 18, 1894, Box 4, Chanute Collection.
12. O. Chanute to L. Mouillard, June 15, 1894, Box 23, Book 31, p. 715, Chanute Collection; O. Chanute to L. Mouillard July 3, 1895, Box 23, Book 32, p. 541, Chanute Collection; L. Mouillard to O. Chanute, May 10, 1895, Box 3, Chanute Collection.
13. O. Chanute to L. Mouillard, Dec. 31, 1895, Box 23, Book 31, p. 948, Chanute Collection.
14. L. Mouillard to O. Chanute, Jan. 5, 1896, Box 3, Chanute Collection.
15. Chanute's correspondence with all figures mentioned is contained in the Chanute Collection. See collection inventory for a guide to the correspondence.
16. Phillip Jarrett, "Pilcher and the Multiplane—a Neglected Aspect of a Pioneer's Work," *Aeronautical Journal* (May 1976), pp. 298–309; Scrapbook, "Materials for the Study of Percy Pilcher," Chanute Collection, John Crerar Library, Chicago, Ill.; see also Chanute Collection, Pilcher correspondence, Library of Congress.
17. L. Hargrave to O. Chanute, Dec. 2, 1892, Box 1, Chanute Collection.
18. L. Hargrave to A. F. Zahm, Feb. 8, 1893, Box 62, A. F. Zahm Collection, Notre Dame University Archive, South Bend, Ind.
19. O. Chanute to R. Thurston, Jan. 11, 1889; O. Chanute to R. Thurston, Dec. 21, 1889; O. Chanute to R. Thurston, Feb. 4, 1889, all in Box 21, Book 25, Chanute Collection.
20. O. Chanute, *Aerial Navigation: A Lecture to the Students of Sibley College, Cornell University* (New York, 1891).
21. O. Chanute to F. H. Wenham, Sept. 13, 1892, Box 22, Book 30, p. 318, Chanute Collection.
22. O. Chanute to M. N. Forney, Jan. 18, 1894, Box 23, Book 31, p. 297, Chanute Collection.

Chapter 5. A Meeting in Chicago

1. A. F. Zahm, "Aerial Navigation," *Journal of the Franklin Institute* (Oct. 1894).
2. A. F. Zahm, "Autobiographical Notes," Box 91, A. F. Zahm Collection, Notre Dame University.
3. *Ibid.*

4. Rossiter Johnson, *A History of the World's Columbian Exposition Held in Chicago in 1893* (New York, 1898).

5. A. F. Zahm, "Diary of the Aeronautical Congress of 1893, by Professor A. F. Zahm, General Secretary," unpublished ms. in Box 91, A. F. Zahm Collection. This document is a precise chronology of all events leading up to the congress.

6. *Ibid.*, May 21, 1892.

7. *Ibid.*, Sept. 10, 1892.

8. *Ibid.*, Oct. 19, 1892.

9. *Ibid.*, Sept.–Dec. 1892.

10. O. Chanute to A. F. Zahm, letter dated only "Spring 1892," Box 62, A. F. Zahm Collection.

11. Zahm, "Diary," July 12, 1892.

12. E. C. Huffaker, "Biographical Notes," in E. C. Huffaker Biographical File, Library, National Air and Space Museum.

13. E. C. Huffaker, "Soaring Flight," in *Proceedings of the International Conference on Aerial Navigation, Held in Chicago, August 2, 3 and 4, 1893* (New York, 1894), p. 215.

14. *Ibid.*

15. Arthur D. Spearman, *John Joseph Montgomery* (Santa Clara, Calif., 1967), p. 17.

16. A. D. Spearman, *John Joseph Montgomery, 1858–1911: Father of Basic Flying* (Santa Clara, Calif., 1967); C. H. Gibbs-Smith, *Aviation*, p. 59; McFarland, ed., *The Papers of Wilbur and Orville Wright*, p. 409; V. Lougheed, *Aeroplane Designing for Amateurs* (Chicago, 1912), pp. 20–21.

17. U.S. Court of Claims, Case No. 33, 852, R. M. Montgomery *et al.* v. the U.S., Complaint's Affidavits, Defendant's Copy, Box 73, Wright Collection, Manuscript Division, Library of Congress.

18. H. Dare, "The Personality of the Man," *San Francisco Call*, May 7, 1905.

19. Chanute, *Progress*, p. 150.

20. *Ibid.*, p. 249; J. J. Montgomery, "Some Early Gliding Experiments in America," *Aeronautics* (Jan. 1901), pp. 47–50.

21. J. J. Montgomery, *The Aeroplane* (Santa Clara, Calif., 1905), p. 21; see also J. J. Montgomery, "Soaring Flight," unpublished ms., Library, National Air and Space Museum.

22. J. J. Montgomery to R. Montgomery, Dec. 22, 1885, in R. Montgomery file, C. D. Walcott Papers, Smithsonian Archive.

23. J. J. Montgomery to James Montgomery, Sept. 7, 1886, in R. Montgomery file, C. D. Walcott Papers, Smithsonian Archive.

24. *The Aeroplane: A Scientific Study* (Santa Clara, Calif., 1905).

25. J. J. Montgomery, "Some Early Gliding Experiments in America," *Aeronautics* (Jan. 1909).

26. J. J. Montgomery, "The Origins of Warping," *Aeronautics* (June 1910), pp. 63–64.

27. Windsor Josselyn, "He Flew in 1883," *Harper's Magazine* (June 1940).

28. *Ibid.*

29. Inscription on Otay Mesa Monument.

30. J. J. Montgomery to J. Montgomery, Aug. 25, 1895, Library, National Air and Space Museum.

31. Zahm, "Diary," n.d.

32. *Ibid.*

33. *Pittsburgh Dispatch,* Jan. 23, 1894.

34. *Engineering News and American Railroad Journal* (July 20, 1893), p. 55.

35. Montgomery Affidavit, p. 329.

36. J. J. Montgomery to R. Montgomery, Aug. 30, 1894, Library, National Air and Space Museum.

37. O. Chanute to J. Montgomery, July 13, 1895, Box 23, Chanute Collection.

38. O. Chanute to J. Montgomery, Aug. 16, 1895, Box 23, Chanute Collection.

Chapter 6. Boston: The Third Circle

1. S. Cabot to O. Chanute, undated letter, Box 1, Chanute Collection; "He Soars Like a Bird," *Philadelphia Press,* Jan. 12, 1894; "Flight in the Air," *Boston Advertiser,* July 22, 1893.

2. S. Cabot to O. Chanute, Jan. 30, 1894, Box 1, Chanute Collection.

3. J. Means, *The Problem of Manflight* (Boston, 1894).

4. J. Meade (J. Means), "The Scientific Value of Flying Models," *Frank Leslie's Weekly* (Jan. 1893), p. 42; J. Means, "Manflight, the Last Mechanical Problem of the Century," *Boston Transcript,* July 17, 1893.

5. *Ibid.;* Means, *Problem,* p. 15.

6. J. Means to J. H. Holmes, June 27, 1893, "Correspondence on Aeronautical Subjects by James Means," in James Means folder, Historical Collection, American Institute of Aeronautics and Astronautics, Manuscript Division, Library of Congress. Hereafter cited as AIAA.

7. J. Means to J. B. Walker, April 29, 1896, "Correspondence." As a result of Means's effort, Walker was to become an aeronautical enthusiast, featuring frequent articles dealing with the subject in *Cosmopolitan* and building a personal relationship with men like Langley and Chanute. Perhaps Walker's most successful venture in the field was his sponsorship of an aeronautical essay contest featuring entries by such well-known figures as John Holland (inventor of the submarine), Mouillard, and Maxim.

8. J. Means to I. Lancaster, Nov. 10, 1894, "Correspondence."

9. J. Means, "Senate Bill No. 302 . . . ," *Aeronautical Annual* (Boston, 1896), pp. 80–84; see also *L'Aérophile* (Feb. 1897), pp. 23–25.

10. W. H. Pickering, "The Vertical Screw or Helicopter," in *Navigating the Air: A Scientific Statement of the Progress of Aeronautical Science up to the Present Time* (New York, 1907), p. 114.

11. David Todd, "Aerial High Speeds," in *Navigating the Air*, p. 195.

12. A. L. Rotch, *Sounding the Ocean of Air* (London, 1900); assorted undated articles in Langley Scrapbooks, 1892–1897, Library, National Air and Space Museum.

13. "Kites and Flying Ships," *Boston Transcript*, March 7, 1896; *Elizabeth* (New Jersey) *Journal*, Feb. 10, 1895; "Aerial Navigation," *New York Herald*, Dec. 23, 1894.

14. "Mr. Lamson's Airship"; C. H. Lamson, "Work on the Great Diamond," in *Aeronautical Annual* (Boston, 1896), pp. 133–137; "Mr. Lamson's Airship," *Portland* (Maine) *Daily Press*, Aug. 21, 1896.

15. "Mr. Lamson's Airship," *New York Sun*, Aug. 24, 1896; C. H. Lamson to H. A. Hazen, June 27, 1897, in C. H. Lamson biographical file, Library, National Air and Space Museum.

16. "Up 100 Feet on His Kite," *New York Sun*, June 21, 1897; "Lamson's Man-lifting Kite," *Aeronautical Journal* (June 1897), p. 20; "Airship on Trial," *New York Herald*, June 27, 1897; Hodgkins Fund Records, Smithsonian Institution Archive.

17. Grace N. Gould, *New York Journal*, July 11, 1897.

18. Constitution of the Boston Aeronautical Society in James Means file, AIAA.

19. J. Means to A. Pope, March 1, 1896, "Correspondence," AIAA.

20. Assorted correspondence of James Means, "Correspondence," AIAA.

21. J. Means to A. A. Merrill, Feb. 13, 1897; Feb. 16, 1897; Feb. 5, 1897, "Correspondence," AIAA.

22. *Ibid.*

23. S. Cabot to O. Chanute, May 7, 1897, Box 1, Chanute Collection.

24. Stella Randolph, *The Last Flights of Gustave Whitehead* (Washington, 1937), pp. 24–25.

25. S. Cabot to O. Chanute, May 18, 1897, Box 1, Chanute Collection.

26. See especially, Randolph, *Last Flights;* William O'Dwyer and Stella Randolph, *History by Contract* (West Germany, 1978).

27. Randolph, *Last Flights*, p. 27.

28. W. J. O'Dwyer, "Did Whitehead Fly before the Wrights?" *American Aircraft Modeler* (Nov. 1968).

29. Stanley Y. Beach, "A New Flying Machine," *Scientific American* (June 8, 1901), p. 19.

30. "Connecticut Night Watchman Thinks He Has Found Out How to Fly," *New York Herald*, June 16, 1901.

31. "Flying," *Bridgeport* (Connecticut) *Sunday Herald*, Aug. 18, 1901.

32. "The Whitehead Flying Machine," *American Inventor* (April 1, 1902), pp. 1–2.

33. C. Manly to F. Hodge, Sept. 20, 1901, "Aerodromics 10," pp. 29, 441.

34. John Crane, "Did Whitehead Actually Fly?" *National Aeronautic Association Magazine* (Dec. 1936).

35. Quoted in C. H. Gibbs-Smith, "The Flight Claims of Gustave Whitehead," unpublished ms., Library, National Air and Space Museum. The author acknowledges an enormous debt to Mr. Gibbs-Smith for his guidance in the study of Whitehead's career.
36. "The Whitehead Flying Machine," "The Latest Marvel in Flying Machines," *Broadway Magazine* (Nov. 1903), pp. 124–127; "Aerial Machines for $2000 Each," *Aeronautical World* (Aug. 1, 1902), p. 21; "Flying Machines Soon at $2000 Each," *New York World* (Nov. 18, 1901).
37. Gibbs-Smith, "Flight Claims."
38. "Last Flap of the Whitehead Machine," *Bridgeport Evening Farmer*, April 5, 1902; "Whitehead Still at Work," *Bridgeport Stoneland*, Aug. 2, 1902.
39. "W. G. Whitehead's New Machine," *Aeronautical World* (Dec. 1, 1902), p. 99; "Gustave Whitehead's New Machine," *Aeronautical World* (May 1, 1903), p. 225; "Whitehead's Experiments," *Aeronautical World* (July 1, 1903), pp. 270–71; *New York Sun*, Aug. 31, 1903. Additional general information on Whitehead's work can be found in assorted general news articles, including "Airships Which Can Navigate the Skies According to the Inventor," *New York World*, March 4, 1898; "Whitehead's Flying Condor," Langley *et al.*, Langley Scrapbooks, Library, National Air and Space Museum.

Chapter 7. S. P. Langley: The Scientist as Engineer

1. S. P. Langley to C. Abbe, Nov. 5, 1868, Allegheny Observatory Papers, Smithsonian Institution Archive. Hereafter cited as Observatory Papers.
2. S. P. Langley to C. Abbe, June 14, 1869, Observatory Papers.
3. S. P. Langley to C. S. Pierce, Nov. 11, 1880, Observatory Papers.
4. Quoted in D. Obendorfer, "Samuel P. Langley: Solar Scientist, 1867–1891," unpublished Ph.D. dissertation, University of California, 1969, p. 232.
5. Henry Adams, *The Education of Henry Adams* (New York, 1931), p. 377.
6. "Notes on Wednesday Evening Meetings," Alexander Graham Bell Papers, Library of Congress.
7. "Biographical Sketch of Dr. Albert F. Zahm," Box 91, A. F. Zahm Papers; A. F. Zahm, "A Crisis in Aeroplane Litigation," *Popular Mechanics* (June 1912), p. 778; "Mattulath Patent Appeal, 1912," *Transcript of Record, Court of Appeals, District of Columbia, January Term, No. 751,* Library, National Air and Space Museum; A. F. Zahm, "Aeronautics at the Catholic University," A. F. Zahm Papers.
8. S. P. Langley, "Aerodromics 10," p. 20, Library, National Air and Space Museum. Throughout this chapter the author has chosen to cite manuscript sources whenever possible. The reader should be aware that the following original published sources have also been consulted: "Experiments with the Langley Aerodrome," *Report of the Board of Regents of the Smithsonian Institution*

for 1904 (Washington, D.C., 1905), pp. 113–125; "The Flying Machine," *McClure's* (June 1897), pp. 646–660; *Researches and Experiments in Aerial Navigation* (Washington, D.C., 1908).

9. *Chicago Tribune,* May 18, 1892.

10. S. P. Langley, "Mechanical Flight," *Cosmopolitan* (May 1892), p. 55.

11. S. P. Langley to J. S. Billings, June 2, 1891; S. P. Langley to Lefferts and Co., March 3, 1891; in Secretarial Papers, Outgoing Correspondence, S. P. Langley, Box 33, "Aerodromics 201, Part 1," Smithsonian Institution Archive, hereafter cited as Outgoing Correspondence.

12. Secretarial Papers, 1891–1906, Administrative File—Hodgkins Fund, Collection 31, Smithsonian Institution Archive.

13. "Aerodromics 10," pp. 67–69; "Aerodromics 23," p. 120, Library, National Air and Space Museum.

14. S. P. Langley to J. E. Watkins, April 30, 1891, Box 33, "Aerodromics 20, Part 1," p. 2; "Aerodromics 10," p. 68; "Aerodromics 23," p. 156.

15. "Aerodromics 4," pp. 27–53; "Aerodromics 23," p. 156; "Aerodromics 10," p. 94.

16. "Aerodromics 10," pp. 92, 101; "Aerodromics 4," p. 27; "Aerodromics 23," p. 156.

17. "Aerodromics 10," p. 107.

18. "Aerodromics 5," pp. 14–24, 185; "Aerodromics 6," pp. 161–285.

19. "Aerodromics 10," p. 110; "Aerodromics 4," p. 195.

20. "Aerodromics 10," pp. 112–114; "Aerodromics 4," pp. 200–201.

21. C. G. Abbot, "Samuel Pierpont Langley," typed ms. in Walcott Papers, Smithsonian Institution Archive.

22. "Aerodromics 11," pp. 206–210; "Aerodromics 10," p. 115.

23. *Ibid.*; "Aerodromics 7, Waste Book 15," pp. 38–80; "Aerodromics 5, Waste Book 7," pp. 221–231; "Aerodromics 6, Waste Book 11," p. 185.

24. "Aerodromics 10," p. 140; "Aerodromics 24," p. 370.

25. "Aerodromics 24," p. 376; "Aerodromics 10," p. 154.

26. "Aerodromics 7, Waste Book 15," pp. 26–32; "Aerodromics 6, Waste Book 11," p. 268.

27. "Aerodromics 5, Waste Book 7," p. 231.

28. "Aerodromics 24," pp. 380–384; "Aerodromics 10," pp. 164–170.

29. "Aerodromics 10," p. 180; R. L. Reed to S. P. Langley, Jan. 25, 1896, in "Aerodromics 24," p. 52.

30. O. Chanute to S. P. Langley, Nov. 24, 1894, Box 17, Incoming Correspondence; S. P. Langley to O. Chanute, Nov. 27, 1894, Box 2, Chanute Collection.

31. O. Chanute to S. P. Langley, Nov. 29, 1894, Box 17, Incoming Correspondence.

32. Adler, *I Have Considered the Days,* p. 211.

33. "Augustus Herring," *Dictionary of American Biography;* James V. Martin, "The Aircraft Conspiracy," *The Libertarian* (March 1924), pp. 120–127; A. M. Herring Biographical File, Library, National Air and Space Museum.

34. Herring-Chanute Correspondence, Sept.–Nov. 1894, Box 1, Chanute Collection.
35. A. M. Herring to O. Chanute, May 25, 1895, Box 1, Chanute Collection.
36. Abbot, "Samuel Pierpont Langley."
37. *The Capital* (Oct. 21, 1893), p. 9.
38. "Aerodromics 24," p. 386.
39. A. M. Herring to O. Chanute, June 25, 1895, Box 1, Chanute Collection.
40. A. M. Herring to O. Chanute, Sept. 6, 1895, Box 1, Chanute Collection.
41. A. M. Herring to O. Chanute, Nov. 10, 1895, Box 1, Chanute Collection,
42. "Aerodromics 24," p. 391.
43. S. P. Langley, memo in front of "Aerodromics 24."
44. "Aerodromics 24," pp. 389–390.
45. *Ibid.*
46. A. G. Bell to S. P. Langley, "Aerodromics 24," p. 1.
47. "Aerodromics 10," pp. 120–126.

Chapter 8. Lilienthal and the Americans

1. All details of this episode are drawn from R. W. Wood, "Lilienthal's Last Flights," *Boston Transcript*, Aug. 16, 1896.
2. Biographical details are drawn from Otto Lilienthal, *Birdflight As the Basis of Aviation: A Contribution towards a System of Aviation* (London, 1911), pp. x–xii; Karl Mullenhaff, "Otto Lilienthal: A Memorial Address Delivered before the Deutschen Verein für forderung der Luftschiffahrt, November 26, 1896," *Aeronautical Annual* (Boston, 1897); C. H. Gibbs-Smith, *Aviation* (London, 1971); Gerhard Halle, *Otto Lilienthal* (Düsseldorf, 1976); Gerhard Halle, *Otto Lilienthal und seine Flugzeug-Konstruktionen* (Düsseldorf, 1962).
3. Otto Lilienthal, "Practical Experiments for the Development of Human Flight," *Report of the Board of Regents of the Smithsonian Institution for 1893* (Washington, 1894), p. 199.
4. Halle, *Flugzeug-Konstruktronen.*
5. "How to Sail through the Air," *New York Herald*, June 24, 1894.
6. All quotes drawn from undated news articles in S. P. Langley Scrapbooks, 1891–1896, Library, National Air and Space Museum.
7. S. P. Langley to A. M. Herring, Aug. 6, 1895, in O. Chanute Scrapbook No. 2, "Otto Lilienthal" John Crerar Library.
8. S. Cabot to O. Chanute, Sept. 28, 1896, Box 1, Chanute Collection.
9. *New York Journal,* May 14, 1896; "Another Successful Trip in the Journal's Flying Machine," *San Francisco Examiner,* May 24, 1896; Accession File, Lilienthal Standard Glider, Registrar's Office, Library, National Air and Space Museum.
10. "America's First Glider Club: From Contemporary Notes of Charles P. Steinmetz," *Sportsman Pilot* (Dec. 1930), pp. 26–27, 46.

11. A. M. Herring to O. Chanute, Dec. 24, 1894; Jan. 1, 1895; Feb. 28, 1895; March 17, 1895; March 28, 1895, Box 1; . Chanute to A. M. Herring, Dec. 3, 1894, Box 23, Book 32, p. 436, all in Chanute Collection.

12. A. M. Herring to O. Chanute, Oct. 1, 1894; Sept. 25, 1894; Nov. 11, 1894, all in Box 1, Chanute Collection.

Chapter 9. Chanute: The Glider Years

1. O. Chanute to C. H. Hastings, Dec. 3, 1888, Box 21, Book 27, pp. 458–466, Chanute Collection.

2. O. Chanute to L. Mouillard, June 20, 1891, Box 22, Book 30, p. 415, Chanute Collection.

3. O. Chanute to F. H. Wenham, Oct. 21, 1892, Box 23, Book 32, pp. 184–189, Chanute Collection.

4. O. Chanute to A. M. Herring, Dec. 31, 1894, Box 23, Book 32, p. 436, Chanute Collection.

5. *Ibid.*

6. *Ibid.*

7. A. M. Herring to O. Chanute, Feb. 17, 1895; March 28, 1895; Feb. 28, 1895; March 20, 1895; March 17, 1895; all in Box 1, Chanute Collection.

8. A. M. Herring to O. Chanute, March 17, 1895; March 28, 1895, Box 1, Chanute Collection.

9. O. Chanute to J. Means, Oct. 29, 1895, Box 23, Book 32, p. 436, Chanute Collection.

10. O. Chanute to A. M. Herring, June 20, 1895; June 25, 1895, Box 23, Book 32, Chanute Collection.

11. O. Chanute to A. M. Herring, June 27, 1895, Box 23, Book 32, p. 523, Chanute Collection; A. M. Herring to O. Chanute, July 7, 1895, Box 1, Chanute Collection; O. Chanute to A. M. Herring, July 18, 1895, Box 23, Book 32, p. 523, Chanute Collection.

12. *Ibid.*

13. O. Chanute, "Gliding Experiments," *Journal of the Western Society of Engineers* (Nov. 1897), p. 601; O. Chanute, "Recent Experiments in Gliding Flight." *Aeronautical Annual* (Boston, 1897), p. 30.

14. Chanute, "Gliding Experiments," pp. 603–606; Chanute, "Recent Experiments," p. 35.

15. O. Chanute to J. Means, Jan. 28, 1897, Box 24, Book 34, p. 32, Chanute Collection; *Boston Herald*, Oct. 4, 1896; *Chicago Tribune*, April 6, 1911; W. P. Butusov affidavits and biographical data in Box 3, Chanute Collection.

16. This quotation is drawn from a small brown pocket notebook in which Chanute recorded the events of the summer of 1896. It is to be found in Box 9, Chanute Collection. Unless otherwise noted, all quotes and data on the 1896 machines and trials are drawn from this document.

17. Chanute, "Recent Experiments," p. 33.
18. *Ibid.*
19. "Diary"; Chanute, "Recent Experiments," p. 605; Chanute, "Gliding Experiments," pp. 34–35.
20. Chanute, "Gliding Experiments," p. 606; Chanute, "Recent Experiments," pp. 37–39.
21. Chanute, "Gliding Experiments," pp. 607–608; Chanute, "Recent Experiments," p. 39; A. M. Herring, "Recent Advances toward a Solution of the Problem of the Century," *Aeronautical Annual* (Boston, 1897), pp. 68–71. H. L. Scamehorn, *Balloons to Jets: A Century of Aeronautics in Illinois, 1855–1955* (Chicago, 1957), contains a good secondary account of the trials.
22. Herring, "Recent Advances"; A. M. Herring, "Dynamic Flight," *Aeronautical Annual* (Boston, 1896), pp. 89–101; Carl Dientsbach, "Invention of the Chanute Glider," *American Aeronaut* (June 1908), p. 165; James V. Martin, "When Will Merit Count in Aviation?" *The Libertarian* (Oct. 1924), pp. 589–609.
23. Frederic Culick, "The Origins of the First Powered Man-Carrying Airplane," *Scientific American* (July 1979), p. 88.
24. O. Chanute, "The Evolution of the Two Surface Machine," *Aeronautics* (Sept.–Nov. 1908).
25. A. M. Herring to O. Chanute, March 17, 1901, Box 1, Chanute Collection.
26. O. Chanute to A. M. Herring, March 24, 1901, Box 25, Book 37, p. 361, Chanute Collection.
27. Herring, "Recent Advances"; Herring, "Dynamic Flight," p. 89; Martin, "When Will Merit Count."
28. "Aerodromics 1895," pp. 70–80. This account and the accompanying drawing of the Herring model are the key bits of evidence supporting Herring's contention.
29. W. P. Butusov affidavits and biographical data, Box 8–9, Chanute Collection; Chanute, "Recent Experiments," pp. 39–41; Chanute, "Gliding Experiments," pp. 609–611.
30. Chanute, "Recent Experiments," p. 39.
31. *Chicago Inter-Ocean,* Aug. 27, 1896.
32. Chanute, "Recent Experiments," p. 47.
33. O. Chanute to J. Means, Nov. 14, 1896, Box 24, Book 33, p. 464, Chanute Collection.
34. *Ibid.*

Chapter 10. Herring Alone, 1896–1898

1. For Edison's aeronautics see *New York World,* June 7, 1896; T. Edison, "Attempt to Solve the Problem of Flight," *Aeronautical World* (Jan. 1903), p. 138; "Edison's Views on Flying," *Aeronautical World* (Feb. 1903), p. 164; "Edison's Ships of the Air," *New York World,* Nov. 17, 1895. For John Holland see J.

Holland, "How to Fly As a Bird," in *Navigating the Air;* J. Holland, "Aerial Navigation," *Cosmopolitan* (Nov. 1892); J. Holland, "Mechanical Flight," *Cassier's* (Feb. 1893), p. 243.

2. *Portland Oregonian,* Jan. 24, 1894; *Boston Herald,* July 18, 1893; *Toledo Bee,* July 17, 1893.

3. Chanute, "Recent Experiments," p. 38.

4. O. Chanute to J. Means, May 31, 1897, Box 24, Book 34, p. 366, Chanute Collection.

5. O. Chanute to J. Means, November 14, 1896, Box 24, Book 34, p. 464, Chanute Collection; O. Chanute to F. H. Wenham, Sept. 24, 1897, Box 24, Book 34, p. 584, Chanute Collection.

6. All details of the short-lived 1896 triplane are contained in A. M. Herring's "Recent Advances toward a Solution of the Problem of the Century," *Aeronautical Annual* (Boston, 1897), pp. 68–74.

7. *Ibid.,* pp. 70–74.

8. O. Chanute to J. Means, July 18, 1897; Box 24, Book 34, p. 463, Chanute Collection.

9. O. Chanute to J. Means, Aug. 10, 1897, Box 24, Book 34, p. 483, Chanute Collection.

10. *Chicago Tribune,* April 16, 1897.

11. For description of St. Joseph, Michigan, in 1897–1898, see *St. Joseph Herald-Press,* Feb. 22, 1964.

12. *Chicago Times-Herald,* Sept. 29, 1897.

13. *Ibid.;* J. Means, Jr., *James Means and the Problem of Manflight* (Washington, 1964), p. 76.

14. *Chicago Times-Herald,* Sept. 8, 1897.

15. Untitled article, Sept. 11, 1897, in Box 16, Chanute Collection.

16. O. Chanute to J. Means, Dec. 5, 1897, Box 24, Book 34, p. 77, Chanute Collection.

17. *Ibid.;* A. M. Herring to O. Chanute, Jan. 5, 1902, Box 2, Chanute Collection; see also assorted correspondence in A. M. Herring Collection, Olin Library, Cornell University.

18. O. Chanute to J. Means, Dec. 5, 1897, Box 24, Book 34, p. 77, Chanute Collection; A. M. Herring to O. Chanute, Jan. 5, 1902, Box 2, Chanute Collection.

19. *Niles* (Michigan) *Mirror,* Oct. 28, 1898; *Elmira Advertiser,* Nov. 18, 1898; *The Horseless Age* (May 1897), p. 7.

20. Herring, "Recent Advances," p. 40.

21. *Ibid.;* A. M. Herring, "Early Herring Correspondence," *American Aeronaut* (Feb. 1908), pp. 154–157. See also ms. in Carl Dientsbach File, AIAA History Collection, Library of Congress.

22. A. F. Zahm, *Aerial Navigation* (New York, 1911).

23. *Benton Harbor* (Michigan) *Evening Star,* Oct. 3, 1898; Martin, "When Will Merit Count"; *Horseless Age,* Assorted issues containing reminiscences; *St. Jo-*

seph Times-Herald, Feb. 22, 1964; "Herring's Airship Actually Flew," *American Aeronaut* (April 1908), p. 6032.
24. *Niles* (Michigan) *Mirror*, Oct. 28, 1898; *Chicago Evening News*, Nov. 17, 1898; Martin, "When Will Merit Count."
25. Herring, "Early Herring Correspondence," pp. 154–157.
26. O. Chanute to A. M. Herring, March 4, 1901, Box 2, Chanute Collection; A. M. Herring to O. Chanute, March 17, 1901, Box 2, Chanute Collection; A. M. Herring to O. Chanute, Jan. 5, 1902, Box 2, Chanute Collection.

Chapter 11. Two Gentlemen from Dayton

1. Wright to O. Chanute, May 13, 1900, in McFarland, ed., *The Papers of Wilbur and Orville Wright*. The Wright papers are housed in the Manuscript Division of the Library of Congress. Most citations in this chapter, however, are made of the published edition to encourage readers to explore the extended quotations and useful footnotes and commentary provided by McFarland.
2. *New York Times*, June 1, 1912.
3. Ivonette Miller, *Wright Reminiscences* (Dayton, 1978), p. 32.
4. *Ibid.*
5. *Ibid.*
6. Wilbur Wright, deposition of April 3, 1912, in *Papers*, p. v.
7. For biographical detail, see Fred C. Kelly, *The Wright Brothers* (New York, 1943). John Evangelist Walsh, *One Day at Kitty Hawk* (New York, 1975), is a biased view of the Wrights' relationship; Harry Coombs, *Kill Devil Hills* (New York, 1979), is a good recent treatment of the Wrights' story.
8. R. Wright to K. Wright, Nov. 1888, in the possession of Mrs. Ivonette Miller, Dayton, Ohio.
9. W. Wright to the Smithsonian Institution, May 30, 1899, *Papers*, pp. 4–5; R. Rathbun to W. Wright, June 22, 1899, *Papers*, p. 5.
10. *Binghamton* (New York) *Republican*, June 4, 1886; James Means, "Wheeling and Flying," *Aeronautical Annual* (Boston, 1896).
11. W. Wright to O. Chanute, May 13, 1900, *Papers*, p. 15.
12. Assession file, Gallaudet Kite, NASM Registrar's Office; "Diary, 1898," Gallaudet Family Papers, Manuscript Division, Library of Congress; E. F. Gallaudet biographical file, Library, National Air and Space Museum.
13. O. Wright, deposition, Papers, pp. 5–12; W. Wright to O. Chanute, May 13, 1900, Box 5, Chanute Collection; O. Chanute to W. Wright, May 17, 1900, Box 17, Wright Papers, Manuscript Division, Library of Congress; "Fragmentary Memorandum by Wilbur Wright," *Papers*, pp. 24–28; W. Wright to K. Wright, Oct. 14, 1900, Box 4, Wright Collection.
14. O. Wright to K. Wright, Oct. 18, 1901, Box 4, Wright Collection.
15. W. Wright to K. Wright, Oct. 18, 1903, *Papers*, p. 367.
16. W. Wright to M. Wright, Nov. 23, 1903, *Papers*, p. 383.

17. W. Tate, "I Was Host to the Wright Brothers at Kitty Hawk," *U.S. Air Services* (Dec. 1943), pp. 29–30.

18. O. Wright to K. Wright, Oct. 18, 1900, Box 4, Wright Collection.

19. For general information on the 1900 flying season see *Papers*, pp. 28–45.

20. W. Wright to O. Chanute, May 12, 1901, Box 5, Chanute Collection.

21. Data on all Wright machines have been drawn from *Papers*.

22. E. C. Huffaker, "Experiments with Gliding Models Conducted by E. C. Huffaker of Chucky City, Tennessee. Under Instructions from O. Chanute of Chicago, Illinois, 1899," John Crerar Library, Chicago, Ill.; O. Chanute to E. C. Huffaker, Dec. 22, 1898, Chanute Collection.

23. O. Chanute to W. Wright, June 29, 1901, Box 5, Chanute Collection.

24. *Ibid.*

25. W. Wright to O. Chanute, July 1, 1901, Box 5, Chanute Collection.

26. Huffaker, "Diary," *Papers*, p. 73.

27. W. Wright to M. Wright, July 28, 1901, Box 5, Wright Collection.

28. W. Wright, Diary A, July 20, 1901, Box 1, Wright Collection.

29. *Ibid.;* see also Huffaker, "Diary," *Papers*, p. 82.

30. K. Wright to M. Wright, Aug. 26, 1901, Box 5, Wright Collection.

31. W. Wright to G. Spratt, Sept. 21, 1901, *Papers*, p. 118.

32. *Ibid.*

33. K. Wright to M. Wright, Sept. 25, 1901, Box 5, Wright Collection.

34. W. Wright to O. Chanute, Oct. 6, 1901, Box 5, Chanute Collection.

35. *Ibid.* The most detailed description of the Wright wind tunnels is contained in Fred S. Howard, "1901 Wind Tunnels," in *Papers*, p. 547; O. Chanute to W. Wright, Oct. 12, 1901, Box 17, Wright Collection; W. Wright to O. Chanute, Nov. 2, 1901, Box 5, Chanute Collection; W. Wright to O. Chanute, Dec. 1, 1901, Box 5, Chanute Collection.

36. W. Wright to O. Chanute, Oct. 24, 1901, Box 5, Chanute Collection; O. Chanute to W. Wright, Dec. 19, 1901, Box 17, Wright Collection; O. Chanute to W. Wright, Jan. 1, 1902, Box 17, Wright Collection; W. Wright to O. Chanute, Jan. 5, 1902, Box 5, Chanute Collection.

37. O. Chanute to W. Wright, Jan. 1, 1902, Box 5, Chanute Collection.

38. W. Wright to G. Spratt, Jan. 23, 1892, *Papers*, p. 205.

39. A. M. Herring to O. Chanute, May 29, 1902, Box 1, Chanute Collection.

40. A. M. Herring to O. Chanute, July 7, 1902, Box 1, Chanute Collection; O. Chanute to A. M. Herring, July 20, 1902, Box 25, Book 38, p. 347, Chanute Collection.

41. O. Chanute to W. Wright, March 4, 1902, Box 17, Wright Collection.

42. W. Wright to O. Chanute, Sept. 5, 1902, Box 5, Chanute Collection.

43. K. Wright to M. Wright, Aug. 20, 1902, Box 5, Wright Collection.

44. W. Wright to G. Spratt, Sept. 16, 1902, *Papers*, p. 253; W. Wright to O. Chanute, Sept. 21, 1902, Box 5, Chanute Collection; O. Wright, Diary B, Sept. 23, 1902, Box 1, Wright Collection.

45. O. Chanute to S. P. Langley, Oct. 13, 1902, Box 34, Secretary, 1891–1906,

Incoming Correspondence, Box 34, Smithsonian Archives; O. Wright, Diary B, Oct. 13, 1902, Box 1, Wright Collection. See also O. Chanute to W. Wright, July 29, 1902, Box 17, Wright Collection; O. Chanute to W. Wright, Aug. 9, 1902, Box 17, Wright Collection; O. Chanute to W. Wright, Aug. 6, 1902, Box 17, Wright Collection.
46. W. Wright to O. Chanute, Dec. 11, 1902, Box 5, Chanute Collection.

Chapter 12. The Great Aerodrome

1. S. P. Langley to O. Chanute, June 8, 1897, Box 2, Chanute Collection.
2. S. P. Langley to O. Chanute, Dec. 1897, Box 2, Chanute Collection.
3. "Memorandum on Enlarging Aerodrome Work to Enable the Machine to Carry a Man," in "Aerodromics 25," p. 2. As in the earlier Langley chapters, the consecutively numbered "Aerodromic" books scattered in the Smithsonian Archive and the Library of the National Air and Space Museum are treated as a unit without reference to location.
4. "Memorandum of Conversation with Mr. Walcott," March 1, 1897, in "Scrapbook Containing a Summary of Principal Events Re to the Aerodromic Work in the Order of Dates Beginning with 1897, Etc.," in Langley Papers, Smithsonian Archive.
5. "Memorandum," April 30, 1897; "Conference Memorandum," March 30; "Memorandum," April 13, "Scrapbook."
6. "Memorandum" April 6, 1896, "Scrapbook."
7. Ibid.; untitled copy of the Army/Navy Board Report, "Scrapbook." Most of the memos cited are to be found in in "Langley Aerodrome and Telescope File," Box 314, Secretarial Correspondence, 1891–1906, Smithsonian Archive.
8. Ninth Annual Report of the Board of Ordnance and Fortification, p. 1; copy in "Langley Aerodrome and Telescope." Russell Parkinson, "Politics, Patents, and Planes: Military Aeronautics in the United States, 1867–1907" unpublished Ph.D. dissertation, Duke University, 1963, is an excellent treatment of BOF aeronautical ventures.
9. "Aerodromics 26," p. 4.
10. S. M. Balzer biographical materials, Library, National Air and Space Museum,
11. S. P. Langley to R. H. Thurston, May 9, 1898, "Aerodrmics 26."
12. Memorandum, Feb. 8, 1898, "Aerodromics 26," p. 64; "Aerodromics 24," pp. 244–246.
13. Memorandum, Nov. 7, 1898, "Scrapbook"; "Notes."
14. "Notes"; Résumé of remarks to BOF, Nov. 9, 1898, "Scrapbook"; "Aerodromics 26," p. 8.
15. Washington Post, Nov. 11, 1918.
16. S. P. Langley to C. Walcott, Nov. 17, 1898, "Scrapbook"; S. P. Langley to I. N. Lewis, Nov. 1898, "Scrapbook."

17. J. E. Watkins and C. Manly to S. P. Langley, Nov. 1898, "Scrapbook."
18. C. Manly to S. P. Langley, Nov. 20, 1898, "Aerodromics 26," p. 10; S. P. Langley to S. M. Balzer, Feb. 7, 1898, "Aerodromics 27," p. 109.
19. "Aerodromics 26," p. 4; S. P. Langley, "Aerodromics 26," p. 36; "Aerodromics 27," p. 384.
20. "Aerodromics 20," pp. 108–120; "Aerodromics 26," pp. 88–90; "Aerodromics 20," pp. 130–140; *ibid.*, pp. 140–155, 178–196; *ibid.*, pp. 214–258. See "Aerodromics 26," pp. 68, 74, 88, for information on the new launcher; also "Aerodromics 19," pp. 358–360.
21. S. P. Langley, *Langley Memoir on Mechanical Flight* (Washington, 1911), pp. 133, 134, 154.
22. "Aerodromics 26," pp. 88–90; "Notes."
23. C. M. Manly to S. P. Langley, April 4, 1900, "Aerodromics 29"; "Aerodromics 24," p. 64; Langley, *Memoir*, pp. 188–205.
24. C. M. Manly to S. P. Langley, July 14, 1899, "Aerodromics 28," p. 41.
25. C. M. Manly to S. P. Langley, July 21, 1899, "Aerodromics 28," p. 54; C. M. Manly to S. P. Langley, Aug. 4, 1899, "Aerodromics 28," p. 64; "Aerodromics 20," pp. 318–328; "Aerodromics 26," p. 222.
26. "Aerodromics 28," p. 119; S. P. Langley to I. N. Lewis, Sept. 12, 1899, "Aerodromics 28," p. 301, "Aerodromics 26," p. 96; S. P. Langley to S. M. Balzer, Oct. 23, 1894, "Aerodromics 28," p. 214.
27. C. M. Manly to S. P. Langley, Jan. 4, 1900, Incoming Correspondence, Box 47; C. M. Manly to S. M. Balzer, Jan. 10, 1900, Balzer Papers in the Aeronautics Department, Library, National Air and Space Museum; S. P. Langley to S. M. Balzer, Jan. 12, 1900, "Aerodromics 28," p. 369.
28. C. M. Manly to S. M. Balzer, March 20, 1900, Balzer Papers.
29. Memorandum, S. P. Langley to C. M. Manly, April 6, 1900; "Aerodromics 29," p. 33; S. P. Langley to C. M. Manly, May 11, 1900, "Aerodromics 29," p. 97; S. P. Langley to C. M. Manly, May 19, 1900, "Aerodromics 29," p. 107; G. B. Wells, Diary, May 20, 21, 30, 1900, quoted in Robert Meyer, *Langley's Aero Engine of 1903* (Washington, 1971), pp. 65–67. Meyer's volume is a source book containing portions of the Langley papers relating to the engine. The book, with its fine appendices, constitutes the best work on the subject to date. The Wells diaries have vanished since 1971, forcing the author to rely on Meyer's quotations.
30. S. P. Langley to C. M. Manly, July 11, 1900, "Aerodromics 26," p. 182; C. M. Manly to S. P. Langley, June 19, 1900, "Aerodromics 29," p. 149; C. M. Manly to S. P. Langley, Aug. 21, 1900, Incoming Correspondence, Box 47; C. M. Manly to S. P. Langley, "Report of Progress As of December 1, 1900," "Aerodromics 29," p. 234; "Aerodromics 29," p. 234.
31. S. P. Langley to C. M. Manly, Sept. 3, 1900, "Aerodromics 29," p. 180; "Aerodromics 29," p. 277; S. P. Langley to C. M. Manly, Feb. 1, 1901, "Aerodromics 29," p. 278.
32. R. Rathbun to I. N. Lewis, "Material for Inclusion in the Annual Report

of the Board of Ordnance and Fortification," Sept. 6, 1900, "Aerodromics 29," p. 197.

33. "Aerodromics 24," pp. 244–246. See Merrill File, Hodgkins Fund, Box 37, Secretary 1891–1906, Smithsonian Archive; "Aerodromics 26," pp. 272, 276; "Aerodromics 24," pp. 244–246.

34. "Aerodromics 29," pp. 346–347; C. M. Manly to S. P. Langley, May 30, 1901, "Aerodromics 29," p. 362; C. M. Manley to S. P. Langley, June 4, 1901, "Aerodromics 29," pp. 367–368; C. M. Manly to S. P. Langley, June 19, 1901, "Aerodromics 29," pp. 379–380; "Aerodromics 26," p. 282; Langley, *Memoir*, pp. 226–234.

35. C. M. Manly to S. P. Langley, June 19, 1901, "Aerodromics 29," p. 379.

36. A. G. Bell to S. P. Langley, June 22, 1898; S. P. Langley to A. G. Bell, June 3, 1890, Incoming Correspondence, Box 45; W. J. Rhees, *The Smithsonian Institution, Documents Relating to Its Origin and History* (Washington, 1904), I, p. 121; Wells, Diary, in Meyer, *Aero Engine*, pp. 107–108.

37. *Ibid.*

38. C. M. Manly to S. P. Langley, Oct. 15, 1901, "Aerodromics 26," p. 289.

39. Wells, Diary, Oct. 2, 1901, in Meyer, *Aero Engine*, p. 107.

40. "Aerodromics 26," April 29, 1902, p. 314; S. P. Langley, *Memoir*, pp. 234–246. Meyer, *Aero Engine*, pp. 130–133, is the finest assessment of the Langley engine.

41. S. P. Langley to I. N. Lewis, Nov. 10, 1902, Secretary, 1891–1906, Correspondence, "Langley Aerodrome and Telescope," Box 314.

42. C. M. Manly to S. P. Langley, undated memorandum in *ibid.*; C. M. Manly to S. P. Langley, March 23, 1903, Incoming Correspondence, Box 47. Much of the material in this section is based on an examination of the original Langley aerodrome now in the collection of the National Air and Space Museum. Original drawings are also available in the Langley biographical files of the National Air and Space Museum Library. Langley, *Memoir*, pp. 207–217. Pp. 164–170 are also helpful.

43. "Aerodromics 26," p. 278.

44. *Ibid.*; C. M. Manly to S. P. Langley, June 1, 1901, Incoming Correspondence, Box 47.

45. C. M. Manly to S. P. Langley, Oct. 15, 1903, Incoming Correspondence, Box 47.

Chapter 13. December 1903: The Month of the Flying Machines

1. C. M. Manly to S. P. Langley, Sept. 9, 1903; Oct. 15, 1903, Box 4, Incoming Correspondence. For details of all flight tests, Sept.–Dec., see *Washington Star* coverage.

2. C. M. Manly to S. P. Langley, Oct. 15, 1903, Box 47, Incoming Correspondence.

3. *Washington Post*, Oct. 8, 1903.

4. The author's judgments as to the structural integrity of the aerodrome, now being restored at the National Air and Space Museum, Silver Hill, Maryland, facility. My thanks to Dr. Howard Wolko, assistant director, science and technology, National Air and Space Museum, for his comments and assistance in the matter.

5. See *Washington Post* and *Star* accounts, Dec. 1–10, 1903, especially *Washington Post*, Dec. 8, 1903; "Aerodromics 26," p. 380.

6. Adler, *I Have Considered the Days.*

7. Ernest Sechler, "Aerodromics 26," pp. 376–380; *Washington Star*, Dec. 8, 1903.

8. *Congressional Record*, Jan. 23, 1904.

9. *Ibid.*

10. *Congressional Record*, Jan. 27, 1904, p. 1364.

11. *Ibid.*, p. 1365.

12. *Ibid.*, p. 1367.

13. *Ibid.*, p. 1366.

14. *Ibid.*

15. *Ibid.*

16. "Fads, Frauds and Follies Cripple Nation's Finances," *Brooklyn Eagle*, March 13, 1904.

17. S. P. Langley, *Memoir on Mechanical Flight* (Washington, 1911), p. 278.

18. W. Wright to O. Chanute, Nov. 8, 1906, *Papers*, p. 736.

19. W. Wright to G. Spratt, Dec. 29, 1902, *Papers*, p. 292; "The Wright Propellers," *Papers*, pp. 594–640.

20. W. Wright to G. Spratt, Feb. 28, 1903, *Papers*, p. 299;

21. Rodney K. Warrel, "The Wright Brothers' Pioneer Patent," *American Bar Association Journal* (Oct. 1979), pp. 1511–1518.

22. S. P. Langley to O. Chanute, Dec. 7, 1902, Box 2, Chanute Papers; O. Chanute to W. Wright, Dec. 9, 1902, Box 17, Wright Collection.

23. O. Chanute to W. Wright, July 27, 1903, Box 17, Wright Collection.

24. W. Wright to O. Chanute, Oct. 1, 1903, Box 5, Chanute Collection; O. Wright, Diary D, Nov. 5, 1903, Box 1, Wright Papers.

25. *Ibid.*

26. O. Wright to C. Taylor, Nov. 23, 1903, *Papers*, p. 385.

27. W. Wright to M. Wright, Nov. 23, 1903, *Papers*, p. 389.

28. O. Wright, Diary D, Dec. 14, 1903, Box 1, Wright Collection.

29. William O. Saunders, "Then We Quit Laughing," *Collier's* (Sept. 17, 1927), p. 24.

30. *Ibid.*

31. O. Wright, "How We Made the First Flight," *Flying* (Dec. 1913), pp. 10–12.

32. W. Tate, "With the Wrights at Kitty Hawk," *Aeronautic Review* (Dec. 1928), pp. 188–192.

33. *Papers*, p. 397.

Bibliography

The following bibliography of materials contains only those items that proved particularly useful to the author during the preparation of the dissertation. It is not intended to serve as a complete survey of the aeronautical literature of the period 1875–1905.

Manuscript Sources

The John Crerar Library, Chicago, Illinois: Octave Chanute Scrapbooks.

The Manuscript Division, Library of Congress: the Octave Chanute Papers, the Papers of Wilbur and Orville Wright; the Charles Zimmerman Papers; the American Institute of Aeronautics and Astronautics Historical Collection.

The Smithsonian Institution: The Samuel P. Langley Papers; the National Air and Space Museum Aircraft and Biographical Files; the Stephan Balzer Papers; the James Means Collection; the Alexander Graham Bell Collection; the Augustus Herring Collection.

Notre Dame University: the A. F. Zahm Papers.

Cornell University: the Augustus Herring Papers (microfilm).

The National Geographic Society: the Alexander Graham Bell Papers.

Bibliographies

While a number of bibliographies and catalogues of collections were consulted, the following have proved the most useful.
Brockett, Paul. *Bibliography of Aeronautics* (Washington, 1910).
Renstrom, Arthur. *Wilbur and Orville Wright: A Bibliography* . . .
U.S. Works Progress Administration. *Bibliography of Aeronautics,* 50 vols. (Washington, 1938–1941).

Primary Sources

Adler, Cyrus. *I Have Considered the Days* (Philadelphia, 1940).
Anonymous. "Dr. Samuel Langley's Experiments in Aeronautics." *Scientific American,* 66 (February 18, 1892), 1–2.
———. "Edison's Views on Flying." *Aeronautical World,* 1 (February 1903), 164.
———. "Gustave Whitehead's New Machine." *Aeronautical World,* 1 (May 1, 1903), 225.
———. "The Holland Airship." *Aeronautical World,* 1 (June 1, 1903), 281.
———. "Langley's Flying Machine." *Aeronautical Journal,* 1 (July 1897), 8.
———. "Lamson's Man-lifting Kite." *Aeronautical Journal,* 1 (October 1897), 20.
———. "The Latest Ludlow Airplane." *Popular Mechanics,* 10 (August 1908), 516.
———. "The Whitehead Flying Machine . . ." *American Inventor,* 9 (April 1, 1902), 1–2.
———. "Whitehead's Experiments." *Aeronautical World,* 1 (July 1, 1903), 270–271.
Cayley, Sir George. *Aeronautical and Miscellaneous Note-Books,* ed. J. E. Hodgson (Cambridge, 1933).
Chanute, Octave. "Aerial Navigation." *Engineering World,* 4 (August 10, 1896), 222.
———. "Aerial Navigation." *Transportation,* 1 (October 1893), 24–25.
———. "Aerial Navigation." *Report of the Board of Regents of the Smithsonian Institution for 1903* (Washington, 1904), pp. 173–181.
———. *Aerial Navigation: A Lecture Delivered to the Students of Sibley College, Cornell University, May 2, 1890* (New York, 1891).
———. "Aerial Navigation: Balloons and Flying Machines from an Engineering Point of View." *Cassier's Magazine,* 20 (June 1901), 111–128.
———. "Conditions of Success with Flying Machines." *American Magazine of Aeronautics,* 1 (July 1907), 7–9.
———. "Evolution of the 'Two-Surface' Flying Machine." *Aeronautics,* 3 (October 1908), 9–10.
———. "Experiments in Flying." *McClure's Magazine,* 15 (June 1900), 127–133.
———. "Exposition de Chicago." *L'Aéronaut,* 27 (February 1894), 28–29.
———. "First Steps in Aviation and Memorable Flights." *Aeronautics,* 4 (January 1909), 24.

———. "Future Uses of Aerial Navigation." *Aeronautics*, 2 (June 1908), 15–16.

———. "How to Learn to Fly." *American Aeronaut*, 1 (June 1908), 199–203.

———. "International Conference on Aerial Navigation." *Aeronautics*, 1 (October 1893), 4–6.

———. "La Navigation aérienne aux États-Unis." *L'Aérophile*, 11 (August 1903), 171–183.

———. "Opening Address: Conference on Aerial Navigation." *Aeronautics*, 1 (October 1893), 4–6.

———. "Pending European Experiments in Flying." *American Aeronaut and Aerostationist*, 1 (September 1907), 13–16.

———. *Progress in Flying Machines* (New York, 1894).

———. "Progress in Aerial Navigation." *Engineering Magazine*, 2 (October 1891), 21–24.

———. "Recent Experiments in Gliding Flight." *Aeronautical Annual*, 3 (Boston, 1897), 30–53.

———. "Sailing Flight, Part 1." *Aeronautical Annual*, 2 (Boston, 1896), 60–76.

———. "Sailing Flight, Part 2." *Aeronautical Annual*, 3 (Boston, 1897), 98–127.

———. "The Secret of Soaring." *Aeronautics*, 1 (November 1893), 25–26.

———. "Some American Experiments." *Aeronautical Journal*, 2 (January 1898), 9–11.

Collins, P. F. "The Latest Marvel in Flying Machines." *Broadway Magazine* (November 1903), 124–127.

Eddy, William. "Experiments with Kite Sustained Airplanes." In *Navigating the Air* (New York, 1907), p. 35.

Edison, Thomas. "Attempt to Solve the Problem of Flight." *Aeronautical World*, 1 (January 1903), 138.

———. "Edison on Flying Machines." *Aeronautics*, 1 (October 1893), 15.

Herring, A. M. "Early Herring Correspondence." 1 (February–March 1908), 154–157.

———. "Recent Advances toward a Solution of the Problem of the Century." *Aeronautical Annual*, 3 (Boston, 1897), 68–71.

Holland, John. "Aerial Navigation." *Cosmopolitan*, 11 (November 1892), 89.

———. "How to Fly." In *Navigating the Air* (New York, 1907), p. 63.

———. "Mechanical Flight." *Cassier's Magazine*, 3 (February 1893), 243.

Lancaster, Israel. "A Communication from Mr. I Lancaster." In *The Seventeenth Annual Report of the Aeronautical Society of Great Britain for the Year 1882* (London, 1883), p. 47.

———. "Flying Birds and the Art of Flying." *Scientific American Supplement*, 57 (April 28, 1904), 23663.

———. "Gravitation and the Soaring Bird." *American Naturalist*, 20 (June 1886), 520.

———. "The Problem of the Soaring Bird." *American Naturalist*, 19 (June and November 1886), 1056, 1167.

Lamson, C. H. "Work on the Great Diamond." *Aeronautical Annual,* 2 (Boston, 1896), 133–137.

Langley, Samuel P. "Dr. Langley's Aerodynamic Experiments." *Aeronautical World,* 1 (January 1902), 104–105.

———. *Experiments in Aerodynamics* (Washington, 1891).

———. "Experiments in Mechanical Flight." *Aeronautical Annual,* 3 (Boston, 1897), 11–25.

———. "Experiments with the Langley Aerodrome." *Popular Science Monthly,* 73 (November 1908), 462–474.

———. "The Flying Machine." *McClure's Magazine,* 9 (June 1897), 647–660.

———. *Internal Work of the Wind* (Washington, 1893).

———. "The Langley Aerodrome." *Scientific American Supplement,* 54 (December 6, 1902), 22512.

———. *Langley Memoir on Mechanical Flight* (Washington, 1908).

———. "Langley's Law." *Aeronautical Annual,* 1 (Boston, 1895), 127–128.

———. "Mechanical Flight." *Cosmopolitan,* 13 (May 1892), 55–58.

———. "Methods of Launching Aerial Machines." *Aeronautical Annual,* 3 (Boston, 1897), 154–155.

———. "The New Flying Machine." *Strand Magazine,* 13 (June 1897), 701–718.

———. "The Possibility of Mechanical Flight." *Century Magazine,* (September 1891), 783–785.

———. "Professor Langley." *Flying,* 1 (December 1901), 7.

———. *Researches and Experiments in Aerial Navigation* (Washington, 1908).

———. "A Rubber Powered Model." *Aeronautical Annual,* 3 (Boston, 1897), 153–154.

———. "Samuel P. Langley." *Aeronautical Annual,* 3 (Boston, 1897), 5–10.

———. "The Story of Experiments in Mechanical Flight." *Aeronautical Annual,* 3 (Boston, 1897), 11–25.

———. "A Successful Trial of the Aerodrome." *Science,* 16 (May 22, 1896), 753.

Le Conte, John. "New Light on the Problem of Flying." *Popular Science Monthly,* 44 (April 1894), 744.

———. "The Problem of Flying Machines." *Popular Science Monthly,* 34 (November 1888), 69.

Lilienthal, Otto. "The Best Shape for Wings." *Aeronautical Annual,* 3 (Boston, 1897), 95–97.

———. *Birdflight As the Basis for Aviation: A Contribution toward a System of Aviation* (London, 1911).

———. "The Flying Man." *Aeronautics,* 1 (April 1894), 85–86.

———. "The Flying Man." *McClure's Magazine,* 3 (September 1894), 1–10.

———. "Lilienthal's Experiments in Flying." *Nature,* 51 (December 20, 1894), 177–179.

———. "Our Teachers in Sailing Flight." *Aeronautical Annual,* 3 (Boston, 1897), 84–91.

———. "Practical Experiments for the Development of Human Flight." *Aeronautical Annual*, 2 (Boston, 1896), 7.

———. "Practical Experiments in Soaring." In *The Annual Report of the Board of Regents of the Smithsonian Institution for the Year 1893* (Washington, 1894), p. 194.

Lougheed, Victor. *Airplane Designing for Amateurs* (Chicago, 1912).

———. *Vehicles of the Air* (New York, 1911).

McFarland, Marvin W., ed. *The Papers of Wilbur and Orville Wright, 1899–1948*, 2 vols. (New York, 1953).

Means, James. "An Editorial." *Aeronautical Annual*, 1 (Boston, 1895), 69.

———. "The Scientific Value of Flying Models." *Frank Leslie's Weekly*, 76 (January 1893), 42.

———. "Senate Bill No. 302." *Aeronautical Annual*, 2 (Boston, 1896), 80–84.

———. "Wheeling and Flying." *Aeronautical Annual*, 2 (Boston, 1896), 25.

Melville, George W. "Aerial Navigation Problems." *Scientific American Supplement*, 53 (February 22, 1902), 21859–21860.

———. "The Engineer and the Problem of Aerial Navigation." *North American Review*, 173 (December 1901), 820–831.

Merrill, A. A. "A New Method of Experimenting with Gliding Flights." *Aeronautical Journal*, 10 (October 1906), 13–14.

———. "Some Simple Experiments with Aero-Curves." *Aeronautical Journal*, 3 (July 1899), 65–67.

Millett, J. B. "Some Experiments with Hargrave Kites." *Aeronautical Annual*, 2 (Boston, 1896), 127–132.

Montgomery, John J. *The Aeroplane* (Santa Clara, Calif., 1905).

———. "The Aeroplane." *Scientific American*, 92 (May 20, 1905), 405–406.

———. "New Principles in Aerial Flight." *Scientific American Supplement*, 57 (November 22, 1905), 24991–24993.

———. "Principles Involved in the Formation of Wing Surfaces and the Phenomena of Soaring." *Aeronautics*, 3 (November, December, January 1908), 39–40, 32–36, 43–46.

———. "Some Early Gliding Experiments." *Aeronautics*, 1 (January 1901), 47–50.

Mouillard, Louis. *L'Empire de l'air* (Paris, 1881).

Newcomb, Simon. "An Astronomer's Indictment of Aerial Navigation." *Cassier's Magazine*, 45 (November 1908), 563–564.

———. "Aviation Declared a Failure." *Literary Digest*, 37 (October 17, 1908), 549.

———. "Is the Airship Coming?" *McClure's Magazine*, 17 (September 1891), 562–565.

Pénaud, Alphonse. *Aviation* (Paris, 1875).

Pickering, William. "The Vertical Screw or Helicopter." In *Navigating the Air* (New York, 1907), p. 114.

Pilcher, Percy. "Mr. Pilcher on Flying Machines." *Aeronautical Journal*, 1 (April 1897), 3.

———. "Soaring Machines." *Aeronautical Journal*, 2 (January 1898), 5.

Proceedings of the International Conference on Aerial Navigation, Held in Chicago, August 2, 3, 4, 1893 (New York, 1894).

Rayleigh, Lord. "Experiments in Aerodynamics." *Nature,* 145 (December 3, 1892), n.p.

Root, A. I. "Our Homes." *Gleanings in Bee Culture,* 33 (January 1, 1905), 36–39.

Rotch, Abbot Lawrence. *Sounding the Ocean of Air* (London, 1900).

Thurston, Robert H. "Problem of Aerial Navigation." *Forum,* 8 (January 1890), 542.

————. "The Status of Aeronautics." *Science,* 5 (April 10, 1885), 295.

Walker, John Brisben. "The Problem of Aerial Navigation." *Cosmopolitan,* 12 (January 1892), 252.

————. "The Problem of Aerial Navigation." *Cosmopolitan,* 12 (March 1892), 624.

Wenham, Francis Herbert. *Aerial Locomotion* (London, 1866).

————. "On Aerial Locomotion and the Laws by Which Heavy Bodies Impelled through the Air Are Sustained." In *First Annual Report of the Aeronautical Society of Great Britain* (London, 1866), pp. 10–46.

————. "On Aerial Locomotion." In *Annual Report of the Board of Regents of the Smithsonian Institution for 1889* (Washington, 1890), pp. 303–323.

————. "Remarks on the Present State of Aeronautical Science." In *Second Annual Report of the Aeronautical Society of Great Britain* (London, 1867), pp. 13–17.

Zahm, Albert Francis. *Aerial Navigation: A Popular Treatise on the Growth of Air Craft and an Aeronautical Methodology* (New York, 1911).

————. *The Aeronautical Papers of Albert Francis Zahm, 1885–1945* (South Bend, Ind., 1950).

————. "Alexander Goupil, Inventor of Three-Torque Airplane Control." *Journal of the Maryland Academy of Science,* 2 (April 1931), 138–139.

————. "A Crisis in Aeroplane Litigation." *Popular Mechanics* (June 1912), 778.

Secondary Sources

Abbot, Charles G. "Samuel Pierpont Langley." *Smithsonian Miscellaneous Collections,* 92, No. 3281 (August 22, 1934).

Anonymous. "America's First Glider Club: From Contemporary Notes of Charles P. Steinmetz." *The Sportsman Pilot,* 4 (December 1930), 26–27.

Bruce, Robert V. *Bell: Alexander Graham Bell and the Conquest of Solitude* (Boston, 1973).

Crouch, Tom D. *The Giant Leap: A Chronology of Ohio Aerospace Events and Personalities, 1815–1969* (Columbus, Ohio, 1971).

Davy, M. J. B. *Henson and Stringfellow: Their Work in Aeronautics* (London, 1931).

————. *Interperative History of Flight* (London, 1948).

Dollfus, Charles, and H. Bouché. *Histoire de l'aéronautique* (Paris, 1932).

Durand, William F. *Robert H. Thurston* (New York, 1929).

Freudenthal, Elsbeth E. *Flight into History: The Wright Brothers and the Air Age* (Norman, Okla., 1949).

Gibbs-Smith, Charles H. *The Aeroplane: An Historical Survey* (London, 1960).

———. *Aviation: An Historical Survey from Its Origins to the End of World War II* (London, 1969).

———. *Clément Ader: His Flight Claims and Place in History* (London, 1965).

———. *The Invention of the Aeroplane, 1809–1909* (London, 1966).

———. *Sir George Cayley's Aeronautics, 1796–1855* (London, 1965).

———. "The Sorry Affair of Gustave Whitehead and His Alleged Powered Flight." *Aeronautics and Astronautics,* 8 (February 1970), 66–68.

Hamilton, John. *Bell and Baldwin: Development of Aerodromes and Hydrodromes at Baddeck, Nova Scotia* (Toronto, 1964).

Hodgson, J. E., ed. *Aeronautical and Miscellaneous Notebooks of Sir George Cayley* (London, 1933).

Horgan, James, Jr. "Aeronautics at the World's Fair of 1904." *Missouri Historical Society Bulletin,* 24 (April 1968), 215–246.

Kármán, Theodore von. *Aerodynamics: Selected Topics in the Light of Their Historical Development* (Ithaca, New York, 1954).

Kelly, Fred C. *The Wright Brothers* (New York, 1943).

Martin, James V. "The Aircraft Conspiracy." *The Libertarian,* 2 (March 1924), 120–127.

Means, James, Jr. *James Means and the Problem of Man-Flight* (Washington, 1964).

Meyer, Robert. *Langley's Aero Engine of 1903* (Washington, 1971).

Millbank, Jeremiah. *The First Century of Flight in America* (Princeton, 1941).

Miller, Francis T. *The World in the Air* (New York, 1930).

O'Dwyer, William. "Did Whitehead Fly before the Wrights?" *American Aircraft Modeler,* 67 (November 1968), 14–17.

Parkinson, Russell J. "Politics, Patents and Planes: Military Aeronautics in the United States, 1860–1907." Unpublished Ph.D. dissertation, Duke University, 1963.

Penrose, Harald. *British Aviation: The Pioneer Years, 1903–1914* (Fallbrook, Calif., 1967).

Pritchard, J. L. "The Dawn of Aerodynamics." *Journal of the Royal Aeronautical Society,* 61 (March 1957), 151–160.

———. "Francis Herbert Wenham, Honorary Member, 1824–1908: An Appreciation of the First Lecturer to the Aeronautical Society." *Journal of the Royal Aeronautical Society,* 52 (August 1958), 571–596.

Randolph, Stella. *The Lost Flights of Gustave Whitehead* (Washington, 1937).

Roseberry, C. H. *Glenn Curtiss: Pioneer of Flight* (New York, 1972).

Scamehorn, H. L. *Balloons to Jets: A Century of Aeronautics in Illinois* (Chicago, 1957).

Spearman, Arthur Dunning. *John Joseph Montgomery, 1858–1911: Father of Basic Flying* (Santa Clara, Calif., 1967).

Vivian, E. C., and W. L. Marsh. *A History of Aeronautics* (New York, 1921).

Walcott, C. D. "Biographical Memoir of Samuel P. Langley, 1834–1906." *National Academy of Sciences Biographical Memoirs*, 7 (April 1912), 247.

Walsh, John Evangelist. *One Day at Kitty Hawk* (New York, 1975).

White, Lynn, Jr. "Eilmer of Malmesbury: An Eleventh Century Aviator." *Technology and Culture*, 3 (Spring 1972), 98.

Index